JOSEPH A. SOARES

The Power of Privilege

Yale and America's Elite Colleges

STANFORD UNIVERSITY PRESS

STANFORD, CALIFORNIA

2007

Stanford University Press
Stanford, California
©2007 by the Board of Trustees of the Leland Stanford Junior University.
Printed in the United States of America on acid-free, archival-quality paper

Library of Congress Cataloging-in-Publication Data
Soares, Joseph A.
  The power of privilege : Yale and America's elite colleges / Joseph A. Soares.
      p. cm.
  Includes bibliographical references and index.
  ISBN 978-0-8047-5637-2 (cloth : alk. paper) -- ISBN 978-0-8047-5638-9 (pbk. : alk. paper)
    1. Universities and colleges--United States--Admission. 2. Education, Higher--United States. 3. Elite (Social sciences)--United States. 4. Yale University--Admission. I. Title.

LB2351.2.S63 2007
378.1'610973--dc22

                                                    2006100226

Typeset by Bruce Lundquist in 10/14 Janson

For Felicitas, Axel, and Isabella

Contents

Tables

Foreword and Acknowledgments

Having spent the better part of two decades at Harvard and Yale, first as a graduate student, then as a senior lecturer in social studies at Harvard, and finally as an associate professor of sociology at Yale, there were abundant personal experiences to draw on for this book. The scholarly research and writing that went into this work, however, stretched over the last five years, and two of those were at Wake Forest University in North Carolina. This manuscript emerged from a "revise and resubmit" that an article-length version of this received from the journal *The Sociology of Education* in 2002. I had written, in response to Nicolas Lemann's *The Big Test*, a critique of the notion that a test-score-selected meritocracy had emerged at Harvard and Yale in the late 1950s and early 1960s. I doubted that the use of the Scholastic Assessment Test (SAT) in admissions had produced a social revolution in the composition of the undergraduate body. Even in 2002, family privileges, in the form of admission perks for the offspring of alumni was an accepted, if little commented on, fact; anyone with half a nose for social distinctions could hardly avoid the fragrance of serious money in town. How was it possible that our most prestigious universities selected so many of their best from rich families? Families of wealth, both old and new, were too well represented among undergraduates for this to be merely a coincidence. If their presence was the inescapable result of the academic competition being won by those who started life well ahead of the pack, then something about educational opportunities in our society was seriously amiss. If this was not, however, because of blind factors beyond anyone's control, then an even more disturbing possibility presents itself. What would it mean if those inequalities were consciously designed by admissions' gatekeepers? Were our most prestigious universities guilty of confusing merit with social class and of passing on the consequences to the rest of higher education?

I delivered an abbreviated version of the article at a regular session of the American Sociological Association's convention in August of 2002, and then sat down to revise the journal submission. The manuscript, however, took on a life of its own that refused compression within the page limits of an article. Three years later, with considerably more research under my belt, this book emerged.

When I began to work on this, I was mindful that there were other sociologists, Jerome Karabel and David Karen in particular, who also held views critical of the widespread belief that the Ivy League had become academically meritocratic and socially democratized in the 1960s. Literally, while I was putting the finished touches on my last chapter, Jerome Karabel's masterpiece, *The Chosen* (2005), came out. Karabel's conclusions are consistent with my own. I think it is fair to say that both of our works show that Harvard, Princeton, and Yale never desired or attempted to create an undergraduate academic meritocracy. There are, however, significant differences between our two books. My central question concerns the social role of America's top collegiate tier, which I explore from the perspective of Yale University, a key actor in the structuring of our very selective and private elite colleges. Although Karabel's work is over 600 pages of detailed history, mine is more specifically focused on the nexus between social class and admissions regime. It is a sociological account of institutional gatekeepers, confident of the validity of what were actually biased measures of merit, seeking to select tomorrow's leadership class from among their economically privileged clientele. By concentrating on Yale, I was able to uncover many documents and reports, particularly from its Office of Institutional Research, that were unavailable to Karabel. Despite differences of evidence and interpretation, I hope that our complementary works can contribute to dispelling the myth of Ivy League meritocracy, of the alleged shift in admissions after 1950 from character to brains. If our most prestigious private universities have failed to deliver on the promise of academic meritocracy, perhaps it is time for us to pursue alternatives?

I would like to acknowledge the graduate student research assistants at Yale who toiled beside me in the archive: David Reisman (now a professor of Islamic studies at the University of Illinois in Chicago), and Ling Tang, a candidate for a Ph.D. in sociology at Yale. She was also the lone researcher on the West Coast, working in the University of California's archives. I need to thank the provost's office at Yale for the faculty research grants that funded my assistants. From Yale's Office of Institutional Research, I am especially indebted to Dr. Russ Adair. From the Yale archive, I would like to express my gratitude to Bill Massa and Richard Scary in particular, but everyone working in the archive deserves acknowledgment for their professional services and personal warmth. At Wake Forest, I want to thank my departmental colleagues and their families for being a nurturing and stimulating community for my entire family; my research assistant, Shaughnessy O'Brien, for working with me to uncover the effects of college tiers from the restricted assess version of the National Educational Longitudinal Survey; and Romina Frank, for Germanic childcare. And I thank Dr. Ann Mullen of the University of Toronto for collaborating with me on papers and articles on cultural capital and professional school matriculation that I drew on for this work.

I would also like to note my appreciation of Kate Wahl, Acquisitions Editor, Stanford University Press, for her support, understanding, and critical guidance through the final stage of this project.

Finally, Dr. Felicitas Opwis was fortuitously distracted from her responsibilities as a professor of Arabic and Islamic studies at Georgetown University by her pregnancy with our second child. While at home in North Carolina, she acted as my best critic and copyeditor during the final stage of this work. I dedicate this book to her and our two children, Isabella and Axel (who were, respectively, four days and four years old when this manuscript was sent to Stanford).

THE POWER OF PRIVILEGE

CHAPTER ONE

Meritocracy and Its Discontents

Even Americans unfamiliar with the word embrace *meritocracy* as if it were a birthright. We believe in the essential goodness of the idea that people should be able to achieve in school and at work to the full extent of their natural abilities and drive. Being rewarded for what one does, rather than whom one is, and being able to rise or fall on one's merits is part of what defines the American dream of individual freedom and personal accomplishment.[1] Our national ethos of self-determination may be a delusion, but its appeal persists, even internationally. A female graduate student, speaking for French youths frustrated by a culture of limited opportunities, lamented to a *New York Times* reporter, "We are never taught the idea of the American dream," the concept of "the self-made man."[2]

For many Americans, schools and colleges are the vessels of our meritocratic aspirations; they provide our primary experience with an institution that evaluates individual performance. Reliable surveys tell us that most adults think of merit in school or college as academic accomplishments; we believe entry to college should be based on grades and test scores alone.[3] Youths applying to college count on the basic fairness of the admissions process, and when it does not appear to be that way, a rejection letter may bring on litigation. If all else is equal between two candidates, is it fair for the applicant whose father went to Harvard, for example, to be admitted there over someone whose parents did not? Should religion, gender, or race matter to one's prospects? Some of the ambivalence that many feel about affirmative action is because it seems unconstitutional that anything other than individual academic merit should count for college admissions.

America has, according to international scholars, seventeen of the top twenty universities in the world.[4] Most of our best universities, as ranked by *Barron's*, the *Princeton Review*, or *U.S. News and World Report*, are private. We take great national pride in our premier universities and like to believe that their academic excellences are matched by a fair admissions process that selects the best brains for their classrooms. Our belief in America as a society where opportunities are open to talent is sustained, in part, by our confidence that our most prestigious universities operate according to the best possible standards of academic meritocracy. One should get into a top university because of one's achievements, not because of accidents of birth.

What would it mean, however, if Harvard and Yale and their peers had a history of excluding applicants based on gender, religion, race, income, and personality? The facts are that colleges like Yale kept a limit on their Jewish students until the early 1960s,[5] females were barred entirely through the late 1960s, Blacks were eliminated from the competition by poverty and inadequate schools until the 1970s, and right up to the contemporary period, one's personality and family income still matter. If those ivied universities pursued, not only in the recent past but at present, admissions policies aimed at capturing youths from families at the top of the income pyramid, and those universities selected students more for personal qualities than for academic accomplishments, would that require us to reevaluate the way we think of educational opportunity and individual merit? What sort of academic meritocracy would we have if one's chances of being in it were substantially determined by extracurricular performance and family wealth?

It is ironic that those top colleges who distance themselves from the pre-professional practices of the National Collegiate Athletic Association (NCAA) provide the greatest boost to athletes in their admissions process.

Neither racial minorities nor alumni offspring receive the preferential treatment given to athletes in top-tier admissions. The academic entry hurdle in the Ivy League is lowest for athletes, a majority of whom are White and from affluent families.[6] And athletes are in a stronger position to influence campus life in ivied colleges than in NCAA state universities because they are a larger percentage of the undergraduate population in the former. Male athletes are just 3 percent of the men at the University of Michigan, for example, although they are 22 percent of Princeton's men.[7] The emphasis placed by American elite colleges on athleticism is a national anomaly. Youths with undistinguished academic records cannot get into England's Oxford University or to France's *Ecole Nationale d'Administration* just for playing soccer. Why should sports matter so much in the Ivy League?

Separate from the significant athletic boost in admissions, there is the benefit of standing on stacks of money. Lawrence Summers, as president of Harvard, expressed dismay with the grip of wealthy families on elite colleges. He reported that at America's most prestigious colleges, approximately 74 percent of undergraduates came from families in the top income quartile, and only 9 percent of undergraduates came from the bottom 50 percent of America's families ranked by income.[8] Is the overlap of economic class and academic prestige merely an unfortunate yet inescapable coincidence? Or are admissions in the Ivy League governed by a logic that rewards socioeconomic status but disguises it as merit? Summers proclaims, "There is no more important mission for Harvard and higher education than promoting equality of opportunity for all."[9] Yet, as his statistics show, unless one believes that only rich people can be smart, we have a staggering distance to travel to achieve a fair opportunity for all to reach every level of our educational system.

President Summers's disclosure on the economic composition of top-tier colleges draws attention to another American irony. America, which we like to think of "as the very embodiment of meritocracy,"[10] is a place where economic class origins largely determine one's educational destiny. Class background influences whether or not one completes a college degree. If one is born into a family in the bottom-income quartile, one's odds of finishing college are nine out of one hundred, whereas the odds for a top income quartile youth are seventy-five out of one hundred.[11] And class origin affects, as Summers noted, whether one attends a top-tier or an unselective college.

For an overview of the national situation, consider the raw percentages of students by their social origin in each college tier. If one divides American colleges into seven prestige tiers and U.S. families into four socioeconomic status (SES) quartiles, the composition of tier 7 is without serious disparities. In tier 7, where colleges have non-competitive admissions, 22 percent of students are from the top SES quartile; 25 percent are from the second SES quartile; 27 percent are from the third SES quartile; and 25 percent are from the bottom quartile. The social composition of the other tiers is not, however, as egalitarian (see Table 1.1).

The least equitable outcomes are in the first tier where 79 percent of the students are from the top SES quartile and 2 percent are from the bottom. Whether one uses Summers's percentages, or these numbers derived from Department of Education data, there is a symmetry between social class and college tier.

Many things beyond brand-name prestige are at stake in attending a top-tier college. The consensus among economists is that college tier corresponds to income; the higher the tier, the higher the lifetime payoff.[12] College graduates earn over their working lives on average one million dollars more than high-school graduates, but tier-one college graduates accumulate an equally impressive one-million-dollar premium over the average earnings of alumni from the bottom tier.[13] The bottom tier enrolls the greatest cluster, 35 percent of all college students, whereas tier 1, where Yale and Harvard reside, includes just 4 percent of America's undergraduates.

TABLE 1.1

Percent of Each Higher Education Tier Occupied by Each SES Quartile.

	% of Tier 1	% of Tier 2	% of Tier 3	% of Tier 4	% of Tier 5	% of Tier 6	% of Tier 7
SES quartiles:							
Top	79	64	51	37	23	36	22
Upper Middle	16	19	24	27	28	21	25
Lower Middle	3	9	14	23	28	24	27
Bottom	2	7	10	13	20	19	25

SOURCE: National Educational Longitudinal Survey, 1988–2000. U.S. Department of Education. Restricted Access Data License Control Number: 06011044.

Students enter the top tier from wealthy families and leave it for the best-paying jobs. How have we gotten to a place where we profess meritocracy but apparently condone the reproduction of class privileges?

Yale's Story

This book explores these questions through a history of admissions at Yale. Why is Yale's story relevant to the whole nation? How does it illuminate the social-class dilemmas of our entire higher educational system?

Yale is one of the oldest and most prestigious universities in America. Its role in our society, from colonial times to the present, has been extraordinary. Founded in 1701 by Puritans who thought Harvard, established in 1636, had gotten lax, Yale's original purpose was the same as its rival, to provide a supply of educated clergy to Calvinist Congregationalists in New England. By the time of the American Revolution, however, Yale was already producing more lawyers than ministers, and careers in industry, trade, and banking took off after the Civil War.[14] Throughout our history, Yale has provided prominent lawyers, doctors, businessmen, and politicians, and perhaps it is for the latter that Yale is best known today.

Yale graduates play an exceptional role in the political life of our nation. First, and most visibly, there is Yale's eminence in presidential politics. When George W. Bush, a fifth-generation Yalie, completes his second term in office and steps down in 2009, a Yale man will have been sitting at the president's desk for twenty years. And the last time there was a presidential election without a Yale man on the ticket for either of the two major parties was in 1968.[15] Since 1974, when Richard Nixon resigned and was replaced by Gerald Ford, we have had only Jimmy Carter's administration when a Yalie was not either the president or vice-president of the country; by 2009, that unbroken occupancy of the White House will have lasted twenty-eight years.[16] Commenting on Yale's presidential record during the Bush/Kerry contest, an author wrote in the *Yale Alumni Magazine*, "The fundamental and clearest presidential pattern at Yale is the extraordinary power of privilege: the intense web of connections knitting together America's upper classes through family ties, business relationships, philanthropic and civic activities, social and recreational life, and of course, education."[17]

The incongruity between Yale's public meritocratic image and the author's reflections on its upper-class networks did not elicit any critical comments from readers of the publication.[18] Apparently, insiders are not surprised by blunt statements on Yale's class composition.

Moving from the White House to the Supreme Court, Yale's record is second only to Harvard's. Yale's two graduates on John Robert's court are outnumbered by Harvard's five (counting Ruth Bader Ginsburg's unhappy time at Harvard, John P. Stevens is the only Supreme Court justice without any student days at Harvard or Yale).

In other branches of government, in the recent past there have been four state governors with Yale degrees.[19] And in 2004, there were thirteen Yalies in the House of Representative and seven in the Senate.[20]

Although Yale's image may be enhanced by its association with those who walk the corridors of power, it cannot take direct credit or blame for the actions of alumni in political or judicial office. Its impact on the world of higher education, however, is another matter. For centuries, Yale has consciously attempted to be a leader to the whole of higher education, and it has enjoyed considerable success in that endeavor. When Yale's president in 1967, Kingman Brewster, Jr., spoke to an alumni officers' convocation on higher education, he expressed the traditional view on Yale's leading role. Mixing terms from the cloister and the boardroom, he told the alumni assembled,

> I think it's fair to say, without being too officious or self-congratulatory, and I hope not smug, that it has been and is the ancient privilege of endowed free universities of this country, particularly in the northeast, . . . [to be] the yardstick, not only for the independent rivals in the Ivy League and elsewhere, but the yardstick for the fast growing and very rapidly improving state institutions in the west and far west. This is an industry in which the yardstick is the independent and the private institution even though quantitatively, it acts for a smaller and smaller share of the total market. . . . Yale University is . . . one of the fortunate few whose tradition and endowed strength has permitted it to have a really discernible impact upon the standards of universities everywhere.[21]

Smug or not, Brewster was right. Many aspects of American colleges, ranging from a liberal-arts curriculum to the use of financial-needs-blind admissions, have derived their legitimacy from Yale. Without Yale, the Scholastic

Assessment Test (SAT) would not have come into such prominence in college admissions across the entire country. There are many educational practices in the United States for which, unlike presidential policies, one can place praise or censure on Yale's shoulders.

The final reason why Yale is the right place for this story is that it has been one of the two colleges, the other being Harvard, featured in histories on the rise of America's meritocracy. No other colleges have been singled out as being as crucial to the abolition of family privilege and to the introduction of academic merit as those two.

Meritocratic Controversies

For decades, Yale and its elder sibling Harvard have taken center stage in tales on the fabled downfall of the old Protestant Establishment.[22] Once, the story goes, America had an inbred upper class. It resided in brownstone townhouses and country estates in the northeast, attended Protestant, frequently Episcopalian, churches, and sent its sons to ivied colleges. Both church and college consecrated, within faux-medieval gothic walls, a stuffy deference to Anglophile tradition. It hired John Singer Sargent to paint scenes of its domestic bliss, and politely objected to unflattering depictions of its clannish customs in novels written by Edith Wharton, Henry James, and F. Scott Fitzgerald. It built yacht clubs, museums of fine arts and symphony halls, and listened to its panegyric in Cole Porter's (Yale class of 1913) Hollywood musical *High Society*. For a time, stretching from just after the Civil War until the late 1950s, America's best colleges and top professions were dominated by old-money Protestant families, WASPs,[23] who cared more about one's listing in the *Social Register* than about one's intellectual competence. Then, according to historians and journalists, meritocratic subversives got into control of admissions at Harvard and Yale, and the world of the WASP was undone.

The tale is told of how Harvard and Yale became meritocratic in the 1950s, admitting the best brains as judged by the SAT without regard to social pedigree; this allegedly produced, as the *Economist* calls it, "an academic and social revolution,"[24] first in the Ivy League and later in America's most powerful and high-paying occupations. Intellectually gifted newcomers elbowed aside the old-money Protestant gentlemen, making their way up in life through educational and corporate institutions rather than by family networks or wealth. Family privilege was dethroned, and self-made meritocrats were now in command. As David Brooks, the newspaper opinion journalist, puts it in his book on the new elite, "Admissions officers wrecked the WASP establishment."[25]

Although skepticism about the historical veracity of the preceding seems in order, accounts of the triumph of meritocracy are too numerous and influential to be ignored. The most recent in-depth version of this story is told by Nicholas Lemann, dean of the Columbia University Graduate School of Journalism, in *The Big Test*. Lemann provides a dramatic narrative, featuring Yale University, on the supplanting of WASPs or, emphasizing its Episcopalian affinities, what Lemann calls "the Episcopacy . . . [by] a new elite chosen democratically on the basis of its scholastic brilliance."[26] By the early 1960s, Lemann argues, the meritocrats had won.

Furthermore, Lemann presents a very strong case for the interpretation that meritocracy came about through the conscious efforts of WASP-insider subversives. Lemann's cabal of class traitors included James Bryant Conant, president of Harvard; Henry Chauncey, Harvard's freshman scholarship dean and founding president of the Educational Testing Service (ETS); Henry "Sam" Chauncey, Jr., Henry's son and special assistant to the president of Yale; Kingman Brewster, Yale's debonair president; and R. Inslee "Inky" Clark, Jr., Yale's young dean of admissions. They all, as Sam Chauncey told the *New York Times*, "believed in meritocracy."[27] Harvard's and Yale's presidents, their admissions deans, and the father-son Chauncey team that bridged Harvard, ETS, and Yale, were meritocracy's midwives. What Lemann said of Henry Chauncey in his *New York Times* obituary may also be attributed to the group as a whole: "Henry was [a] creature of the old elite. . . . There's some irony in the fact that he . . . work[ed] ceaselessly to replace the elite he grew up in with a new elite that he probably wouldn't have been in."[28]

Lemann's history has respectable company. Venerable sociologists, such as E. Digby Baltzell, S. M. Lipset, and David Riesman,[29] were among the first to identify the meritocratic tide, and contemporary economists and sociologists, including the editor of the *American Journal of Sociology*, continue to frame research questions with reference to meritocracy's alleged accomplishments.[30] The quality press, such as the *New York Times*[31] and the

Economist, hardly miss an opportunity to use filler from the meritocratic narrative in a range of articles, not just in those on admissions or standardized tests.[32] Major historians of higher education, such as Roger Geiger, concur on the timing and trajectory of meritocracy's ascent.[33] Even the authors of the controversial *Bell Curve* provided a brief historical sketch[34] on the victory of meritocracy that, unlike their claims on race and I.Q., was not disputed.[35] The triumph of the test-takers is part of the conventional wisdom of our age.

It is fair to say that there is a widespread consensus on the timing (the decade of the 1950s), point of origin (Harvard and Yale), and significance (the shift from social to academic selection) of higher education's meritocratic makeover. The only issue in dispute among those who subscribe to the meritocratic narrative is whether the change in the nature of admissions produced a minor or major change in the social composition of elite colleges. There are two schools of thought on the social effects of meritocratic admissions.

Those most optimistic about meritocracy, including Lemann and Brooks, believe that the Ivy League and kindred colleges were the venue where old socially selected elites were displaced by a new academically selected one in the late 1950s and early 1960s. The shift from "character" to "intellect" by the gatekeepers of academia produced a social revolution. The struggle over merit was not a sibling rivalry fought out within WASP families in which affable but dim-witted brothers in WASP families were left behind by their egghead siblings; rather, it was a conflict between families on different sides of a social divide. Meritocracy allegedly cancelled the "Episcopacy" supremacy.

There are, however, those who find this tale too optimistic. Those cautious about the impact of meritocracy, and their ranks would include Geiger and Riesman, acknowledge that all is not bright and new in the land of merit. These cautious authors offer a historically nuanced argument that places the emphasis on changes in the mechanics of elite selection. Their account may be summarized as this: the admissions process changed in the 1950s from being one determined by particularistic social connections to one driven by universalistic academic criteria. WASP families may have continued to have gotten a disproportionate number of their youths into elite colleges, but they did so thanks to the benefits of an affluent and cultured home environment and the best preparatory schooling that money could buy, whether as housing in the right neighborhood or tuition at a private school. The mechanism of selection effectively changed, from social pedigree to academic profile, and that was as far as any reasonable person could expect things to go. Children of privilege may still be winning the competition, but the rules of the race were rewritten in the 1950s and the academic contest is now essentially fair.

Meritocracy, however, also has its discontents who judge both the optimistic and the cautious versions of the story to be more myth than historical fact. A school of thought that originated with the French sociologist Pierre Bourdieu (1930–2002) finds both versions of the rise of meritocracy tale naive. Bourdieu articulated a type of symbolic competition theory of society, using baroque statistics and opaque communication skills. As Brooks pithily puts it, Bourdieu had mostly "his atrocious prose style" to blame for not being known "as the Adam Smith of the symbolic economy."[36] Bourdieu does, nonetheless, offer a sophisticated explanation as to how both families and colleges at the top manage to remain there, generation after generation.

Bourdieu's departure point is the post–Second World War expansion of higher education and the ensuing importance of educational credentials to occupations. Privileged social groups, in particular managerial and professional career families, strive to stay ahead by equipping their young with educational credentials that are more elite than those widely attained by middle- and working-class youths. The best insurance the professional/ managerial strata have that their investments in education will pay off is their patronage of a distinctly elite sector in the educational system.

Bourdieu sees every modern educational system as having a separate elite sector, whether formalized, as in France, or informal, as in the United States. At the level of higher education, in France they have the *grandes ecoles*,[37] but in the United States we have the Ivy League and its kindred private universities and liberal arts colleges. In both countries, the elite tier enrolls exactly the same relative amount, just 4 percent, of the student population. And naturally, the requirements of an elite sector presuppose the existence of a distinct non-elite sector for the unprivileged.

Bourdieu finds that prestigious colleges will protect their elite status by differentiating themselves as much as possible from their non-elite rivals. Elite colleges have a market niche and brand name to defend; in the course of doing so, they will place a different emphasis than non-elite universities on admissions criteria, the curriculum, and the extracurricular experience. If state universities, such as Michigan, have historically admitted students based on their subject-specific competence, to study mostly in the sciences while living either at home or in beehive dorms, elite private colleges, such as Yale, have selected students using aptitude tests, to study the liberal arts in residential country-club like surroundings.

Students from families with different economic and cultural resources are, according to Bourdieu, everywhere systematically sorted into elite and non-elite educational institutions. Although it was for Bourdieu a simplification, nevertheless, one could say, "students generally tend to choose the institution . . . that requires and inculcates the (aesthetic, ethical, and political) dispositions that are most similar to those inculcated by their family."[38] There is a structured harmony of student aspirations and institutional selection. For example, in the ostensibly open, yet highly stratified system of higher education in the United States, approximately 74 percent of all undergraduates attend their first-choice, and 20 percent their second-choice college—leaving minor difficulties with matching individual preference and institutional choice to a mere 6 percent.[39] It is not an exaggeration to say that college-bound youths in the United States know where they belong. And our youth's sense of place is, according to Bourdieu, determined by their inheritance of what he calls "cultural capital."

Professional/managerial strata families have the cultural capital to instill in their children the capacity and drive to succeed in schools. By cultural capital, Bourdieu means a familiarity with highbrow-cosmopolitan culture and the possession of a personal style and aspirations that resonate with teachers and admissions officers as signaling sophistication, talent, and intellectual promise. Cultural capital has been shown to enhance one's academic performance,[40] and to increase the likelihood that one will apply to, and attend, an elite school.[41]

With the benefit of Bourdieu's intellectual framework and research findings, one would not expect that either the logic of Ivy admissions or the composition of elite colleges would have changed significantly during or after the 1950s. Bourdieu would anticipate that the overriding imperative of elite admissions would be to maintain the market position of top-tier colleges by sustaining their intimate relation to upper-class families. Elite private colleges are like luxury goods firms that must sell status intangibles to a clientele rich enough to purchase the indulgence. The ultra-quality of the good and the exquisite sensibilities of the consumer are interdependent; the transaction validates both the academic excellence of the seller and the best-of-the-brightest status of the buyer. Although the cosmetic composition of students in the top tier may alter to disguise the continuity at its core, top colleges will never divest themselves of their traditional clientele. Nothing—not SAT scores, or the admission of Jews, women, or Blacks—will get in the way of the exchange between elite colleges and wealthy families.

In sum, Bourdieu would see a harmony between the market needs of elite colleges and the class interests of their clientele. The criteria used in admissions will match the qualities that privileged groups carry with them, and the result of this mutual recognition will be social reproduction disguised as a fair and meritorious academic competition. Bourdieu gives us a third way of thinking about the history of elite admissions in the United States.

In the rest of this book, we will weigh the evidence in light of these three perspectives: the optimistic, cautious, and critical visions of meritocracy. Perhaps none of them has gotten the history and sociology right, but they ask the right questions. Did the admissions' criteria or the application of it change in the 1950s or subsequently? What was the impact of the SAT on admissions? Whether or not the rules for admissions changed, were the WASPish ranks of the upper-class reduced or eliminated in elite colleges? Did alumni offspring lose their privileges? And if anything changed, was that because of internal subversives or because of external trends that elite colleges had little control over? In sum, how much inherited privilege or equal opportunity has there been in elite admissions? How responsible are elite colleges for their own performance records on privilege and opportunity? And what is the social role of America's top college tier today?

CHAPTER TWO

Elite Colleges and the Search for Superior Students

Although elite colleges in the United States are almost all private, many European countries have only public universities. With inconsequential exceptions, universities in Denmark, England, France, Germany, the Netherlands, and the Scandinavian countries, for example, are public. Elite sectors in those nations exist, yet they function within a public educational system. For example, in France, the *grandes ecoles* have always been state institutions, a step above, much smaller in size, and with substantially more difficult entry requirements than France's universities; in England's post–1946 public system, the universities of Oxford, Cambridge, and London live in a world apart from the rest. They attract a grossly disproportionate share of the most distinguished students and staff and receive significantly more funding than other public universities.[1]

Elite public institutions tend to draw from a broader social stratum than private ones do. Being dependent on the public purse, rather than on affluent families' personal savings, public elite universities can truly admit students without any regard, no matter how surreptitious, to ability to pay. They tend to be more middle class, and some even have larger representation from the working class than America's private elite colleges; for example, after the 1960s, Oxford University had four times Harvard's percent of youths from blue-collar families.[2] All of this is not to say that Oxford and other public elite universities are not skewed toward the top of the socioeconomic pyramid—they are, but less steeply than America's private elite colleges. For a comparison, look again at England's Oxford and America's Yale. The top 25 percent of American families, ranked by socioeconomic status, supply 79 percent of Yale's undergraduates; to get the same percentage of undergraduates at Oxford, one must move down England's socioeconomic status scale to include families from their top 40 percent.[3]

Public elite universities also have a different sense of mission than private ones do. Being less upper class, and more dependent on the taxpayer's favor, public elite universities tend to focus less on old traditional humanities subjects, and more on modern natural science and technology. Political and bureaucratic paymasters care less about poetry than about technology transfer. So contrary to some outdated misperceptions, the natural sciences are the largest single subject group studied at the University of Oxford, but not at Yale. Although 39 percent of Oxford's undergraduates work in the natural sciences, undergraduate science majors are approximately 17 percent at Yale.[4]

Most importantly from the standpoint of meritocracy, youths in Oxford are there because of academic scores on subject specific tests, not because of family connections or extracurricular résumés documenting an adolescence crammed with Herculean projects. Critical sociologists at Oxford, looking for the slightest signs of privilege, have thoroughly investigated the university's admissions policies and practices. They have found no advantages in admissions given to sons or daughters of alumni. Scores on subject-specific nationally standardized tests, known as "A levels," determine admissions more than any other factor. Working-class and professional-class youths with three "A" grades on their "A level" exams have statistically the same odds of getting into Oxford.[5] The same cannot be said of America's elite private colleges.

The dominance of private colleges in America's top tier is due, in the first instance, to the U.S. Constitution's delegation of the responsibility for education to the separate states.[6] We have state universities, none of which can lay claim to the nation's loyalties or to the right to set national standards. Youths in Florida do not grow up dreaming of attending the University of Wisconsin, and even if they did, Wisconsin's taxpayers would not happily subsidize a university whose composition was more national than local. Furthermore, Wisconsin cannot establish admission, curriculum, or grading criteria that will set standards for the rest of the nation; universities in California and Texas have their own ideas about how best to select and to educate undergraduates. Hobbled by the constitution, our state system has proven, so far, incapable of having as much prestige as the private sector.

Our state university system had a very promising, even noble, launch. It arose out of America's bloodiest conflict, the Civil War. In 1862, Abraham Lincoln signed the Land-Grant Act, empowering the states to use public resources to set up universities for ordinary citizens that would concentrate more on the challenges of economic development than on Latin rhetoric. The bill was originally submitted in 1857 by Congressman Justin Smith Morrill of Vermont, but it was blocked by the slave-master class in the south.[7] Between the first passage of the Land-Grant Act, when southern opposition was rendered mute by the Civil War, and its extension in 1890, the foundations for public universities were laid in every state.

The first challenge facing those universities was to find suitably prepared prospective students. One could not simply turn to local secondary schools because outside the Northeast, there were at the time very few. The public high school had to be invented as an institution to bridge the gap between state universities and primary schools. Land-grant universities, with Michigan leading the way, played a central role in the movement to build public high schools. In 1871, Michigan pioneered the certification system that set the pattern for state universities, particularly in the Midwest and West, to help create, certify, and inspect high schools with a college preparatory curriculum so that their seniors, like the products of a German *Gymnasium*, would be on graduation granted entry to land-grant universities. After the Michigan Supreme Court ruled in 1874 that tax money could be spent on high schools, the institution started to spread within and beyond the state. In 1870, only 2 percent of America's seventeen-year-olds had a high-school education, by 1919 that percentage had leaped to 17 percent, and by 1930 to 32 percent of the youth cohort.[8] We largely owe the existence of public high schools across the nation to the certification campaign pushed by state universities.[9]

Certification put public universities and public high schools into a working relationship that benefited both; universities set the standards and monitored compliance, and high schools sent academically prepared youths to the universities. When the American Council on Education held a conference on admissions in 1932, it noted that certification "is followed in more than 90 per cent of American college admissions."[10] Between 1871 and the 1960s, most students at a university or a four-year college gained admission by graduating from high school with good grades in specified courses, not by taking any type of entry examination.[11]

The certification system, despite its many virtues, was not uniform or durable across the nation. It broke down under the weight of numbers. It was one thing for state universities in 1890 to monitor the education of approximately 22,000 public high-school seniors in the whole nation, but quite another to cope with the 1,435,000 public high-school graduates of 1959.[12] When the systems broke down, standardized tests of the sort preferred by the private sector assumed a much larger role nationally than before in college admissions. In the Midwest and the South, state universities started using standardized tests after 1959, when a University of Iowa psychology professor, E. F. Lindquist, launched American College Testing (ACT) achievement exams as a curriculum-based alternative to the Scholastic Aptitude Test (SAT). On the West Coast, certification lasted longer, but when the University of California began using standardized tests in 1968, it adopted the SAT.[13] It remains unresolved just how much educational standards have suffered nationally since the 1960s rupture between state universities and public high schools.

Although state universities failed to serve as national institutions, there were two alternative candidates: military schools and private colleges. It is an irony of our republic that our only truly national public universities have been military academies. We have the Army's West Point, the Navy's Annapolis, the Coast Guard Academy, and the Air Force Academy; all but the last one are in America's most selective and prestigious elite tier. Given their military callings, those academies could not be the models for universities across the nation; however, neither state's rights nor military obligations prevented our private colleges from successfully performing a premier national role.

The Consolidation of the Private Sector

Our private colleges and universities mostly grew, like Yale, out of the nation's religious diversity. Each competing church, from Calvinist to Southern Baptists, started its own college between the seventeenth and nineteenth centuries for the education of its clergy. Then worldly success, secularism, and privileged social groups overtook most of them by the end of the nineteenth century.

Private colleges tried to keep their distance from public high schools and the certification method of college entry. Northeastern colleges, with Harvard and Yale in the lead, imitated the universities of Oxford and Cambridge by requiring their own entry examinations.[14] To pool their efforts, those colleges established the College Board (CB) in 1900, as a private association for the design and administration of admissions tests.[15]

In the early stages of the College Board's history, not every private college relied exclusively on its examinations. Some, including Amherst, Dartmouth, and Williams, accepted certificate candidates, but they were disparaged by Yale, Harvard, and Princeton (known as "the Big Three") for doing so.[16] As Yale's dean of admissions explained, "It is easier for a boy to enter another college for which examinations are not required than it is to get into Yale." The dean believed, "The majority of the boys who shift [their application] from Yale to a certificate college [like Dartmouth] are not very strong candidates."[17] Not wanting to be seen as academic lightweights, Dartmouth and the others fell in line with Yale's preference for exams. Competitive pressures from the Big Three persuaded the rest of the private sector of the idea that exams were superior to high-school certification as a way to judge a youth's academic merit.

There were social-class and market reasons for the divide between a private-college/entry-examination system, on one side, and a public-university/high-school certification system, on the other. Public universities were more middle class and local than were private colleges that attracted a socially privileged and, if not national, at least regional student body. And after 1890, public institutions could depend on annual appropriations of federal and state funds[18]; private ones had to rely on the tuition fees and endowments contributed by their affluent constituents.

Although public universities were, with oversight, delegating the responsibility to public secondary schools to evaluate fitness for higher education,

CB exams sustained the prerogatives of private colleges to make all of their own choices. Private colleges could assert that their exams set higher and more impartial standards of evaluation than high schools, which helped to ensure that when individuals from privileged class backgrounds were being selected, they could claim academic merit rather than ability to pay was what really mattered.

Separate from the exam's usefulness for disguising social selection as selection for academic superiority, there were market reasons for private colleges to retain control over admissions. There were more physical and economic constraints on the size of undergraduate classes at private than at public institutions. As residential institutions with limited space and without a legislative and tax-based mandate supporting the accommodation of additional qualified applicants, private colleges wanted individual exams as a sorting tool to justify the exclusion of any particular individual.

The School and Highbrow Nexus

Private colleges were remote options for most Americans because of their cost. If one's family could afford a private prep-school education, then, when the time came, one might be in the market for a private college. Fortuitously for Yale and its peers, the private-school market had a mini boom at the end of the nineteenth century.

The social demand for prep schools was created partially in response to the certification campaign to build public high schools, but the more proximate stimulus for boarding schools came from the recent growth of wealth at the top of our society. It was a time in American history when wealthy families were sufficiently affluent to reach beyond local boundaries to those similarly privileged elsewhere through a network of clubs, cultural institutions, schools, and colleges. In the process, they gained a sense of themselves as a national upper class.

Boarding schools were built when America's old-money families sought to consolidate themselves as a cohesive group in contrast to the *nouveaux riches* thrown up by post–Civil War industrialization.[19] Prep schools were part of a class wall separating old privilege from upstarts. All of America's top-twelve boarding schools were founded or reconstituted between 1883 and 1906.[20] Private schools prided themselves on their large number of graduates who went on to elite colleges, and those colleges were pleased to return the esteem. Yale was quite happy to nurture warm relations with boarding "feeder" schools, particularly Andover, Choate, Exeter, Hotchkiss, Lawrenceville, and St. Paul's, which supplied many of Yale's undergraduate gentlemen.

The examination system organized by the College Board was a bridge between boarding-school students and private colleges, and a barrier to public-school youths. Private prep schools prepared their students for their college boards; there was a tight fit between their curriculum and the tests. And many, if not most, of their seniors would participate in the week-long exam marathon. One's parents factored in the examination expenses as part of the cost of a private education. In contrast, if one were a public high-school student thinking about taking the CB tests, one had to prepare for exams that were foreign to one's school culture, travel to a test site, and pay the unusual fees and expenses of the procedure. Very few, if any, of one's peers would be sharing the experience, and one's teachers and counselors were not well informed or particularly encouraging about that path. The distance between public schools and the exam system was still being felt a half century later by the College Board's director, Frank Bowles, when, on taking office in 1948, he faced the "built-in hostility from the majority of the public secondary school administrators . . . [who resented] the Board as agent and symbol of the so-called exclusive private colleges."[21]

The late-nineteenth-century emergence of a self-conscious upper class required, in addition to boarding schools, visible displays of social pedigree and cultural superiority. The *Social Register* was created in 1886; being able to trace a family's lineage in its pages, including degrees from elite colleges, became part of what was expected of members of the upper crust. Between the 1880s and the 1920s, families listed in the Boston or New York *Social Register* with college-educated sons sent, respectively, 91 percent and 83 percent of them to one of six private colleges: Columbia, Harvard, MIT, Princeton, Williams, or Yale.[22] But elite colleges were just part of a cultural complex conferring a sense of collective identity on the privileged class. Museums, concert halls, and theaters were their new temples of highbrow Europhile culture.[23] In major cities, during the 1870s and 1880s, fine arts museums and symphony halls were built for gentlemen and their families;

the unwashed were kept out by a variety of means, including exclusionary codes of dress and etiquette. The most dramatic case of usurping a popular form of entertainment to transform it into an element of highbrow culture was the fate of Shakespeare in America. Once, to judge by authorities as various as John Quincy Adams and Alexis de Tocqueville, Shakespeare's works were nearly as common in American homes as copies of the Bible.[24] He was even part of the everyday cultural repertoire of our urban working class. Attending a Saturday night play by Shakespeare with one's work-mates, drink and food in hand, was a regular feature of masculine, urban, working-class culture from the 1820s through the 1850s. Workers in the theater's pit would control the action on the stage, demanding repeats of lines delivered well or dismissal of wooden performers. Then, beginning with the Astor Place Opera House massacre in New York, when ten thousand turned out to protest the arrogance of British actors, and twenty-two workers were shot down by the police, the rowdy common man was removed from the theater.[25] By the 1870s, Shakespearian actors had been rescued from food-throwing-Richard-III-quoting urban workers and ensconced in respectable theaters for the edification of the well off. Cultural hierarchy was matched by geographic and social segregation. New palatial mansions went up in Newport, Rhode Island, and other coastal enclaves, and survival-of-the-richest social Darwinism had its American spokesperson William Graham Sumner, Yale's first professor of sociology, to explain how welfare was immoral and ineffective, and why the upper class owed the lower social classes nothing.[26]

Eugenics and IQ Tests

Sumner was one of Yale's most popular professors; in the 1880s, very few Yale men could consider their education complete without at least sitting in on his lectures.[27] His survival-of-the-fittest social doctrines, published in 1883, coincided with the creation in England by Charles Darwin's cousin, Sir Francis Galton, of a new science. Galton called it *eugenics;* it was to be a science of genetic selection to ensure the upward evolution of the race. The socially unfit, congregated in "inferior" ethnic groups, were to be restricted and discouraged from reproduction, by sterilization if necessary, and the superior race, frequently referred to in America as the "Nordic race," were to be given the laws and schools that would allow them to flourish.

In the United States, the eugenic message was well received by many members of the White Anglo-Saxon Protestant (WASP) establishment. It harmonized with their sense of social and cultural superiority and fit so perfectly with anti-Black and anti-immigrant prejudice that prominent American scientists and politicians took up the cause with religious-like fervor. Daniel G. Brinton, president of the American Association for the Advancement of Science, located Negroes "midway between the Orangutang [*sic*] and the European White," and, in 1895, he pronounced that it was the task of science to supply "a positive basis for legislation, politics, and education as applied to a given ethnic group."[28] The next year, the Supreme Court performed its part by making racial apartheid the law of the nation in *Plessy v. Ferguson* (1896). In 1918, New York eugenicists formed the Galton Society, whose monthly meetings took place in the office of its co-founder, Henry Fairfield Osborn, the president of the board for the American Museum of Natural History. The other founder, Osborn's dear friend and champion of the Nordic race, was Madison Grant, author of *The Passing of the Great Race* (1916). Although the first, 1912, International Congress of Eugenics met in London, the New York museum hosted the second, 1921, and third, 1932, congresses.[29] Restricting immigration, sterilizing the unfit, and measuring racial intelligence through head size or intelligence quotient (IQ) tests were the passions of New York's Galton Society.

Eugenicists scored some important victories in the 1920s. The 1924 immigration bill that excluded Jews and Japanese, and cut to a trickle the flow of Mediterranean and Eastern European families, was "the brainchild of Albert Johnson, a Washington State Republican and the honorary president of the Eugenics Research Association."[30] As the *New Yorker* author Claudia Roth Pierpont reports, "The bill passed in the House by a vote of 326–71 and in the Senate by 62–6; it was signed into law by President Coolidge with the words, 'America must be kept American.'"[31] In 1927, the Supreme Court ruled in favor of compulsory sterilization for the unfit. Associate Justice Oliver Wendell Holmes, a Boston Brahmin and Harvard graduate, uttered from the bench the infamous, "Three generations of imbeciles are enough." The designation "imbeciles" was, Pierpont notes, "derived from supposedly precise categories established by the new I.Q.

tests; that year, hospitals throughout the country began to perform the operations."[32]

Eugenicists loved the new IQ science that blossomed in the 1920s. Before IQ exams, the intelligence of racial groups had been measured by head sizes; it was called the science of craniometry. "Nordic" brains were allegedly bigger than "Mediterranean" or "Negro" ones, but the research associating head size with intellect and racial type was shaky even by the standards of the time. There were big-brained criminals and small-brained famous men.[33] IQ tests seemed to offer more reliable and consistent measures of differences between racial groups than clumsy craniometry. Alfred Binet in France gave birth to the concept of an IQ in 1908[34]; and shortly afterwards, during the carnage of the First World War, Harvard's Robert M. Yerkes administered "mental tests to 1.75 million [army] recruits" to lay the foundations for an empirical science of IQ.[35]

A dedicated eugenicist at the College Board, Carl Brigham, saw the relevance of the new science to college admissions. Brigham was a leading member of the board. He was a professor of psychology at Princeton, and his credentials as someone who worked on the science of IQ testing were established in 1923, when he published under the university's imprimatur a eugenicist book, *A Study of American Intelligence*. Brigham's book bemoaned the downward trajectory of American intelligence because of the "promiscuous intermingling" of America's four racial groups.[36]

Brigham saw himself as a scientist on a scientific mission. His work drew on Yerkes' Army tests, which reportedly revealed the racial rationing of intelligence in the United States. According to Brigham, "At one extreme we have the distribution of the Nordic race group. At the other extreme we have the American [N]egro. Between the Nordic and the [N]egro, but closer to the [N]egro than to the Nordic, we find the Alpine and Mediterranean types."[37] "Nordic" for Brigham and the other American eugenicists did not mean German, they were classified as Alpine; Brigham's and others' Nordic race came out of northwest Europe and included the British Isles. The term *Nordic* changed its meaning after the rise of Adolf Hitler, but one may see Brigham's and other eugenicist's use of the word as synonymous with *WASP*. In summing up his findings, Brigham wrote,

> According to all evidence available, then, American intelligence is declining, and will proceed with an accelerating rate as the racial admixture

becomes more and more extensive. The decline of American intelligence will be more rapid than the decline of the intelligence of European national groups, owing to the presence here of the [N]egro. These are the plain, if somewhat ugly, facts that our study shows. The deterioration of American intelligence is not inevitable, however, if public action can be aroused to prevent it. There is no reason why legal steps should not be taken which would insure a continuously progressive upward evolution.

The steps that should be taken to preserve or increase our present intellectual capacity must of course be dictated by science.[38]

The science of intelligence testing revealed for Brigham the superiority of the Nordic race, and now scientific intelligence tests should help ensure their social health through various legal and institutional measures, including the selection of their best for the benefits of an elite education.

Brigham's home college, Princeton, was first to register, in the same year as the publication of his book, a request with the College Board for the creation of an IQ admission test.[39] Yale's call for one came on February 16, 1925, after its admissions board listened to a report from Dr. Anderson of Yale's psychology department detailing the virtues of intelligence tests as aids in selecting students. The board's minutes show, "Voted: That the Board of Admissions favors the preparation and setting of Intelligence Tests by the College Entrance Examination Board."[40]

The search by the College Board for an IQ admissions test became under Brigham's direction the project to create the SAT.[41] The SAT was to be a tool of scientific social selection. It was logical that if intelligence was inheritable and tied to race, then a scholastic aptitude test for college admissions would work to select for Nordics and against all other ethnic groups.

The social exclusionary effects of the College Board's exams were never a higher priority for Yale, Harvard, and Princeton than when the SAT was introduced in 1926. Administrators and admissions deans at private colleges across New England hoped that the SAT would be an IQ test on which WASPs would do well and Jews would do badly.[42] Even though it may be hard for us to imagine, anti-Semitism was an accepted attribute of WASP society in the first half of the twentieth century. Eugenicists and social Darwinists both saw Jews as an inferior race. And in the 1920s, Jews, not Negroes, were the pressing threat.

European Jewish families who arrived in the New York metropolitan area before the 1924 immigration bill had raised boys who did exceptionally well in public schools and they were now, in the 1920s, knocking on the doors of private colleges. CB tests on particular subjects, such as chemistry, were not an insurmountable obstacle to bright and hard-working Jewish boys. Columbia University was the first to suffer from the Jewish meritocratic invasion. Within a decade, Jewish youths went from an insignificant percentage of Columbia's undergraduates to more than 40 percent.[43] The Jewish influx brought a precipitous drop in Social Register and other WASP families as they fled Columbia for racially purer bucolic colleges.[44] Yale, Harvard, and Princeton were appalled by the prospect of suffering a similar fate. Like Columbia University, the Big Three had been using CB subject entrance exams since 1915, and they thought that if subject exams could not keep Jews out, then IQ tests would.

When the SAT was introduced, its single biggest customer in the 1920s was Yale. Between 1926 and 1929, nearly 20 percent of all students taking the SAT each year gave Yale as their college choice.[45] In those days, test scores were reported only to institutions, never to individual students.

Yale obliged all applicants, not just scholarship candidates, to take the SAT because of Brigham's classification of Jews as Mediterranean types, and his "scientific" finding that they performed less well than Nordic types on IQ tests. As Dan Oren, a historian of Jews at Yale, explains,

> In 1926 the board [of admissions at Yale] adopted the last of Corwin's [the admissions dean] "Jewish Problem" recommendations . . . and voted to require that applicants sit for the new "scholastic aptitude test" . . . [T]he aptitude tests were expected to weigh more heavily against Jewish examinees than against non-Jews.[46]

The SAT was embraced by Yale's leaders because it fit their cultural mindset. They subscribed to the notion that Protestant, and usually wealthy, boys were genuinely more intellectually gifted than other social groups, and the administration's experience with the science of assessing intelligence confirmed for them the correctness of that belief.

Before the invention of the SAT, Yale kept track of the performance of alumni sons, legacies, its tribal version of pure-blood Nordics, on tests and grades in comparison with everyone else in the class. For the entry years of 1920 to 1923, legacies consistently achieved higher test scores and scholastic averages than non-legacies. Those statistics were taken as "objective" evidence that Yale's sons were smarter than the rest.[47]

Yale's leaders were convinced, culturally and scientifically, of the superiority of their own kind. They were, however, also aware of the conflicting reality that ambitious and hard-working Jewish and non-Jewish lower-class youths could, by virtue of what Yale disdainfully dismissed as rote memorization by "grinds," master the materials of an academic subject. Yale wanted an IQ or psychological aptitude test that would separate the truly brilliant Nordic stock from Alpine or Mediterranean individuals who were academically deviant from their racial types by virtue of hard work. Yale wanted a test to sort between those with gifts and those with mere academic cramming. And an IQ-type aptitude test would differentiate Yale from public universities that relied on grades in particular high-school subjects. Only an IQ type test would do because an achievement test demonstrating what one learned in high school was for Yale too narrow to reveal the qualities desirable in a liberal arts community.

At the Yale Admission Board meeting that endorsed IQ tests, board members also voted to place a cap on the size of incoming freshman classes. Yale's restriction on class size was a first, and it was intended as a policy, along with the IQ test, to keep out socially undesirable students. The board was not, however, going to take chances with the sons of alumni being excluded, so it decided to exempt them from any numerical restrictions.

This vote created another first, the official policy of giving "legacy" advantages to sons of Yale graduates. The board recorded, "Voted: That limitation of numbers shall not operate to exclude any son of a Yale graduate who has satisfied all the requirements for admission."[48] This double move was typical of Yale's institutional posture toward merit and privilege. Yale desired "scientific" proof of the superiority of its traditional clientele, but it would not rely exclusively on objective scientific devices to take care of its own. Separate standards to advantage their sons were used from the very beginning of selective admissions in the 1920s.

The SAT and CB exams were tools for drawing boundaries between Yale's Protestant clientele and, as Yale's historian George Pierson put it, "the ignorant many [who] were coming out for their letters."[49] CB exams helped hold back the tide of "immigrants and the children of immigrants, who because of their humble origins knew nothing of the liberal arts or regarded them as aristocratic." Pierson did not call the immigrants Jews; he did not have to for his audience. In Pierson's opinion, CB exams saved Yale from the fate of "state universities, dependent as they were on legislative support, [who] had to accept the high-school certificates for admission."[50] Even halfway measures between certification and examination, such as uniform state exit exams, would not do; they would connect too directly to the weak standards and lower-class constituency of public high schools. When a state-exam option was placed on the agenda at Yale, it was rejected. Yale's admissions board voted, "New York State Regents certificate [was] not acceptable as substitute for CB exams."[51]

The SAT gave Yale a seemingly meritocratic way to exclude undesirables on top of a variety of other tools of discrimination. Yale's President James Rowland Angell, quite familiar with Brigham's theories, used eugenicist racial categories when he offensively joked in a letter to the admissions dean, Robert N. Corwin, about Yale's "Jewish problem." Angell's letter was written in 1933, after Hitler had come to power in Germany; he referred to Armenians as a historic reference point, but clearly he had Jews in mind. Angell wrote, "If we could have an Armenian massacre confined to the New Haven district, with occasional incursions into Bridgeport and Hartford, we might protect our Nordic stock almost completely."[52] Yale kept track of those Jews who slipped past its gatekeepers. The admissions office and the president's office knew that most of Yale's Jewish students were from Angell's three massacre-wish-list cities in Connecticut. Yale's drive for a wider geographical distribution in the 1920s was in part an anti-Semitic tactical maneuver.

Yale devised various supplemental methods after the introduction of the SAT for identifying and rejecting Jewish applicants in the 1920s and 1930s. One means was to compel disclosures on the application form. As Dean Corwin stated in a letter to President Angell,

> The blanks as they now stand require the full name and birthplace of the father of each applicant and the maiden name of the mother. These items, together with the comments of principals and headmasters, rarely leave us in doubt as to the ethnological classification of the applicant. It seemed best, therefore, for the present at least, not to alarm our public by asking questions [about religion] which might seem to indicate a sudden anti-Semitic attitude.[53]

Corwin wrote "sudden," but the point was not the age of the policy but, rather, its visibility. It was part of the admissions office's job to disguise social exclusion. Yale also refused to even consider college transfer applicants if their home addresses were in any of the three cities selected by Angell for hypothetical ethnic cleansing.[54] Those simple methods of exclusion were efficient. When Corwin provided the president with a table titled, "Distribution of Jews in Connecticut in the Classes of 1930–34," he could write,

> I trust that you will be favorably impressed with the figures for the Class of 1934. In this connection it might be stated that the result shown, . . . was attained without hue and cry and without any attempt on the part of those chiefly affected to prove that Yale had organized a pogrom.[55]

Although anti-Semitic searches through applicant files worked, Yale's leaders noticed that there were difficulties with the dual roles assigned to the SAT. It was designed to screen out Jews and to predict freshman grades. It did neither. Not catching Jews was bad enough, but test scores were also not strongly correlated with college performance. The SAT was not the scientific IQ instrument they hoped it would be.

Yale's "Predicted Grade" Formula

Yale kept track, beginning with the first class required to take the SAT, of how well various measures of academic ability correlated with grades received in the freshman year. By 1929, enough data had accumulated that a study was produced by a member of Yale's admissions board showing that SAT scores poorly matched college classroom evaluations.[56] In response to the problem, Yale devised its own "scientific" system for predicting academic performance. The dilemma was that, in addition to social exclusionary concerns, Yale did care about the intellectual validity of its selection procedures. Yale's administration and admissions staff felt a need to devise their own in-house mathematical formula for picking academic winners and excluding losers to surpass what the College Board could offer.

Given the failings of the SAT, Yale had ideological, status, and economic reasons for wanting to develop its own system for predicting how candidates for admission would do academically in their first year. First, the ideology of academic "excellence" was an element in Yale's institutional culture in the 1920s. The Nordic race was supposed to be smarter than the rest. The administration viewed Yale as one of the great universities of the world, entitled to the highest academic standards. Being able to predict what a boy would be able to do academically in his freshman year and picking undergraduates by that forecast was, in the minds of administrators and faculty, a legitimate way to sustain Yale's excellence. Second, regardless of the SAT's weak predictive record, Yale could not just use the more reliable indicators of school grades and school rank for entry because that would remove a key status-market distinction between it and public land-grant universities. To abandon aptitude tests for high-school grades would put private colleges and public universities into competition for the same student market, and that would erode the exclusive status pretensions of the private sector. Third, there was a financial incentive in being able to recognize and exclude poor performers.

As a private college, Yale wanted to do what it could to avoid admitting boys who would drop out or flunk out and stop paying fees. Yale's budget required a fixed number of boys in each year paying full tuition. State universities could afford to admit poor bets. Being subsidized by the taxpayer, it was politically more acceptable to fail youths who could not measure up, or to allow them to drop out, than it was to exclude them at the front gate. A study sponsored by the National Educational Association in 1927 found that at state universities, "We have but a half of our entrance group remaining until graduation."[57] Private colleges were compelled by their finances to follow the reverse strategy: exclude at the gate, select for those who will last to pay four full years worth of tuition, room, and board.

The prospect of undergraduate shrinkage was especially alarming in the early years of the SAT because of the Great Depression. At the time, Angell went on a campaign to cushion the financial blow by casting a wider admissions net than usual. Angell was probably aware that except for a few unusual years, Yale had always received more income from tuition, room, and board than from any other source.[58] He wrote to the Yale college dean,

> The University is sufficiently dependent upon its income from tuition to make any large shrinkage at this point a matter of grave financial consequence. I am writing to ask you, as Dean of Yale College, to deal with applications for transfer from other colleges as leniently as you conscientiously can, and for the same reason. I am naturally entirely averse to any relaxation of our essential academic standards, but there are always border-line cases which hitherto we have been glad to decline for entrance by standing on our technical specifications, and in a certain percentage of these instances the

men concerned would probably have proved perfectly safe and reputable investments.[59]

The Dean's response brought Angell up short because of the ever-present Jewish peril. Dean C. H. Warren replied,

> I have . . . some misgivings about increasing very much the admissions by transfer. For the last two or three years at least the great majority of these applications have been from young gentlemen of Hebrew persuasion who are anxious to come here for the purpose of preparing for medical work. In my opinion there are very few of these who are really desirable students, and among those who appear to be fairly desirable, there are almost none who do not apply for substantial scholarship aid.[60]

Although Yale perceived Jews as poor material intellectually and financially, it also did not want to pick deficient WASPs. Yale wanted to embrace just those WASPs who would stay the course—and pay their bills. And it needed a more accurate way than the SAT to identify academically strong WASPs. Consequently, Yale constructed its own method of predicting freshman grades.

Yale was not the only elite college to notice problems from its inception with the SAT as an admissions tool. While Yale was busy devising a "predicted grade" formula, Princeton was for identical reasons working on what it called a "bogey" system. Both methods were ways of mathematically attributing to each applicant a score that would predict his grade point average at the end of his first year in college. Princeton's bogey and Yale's predicted grade quickly became a regular step in the admissions evaluation process.

Six years after the introduction of the SAT, in November 1933, Professor Brigham, the eugenicist, delivered a talk at a CB meeting on whether various measuring sticks, including CB tests, could predict academic performance. He said,

> As everyone knows, all correlations which have ever been found between examinations and college standing are too low to give any feeling of certainty. The low correlations obtained from single tests and examinations led people to try to combine the results of several kinds of evidence into a single index by the use of multiple correlation methods. The Princeton "bogie" and the Yale "predicted grade" are typical of such combinations.

These indices correlate about .65 or .70 with college standing, and thus provide usable betting systems, . . . Professor Crawford can explain the Yale method and I will explain the method used at Princeton. The Yale method is better.[61]

The Yale "predicted grade" algorithm, its measuring stick, was used by its admissions office to give each applicant an academic score, beginning in 1930 with the Class of 1934.[62] The algorithm weighted the school records, CB subject exams, and the SAT to derive a number usually between 50 and 100 that would be written on the applicant's record as his academic score. (The scale's scores translated into letter grades, with 100–90 = A, 89–80 = B, 79–70 = C, 69–60 = D, and 59 and below = F.)[63]

The formula for calculating a candidate's school record was incredibly elaborate. From 1926 forward, records were kept grouping each boy admitted to Yale with his secondary-school cohorts for the last five years. Their freshman college grades were compared with their high-school grades and class rank, enabling Yale to see how well those measures correlated. A statistical adjustment was assigned to each school with at least five boys attending Yale that reflected how reliable that school's records were in predicting performance, regardless of whether that freshman's performance was poor, average, or superb. This was a form of behind-closed-doors audit of individual secondary schools. Rather than do what public land-grant universities did, which was to inspect and certify the high school itself, Yale evaluated how each school's grading scale compared with its own and then kept the results to itself.

Paul Burnham, the research director on Yale's admissions procedures, explained the process to an administrator at Vassar College when, in 1947, they were considering adopting something similar. Burnham told her,

> We have been using multiple regression forecasting procedures to predict the freshman averages of applicants to Yale for a period of well over 15 years. . . . We have been analyzing the records of our own applicants from one year to another and thus building up a body of experience including forecasting formulae based upon actual data. . . . Our experience has been that analyses have to be made yearly in order that our forecasting formulae may be kept up to date, . . . in other words, this process of prediction is a continuing process based not upon subjective opinions but upon analysis of actual data. . . . The success of any method of prediction for college

entrance is partly dependent upon the reliability of the college grades which one is trying to predict. . . . [O]ver the years since about 1930, when we first started making predictions here at Yale, our predictions have correlated approximately .70 with subsequently achieved freshman averages. . . . [O]ur particular formulae might be of little use to you simply because your academic situation may be different from ours.[64]

The Vassar administration was invited to send someone down to New Haven to study Yale's methods in detail.

Burnham, in a memo to Donald Walker in the admissions office, provided the approximate formulae used to calculate each applicant's academic score. Burnham warned, "This is an oversimplification but probably will serve." And then he offered a short text and a table showing three models with different data weights:

With reference to your inquiry about the relative weights of different factors entering into our scholastic predictions, I think these can most simply be expressed by the table below. Group A includes boys from schools where the adjusted rank in class data have proved, from past experience, to be the most reliable; Group I those for which they are next most reliable, and Group II and III those from schools where rank in class or average grades are most difficult to evaluate with assurance. Naturally the relative weight accorded to SGA (School Grade Adjusted) is highest for the first and lowest for the second and third of these groups. SAT refers to the Verbal section of the Scholastic Aptitude Test and the sum of 4 CB [refers] to the average of the four other College Board tests [including the math section of the SAT]. It is obvious that the weight accorded these varies inversely with the dependence we can place upon school grade data. [See Table 2.1.]

TABLE 2.1

Approximate Weights in Grade Prediction.

Factor	Group A	Group I	Group II & III
SGA	.70	.66	.50
SAT (Rounded)	.16	.16	.10
4 CB (Rounded)	.14	.18	.40
	1.00	1.00	1.00*

* Paul Burnham, "Memo to Donald K. Walker, 3 March 1949," *Old Bogey Book* (New Haven, CT: Office of Institutional Research, 1950).

Contrary to all the emphasis Yale placed publicly on entry exams, it is significant that internally it had more statistical confidence in secondary-school grades than in any other single source of data. Even if one came from a relatively unreliable or new-to-Yale's-list school, one's grades carried the most weight. If previous cohorts from one's school performed at Yale consistent with their school grades, then 70 percent of one's academic score would be based on one's transcript, 16 percent based on the verbal SAT, and 14 percent on four other CB tests. However, if one came from a school with an unreliable grading record, then 50 percent was calculated from one's transcript, 40 percent from four CB tests, and 10 percent from the verbal SAT. The better Yale's track record was at matching a particular school's students' grade point averages with their freshman grades, the more Yale treated the school as being, in a sense, "certified" to grade. Secondary school performance was for Yale the most crucial measure of academic merit. As early as 1935, Albert Crawford in the admissions office reported to President Angell, "Our records entitle us to the generalization that a boy ranking in the top 1/10 of his class in almost any school is likely to produce a creditable record at Yale."[65] And twenty years later, Burnham was still explaining the importance of school record at a convocation of Yale alumni serving on admissions interview committees across the nation. In a talk titled, "The Statistical Evaluation of Academic Ability," he told them, our

> adjusted secondary school grade correlates reasonably well with college work. Indeed, the general finding of many years of research here and at other institutions is that the secondary school record, when properly handled, provides the best single indicator of potential success in college.[66]

It is quite striking that the predicted grade formula in use since 1930 gave the verbal SAT its own weight, whereas the math part of the SAT was folded in with three CB subject tests. Perhaps because Yale viewed itself as a liberal arts community, it valued the verbal SAT score as a more reliable measure of intellectual fitness than the math score. Regardless of conscious intent, however, the impact was discriminatory.

Intellectual ability is not reducible to one's vocabulary. Social-class origins and ethnic communities are powerfully reflected in one's language.[67] In time, critics would point out that the verbal section of the SAT was more contaminated than the math section, or even the subject SAT II tests, by cultural bias.[68] It is easier to embed the cultural references of a particular social group in the meaning of words, in vocabulary, than in mathematical equations. If one wanted to design a test to sort for family SES background, a verbal aptitude test would do a better job at that than would a math achievement test. For the 1930s, however, there is nothing in the archive that suggests that Yale consciously understood the social-class disparities contained in the verbal section of the SAT. Decades would pass before researchers would display the full extent of SES distortion in the verbal SAT. Yale's early decision to prioritize the verbal score fit the cultural biases of a socially privileged liberal arts community, and that choice sat nicely with Yale's WASPish clientele.

The practice of counting the verbal SAT more than the math exam in the 1930s was carried over well into the allegedly meritocratic 1960s, under both Arthur Howe, Jr.'s and R. Inslee "Inky" Clark, Jr.'s admissions deanships. In September 1960, for example, Howe explained in a report to the Yale faculty on admissions, "Every analysis of [Yale] college performance in relationship to aptitude suggest[s] that, regardless of the field of major interest, greater significance should be assigned to the verbal score."[69] Howe shared that information with the executive committee of the Alumni Board, in October of that same year.[70] And, during Clark's time in office, the Chairman of the Alumni Schools Committee on Admissions, George Cook, repeated the point to the Executive Committee of the Alumni Association, that the "verbal score [was] . . . the test score given the greatest weight by the Admissions Committee."[71] In the 1990s, if account of the former assistant director of admissions at Dartmouth, Michele Hernandez, is correct, it was still common in the Ivy League to value the verbal over the mathematical SAT.[72]

Character and Connections in Admissions: The Allegedly Bad Old Days

Predicted grade scores were taken so seriously by the Yale administration that even in the dark days of the Great Depression, nothing could get a boy into Yale if its academic formulae put him below the line—not legacy status, or prep school records, or personal ties to administrators, or even White House connections. Contrary to the optimistic and cautious versions of the meritocratic tale, "character" did not trump "intellect" even when Yale was most in need of fee-paying boys. Admissions in the allegedly bad old days before the 1960s rise of meritocracy were not all about social status.

Yale's intellectual standards and financial interests combined to force it to exclude even its own legacy applicants when they were sub par. For example, in 1930, Angell wrote a distraught Yale man[73] whose son was rejected,

> I am extremely sorry that your boy should have had so unhappy a time about his college entrance, and I am only able to assure you, as you already know, that the Board of Admissions gave the most careful and extended consideration to the young man's application. . . . Our experience over many years makes it as nearly certain as anything human can be that a boy coming in with an entrance record of that kind would inevitably be dropped early in the Freshman Year.[74]

The father, wanting a chance for his son, saw an important "difference in having the boy dropped after entrance [rather than] . . . rejected before entrance." Referring to Yale's formulae for admissions, he wrote, "Of course, I know how busy the 'Board of Admission' must be during the period the boys are being chosen, and the work is made easier by having a fixed measuring stick, but I do think that the first consideration should be 'Yale for Yale men.'"[75] Angell offered to cancel the father's subscription to the endowment fund, if that would make him feel any better, but Yale was not dropping its measuring stick.

Legacy status did not help even if one had a "good record at Hotchkiss," one of the private prep-school feeders to Yale, and a rich banker for a father. On September 17, 1934, the president's office at Yale received a Western Union telegram from a Yale graduate on behalf of a classmate's son. The telegram stated,

> In view of his three brothers being all Yale graduates as well as his father who is one of the leading financial men of the country and because as I understand the boy has a good record at Hotchkiss . . . [his father] was my classmate and personal friend and I would like very much to see his youngest son complete the family group as a member of the Yale family.[76]

The Admissions Board held a private conference with the father, but his son was still denied a place in the freshman class.[77]

The Special Assistant to the Secretary of State, writing a personal appeal to President Angell on White House stationary, could not get his boy into Yale. The Special Assistant argued against what he saw as an excessive reliance on academic criteria in admissions. He pleaded,

> I did not for a minute mean to suggest that the College pick out one boy and make a particular ruling in his case. What I had in mind was a general

principle which I thought applicable in the case of my son and which I am positive from the talks I have had with other fathers could be applied with equally desirable results in many other cases. The principle is simply that at Yale recognition could be given to a boy's general character and worthwhileness [sic] in addition to marks arising strictly from his studies. I feel that Yale does not exhaust its possibilities for contributing to the national welfare by confining the test of undergraduates to marks alone.[78]

The appeal fell on unresponsive ears.

Personal ties also could not do what political connections failed to accomplish. The admissions request from the president of a Philadelphia engineering company, who worked in the U.S. War Department with Yale's president, was turned down. He wrote, "My dear Angell: When you and I were in the War Department, you said, 'If there is anything I can ever do for you, let me know, and I will be glad to do it.' Of course this is so many years ago, you may have forgotten it, and not until the present have I wished to cash in on your promise."[79] Time spent in bureaucratic war trenches, however, did not bind; Yale's president put intellectual standards above a personal pledge.

Many fathers and their classmates in the 1930s pressed the same argument as the Special Assistant from the State Department in response to a rejection letter or suspension from Yale. They argued character against intellect. Speaking especially for Yale fathers in the New York area, one alumnus wrote a letter about a classmate's son to Dean Percy T. Walden. The alumnus explained,

> The family [in question] have always been loyal and faithful Yale adherents, and young [boy's name] has always stated he would go to Yale or nowhere.— He is a fine youngster and will, I think, turn into a useful citizen—and a loyal Yale man, if permitted to go through Yale. Is there not some way by which young [boy's name] can go through?
>
> I think, Percy, that there is a tendency at Yale to put too much emphasis on passing examinations and too little on the character, background and promise of future usefulness to Yale and the nation.—I believe that boys of fine character and fine background, who may have trouble in learning from a book, if helped through Yale by a sympathetic faculty, will prove far more useful citizens than . . . boys who learn from a book easily, and who are often referred to as "grinds." I feel sure the records of the past prove this to be true.
>
> I hope you will understand the spirit in which this letter is written. I am

not writing in a spirit of criticism. I am trying to be constructive and to let you know the feelings of quite a number of Yale graduates in and around New York. . . . These fathers are losing interest in Yale, their loyalty is dying, and they talk and criticise [*sic*] Yale a great deal.—It is doing Yale a lot of harm and I am worried about it.[80]

The complaint that examination grinds, those four-eyed eggheads with good grades and test scores, were shoving aside at the entrance gate boys of character from old Yale families was being made extensively in the 1930s.

From the anti-scholastic complaints of Yale fathers one should not infer either that gatekeepers enforced meritocracy after 1926 or that character counted for nothing. It would be as wrong to imagine that personal qualities were not factored in as to assume that family background determined admissions. But the central point is that character did not trump intellect in the bad old days, from the 1920s to the 1940s. From the origins of SAT selective admissions in 1926 to the Second World War, Yale wanted the sons of Protestant gentlemen who were intellectually capable of performing at what was thought of as a high academic standard. A weak intellect disqualified one no matter how sterling was one's character, no matter whether one's father was a Yale man, no matter whether one went to Andover, and no matter how large the bank account or extensive the social networks.

Post–World War II Changes: Applicant Pool, Arthur Howe, and Yale's New Emphasis on Personal Promise

After the Second World War, the applicant pool presented few problems that had to do with intellectual caliber. As the *Bell Curve* authors say in their summary on the rise of meritocracy, the quantity and scholastic quality of the applicant pool rose higher and higher in the 1950s and 1960s all by itself.[81] The response of the admissions office was to focus its attention on personal, not academic, promise.

The admissions dean who had to cope with the post–war applicant boom was Arthur Howe, a Yale man, class of 1943, appointed by Yale's president, A. Whitney Griswold. Howe was acting head of admissions from October 1953, and officially in charge from April 1954 to October 1964.[82]

Howe faced a very different environment from his predecessors. By the

1950s, Yale was receiving nearly four times as many applications as it had in the 1930s. In the 1930s, Yale rejected approximately one-fifth of its candidates; by the 1950s, it would have to turn away approximately three-fifths. In twenty years, the ratio of "rejects" to "admits" had swung around in the reverse direction. Howe reviewed those facts at the Yale 1957 convocation for alumni, staff, and faculty with responsibilities for admissions. He said,

> You know, as I do, that the admissions problems of today are primarily ones of abundance, and abundance of strong candidates, . . . To describe our abundance, I am comparing classes which entered Yale in the mid-1930s with classes entering twenty years later in the mid-1950s. . . . Quantitatively, there were approximately 1,450 candidates for the classes of 850 students that were entering Yale twenty years ago. Now we have nearly 4,500 candidates per year for 1,000 places in each Freshman class.[83]

The rising tide of applications would not matter if their quality was poor, but the opposite was the case. Howe continued to explain, "Our problem today, insofar as we are permitted to call abundance a problem, lies in the fact that about 85 percent of our 4,500 candidates seem to be qualified."[84] Harvard had the same problem. Two years earlier, in 1955, Harvard's *Alumni Bulletin* reported, "Ninety-five per cent of its candidates were 'admissible.'"[85]

Howe could report that quality was going up, because, he explained, "all of the evidence at our disposal supports these comments."[86] By using Yale's predicted grade score to illustrate this, one can see that of total applicants with a predicted performance score of 80 or higher, which would identify them as academically safe bets for "B" or "A" range Yale grades, in 1935 they were 175 or 16 percent of total applicants; in 1947 they were 550 or 19 percent of applicants, but in 1955 they were 1,100 or 26.2 percent of all applicants. The pool got bigger, and it was academically performing better than before.[87]

Changes in the size and quality of Yale's applicant population had the effect of eroding the percentage of the freshman class at the bottom of the academic ability scale, and of expanding the percentage of those at the top. Yale was quite happy to ride the tide as high as it would go, so long as doing so did not undercut the importance of character. One can illustrate the rising wave of ability by looking at a table covering several years that stretch between the times when Howe and Clark were in office. Table 2.2 includes four years (1961 to 1964) when Howe was dean and two years (1965 and 1966) when Clark was dean. From Table 2.2, we can see that the numbers of applicants with verbal SAT scores of 700–800 increased by a multiple of 2.7 from 1961 to 1966.

The intellectual records of Yale's undergraduates went up because of the quality of the applicant group. As Howe explained to the Executive Committee of the Yale Alumni Board in 1960, "Speaking of . . . academic promise, the boy . . . must meet the standards set by his classmates."[88] What significantly changed was neither the size of the freshman class nor the tools for academic selection, but the average quality of the application pool.

Howe spelled out the new situation in an exchange of three letters in February 1957 for a person at *Reader's Digest* responsible for editing a reprint of a *Time* magazine article on college admissions. The *Digest* editor wrote, "Is it true that so far only the big-name colleges, mostly those in the East, have really felt the impact of increased enrollment?" Howe responded,

> As worded, the answer is "No," but I suspect that there is confusion here because of your use of the words "increased enrollment." The point is that the big-name colleges have not to any significant degree increased their enrollments but that there has been an extraordinary increase in the requests for admission. It is true, to the best of my knowledge, that not more than 75 of

TABLE 2.2

Matriculants by SAT Verbal Scores, Yale College 1961–66.

Admit Year	Percent of Each Year Matriculating with SAT Verbal Scores Under 599	Percent of Each Year Matriculating with SAT Verbal Scores 600–699	Percent of Each Year Matriculating with SAT Verbal Scores 700–800	Total Class Size
1961	25	55	20	1018
1962	23	52	25	1015
1963	14	53	33	1022
1964	16	52	31	1054
1965	14	52	33	1048
1966	9	38	52	1012

SOURCE: *Brewster Papers* (Yale Archive, Box 2, Folder 10), "CEEB Test Data for Yale Matriculants."

the approximately 1800 American institutions of higher learning are under real admissions pressure, by which I mean that a situation exists where there are more qualified candidates for admission than the institutions can accept.

Then the editor asked whether those new developments brought about any changes in the privileges enjoyed by legacies: "Is it true that the child of the old grad is losing his advantage?" Howe's reply:

> No. At least at Yale, and I suspect at most similar institutions, the standard which has been and continues to be applied to the sons of graduates is that the candidate must display in his previous academic and personal record promise of a successful career at college. As we annually receive applications from several thousand people who meet this standard, the son of the alumnus might be said to be receiving a greater advantage than ever.

Finally, the editor asked a follow-up question on legacies that fully anticipated the meritocratic interpretation being offered today. The editor wondered if there had been a decline in the number of legacies because of the SAT: "Has the emphasis on College Board aptitude tests hastened the change?" Howe's response was dismissive. "This question becomes illogical in the light of the above statement that there has not been a change in the last ten years."[89] In other words, at Yale there was no falloff in legacy admissions, or change in the role played by the SAT.

One should not imagine that Yale was capturing all of the best brains it could, or that it was outdistancing the competition in a race for high SAT scores. Yale was not then, any more than it is today, obsessed with enrolling all of the top test-scoring students in the applicant pool.

The fact that Yale neither desired to round up, nor by default ended up with, an excess of high-SAT-scoring youths was revealed in its research on where candidates who rejected Yale's offer went instead. In the 1960s and 1970s, it was not uncommon for 40 percent of those admitted to Yale to go elsewhere. From surveys of those who turned down Yale, it knew that the alternatives, in order of popularity, were Harvard, Princeton, Stanford, MIT, and Brown. Harvard was preferred by youths wanting urban culture; Princeton was attractive to those most comfortable in suburbia; Stanford was for some closer to home; MIT engaged those focused on science and technology; and Brown attracted those who desired a less academically demanding environment.[90]

Yale and Harvard monitored the competition; they kept track of the admissions' records of selective institutions in the country. As previously mentioned, in 1957, Howe estimated there were approximately seventy-five selective colleges in the land; in 1968, research conducted by Harvard's admissions dean put the precise number at sixty-nine.[91] Using the Harvard list, Yale's Office of Institutional Research (OIR) circulated a confidential report on each of the sixty-nine colleges, grouped by cross applications over a six-year period, and ranked by entering SAT scores. What was most interesting about this particular study was that it pointed out that Yale and Harvard were not at the top of the SAT pecking order—and the rest of the Ivy League schools were even farther from the summit. Institutions were rated "A" to "F" with fifty SAT points separating each letter on the scale, and, as John H. Hoskins in the OIR said, "The most obvious finding is that neither Harvard nor Yale are in the 'A' (highest) group."[92] In the "A" group were Cal Tech, Carnegie-Mellon, MIT, Stanford, Swarthmore, the University of California at Berkeley the University of California at Los Angeles, and the University of California at San Diego. (Most of the "A" list were in California, not New England.) In the "B" group were Amherst, Harvard, Yale, and the Webb Institute (a private engineering college in Glen Cove, New York). In the "C" group were Brandeis, Bryn Mawr, Harvey Mudd, New College, Pomona, Reed, and Wesleyan. The "D" group included Barnard, Brown, Cornell, Haverford, Middlebury, University of Pennsylvania, Princeton, St. John's in Maryland, Trinity in Connecticut, and Williams. The rest of the sixty-nine, including the two remaining Ivy League members, Columbia University and Dartmouth, were "E" or "F" grade. Most Ivy colleges fell into the "D" or "E" categories. During and after the days of its hypothetical meritocratic makeover, the Ivy League was not anywhere near peak capacity for high SAT-scoring students. Even by the end of the twentieth century, Harvard and Yale each had fewer students with combined SAT scores above 1,400 than any of four state institutions: the University of California at Berkeley, the University of Illinois at Urbana-Champaign, the University of Michigan at Ann Arbor, and the University of Wisconsin at Madison. Those four state universities have the most "super students"[93] in the entire United States because unlike the Ivies they do admissions at the top end of the ability pool based on academic, not personal, qualities.

Selecting for Leaders

Although Yale was happy to let entering verbal SAT score averages for each class rise from the 1950s all the way to 1970 when they peaked,[94] its attention to selectivity was not on academic meritocracy, but on leadership. Selectivity after the late 1940s meant deciding between academically strong candidates on the basis of personal characteristics. During Howe's time in the admissions office, the importance of the personal side of the admissions equation was formalized and proclaimed without inhibition. Whether at internal alumni events or at external radio broadcasts, Howe would say, "Far and away the most important factor in any boy's chances of admission is what we consider his personal promise."[95]

In the 1950s and 1960s, whenever someone at Yale talked about "personal promise" he was speaking about "leadership" potential. And selecting for leadership was widely understood to be Yale's special mission. As President Griswold explained to an alumnus vice president of Pan American World Airways,

> Our admissions policies are under constant scrutiny, . . . Of course, we have no foolproof system for divining which boys will become leaders in later life, but it is interesting to note that, according to a survey reported in *Newsweek* two years ago, Yale, with one out of every twenty-two men in the classes of 1920 through 1949 listed in the 1956–57 *Who's Who*, stood ahead of every other college in the country. I can only assure you of our continuing efforts to discover what are the qualities characteristics of prospective leaders and to improve in every way the educational opportunities for the men who possess them.[96]

Academic promise was quantified through Yale's predicted grade formula and recorded as a number on each applicant's file. But how could the admissions office evaluate and rank "personal leadership" promise? Personal character could not be easily computed from standardized tests like a predicted grade point average; character appeared to be something that had to be subjectively judged. Yale's admissions officers were practiced at the art of evaluating boys for the men they could become, but they wanted whatever assistance empirical science could lend to the effort.

The desire in the 1950s and 1960s to bring science to bear on the problem of reading character repeated the logic behind Yale's adoption of the

SAT. Just as Yale's leaders in 1926 were convinced that Protestant boys were superior to Jewish ones, but they wanted a test to prove it, in the post-war period, Yale's administrators and admissions staff thought they knew what embryonic leaders looked like, but they wanted ways to measure that. Yale wanted, if possible, a scientific way to validate and expedite its selection process. The eugenic impulse behind the introduction of the SAT was also present in the search for the criteria that predicts leaders.

Yale willingly participated in eugenic schemes to measure personal character, in particular the infamous practice that lasted until 1968 of taking nude "posture" photographs to study the relation of body type to personal abilities.[97] Cohort after cohort of Yale men would walk from their freshman dorms on old campus over to Payne-Whitney Gymnasium, stand in line on the fourth floor, and enter one at a time into a room without windows. Inside, two technicians would instruct the youth to disrobe before they would place metal pins against his spine that would both measure and hold each youth in position while three photographs were taken. One need not imagine the experience generated more, or less, anxiety than an army induction physical, and the unpleasant registration procedure may have played some ritualistic role for the youth demarcating, like a military hair cut, the transition from secondary school to Ivy League status. The practice, begun at a few elite colleges in the 1930s, was required at all of the Ivy League colleges (Brown, Columbia, Cornell, Dartmouth, Harvard, Pennsylvania, Princeton, and Yale) and the Seven Sisters (Barnard, Bryn Mawr, Mount Holyoke, Radcliffe, Smith, Vassar, and Wellesley) from the 1940s to the 1960s. The results of this procedure were obscure and publicly uncommented on, except when someone in authority would report a fact gleaned from the project. For example, when the dean of Yale College, George May, spoke to the new class on September 16, 1963, he reported, "Yale Freshmen of the Class of 1967 average one inch taller and 12 pounds heavier than members of the Yale Class of 1938." One hopes Dean May's comments drew a few chuckles, but his next point was no doubt taken seriously by most of those present. He went on from his reference to their increased body mass to compliment Yale's new students on their enhanced academic performance in comparison with predecessors. As the press release on the talk put it, "In 'significant and measurable' ways, said the Dean, present-day students have improved in a 'quite spectacular' manner" over older classes.[98] In hindsight, the posture photos seem bizarre, but at the time they were consistent with an upper-class mentality that thought it could produce objective measurements of its superiority.

At Harvard, where an identical search was underway for calibrations of leadership material, the posture photographs were part of a formal medical discourse on "character."[99] Every new Harvard undergraduate would be photographed naked and then, on a separate occasion, subjected to a medical exam by a member of the department of hygiene.[100] The doctor would have to observe and engage the freshman in a conversation about feelings, attitudes, and activities. The doctor was supposed to use a diagnostic tool that presumed to evaluate individuals against a normative standard of what constituted a healthy masculine male. It was a perfect example of what Michel Foucault called "bio-power"; the power of social norms, professional experts, and institutional authorities to mold human subjects as bodies and mentalities in conformity to a type. Foucault's notion is summarized well by the Berkeley anthropologist Aihwa Ong. As Ong says, bio-power "makes strategic use of bodies of [scientific] knowledge that invest bodies and populations with properties that make them amenable to various technologies of control. This power . . . is exercised with the purpose of producing subjects who are healthy and productive."[101] Harvard's medical exam, regardless of intent, was a technology that validated particular masculine cultural stereotypes, while stigmatizing others as deviant.

Students had to arrive for the doctor's examination with a five-page questionnaire filled in, which included thinly disguised ethnic inquiries, requesting that one list one's religious denomination, as well as one's father's and mother's birthplaces. Just as at Yale, answers to those questions helped Harvard keep track of its Jews. And there were a number of questions on social class. One had to list the occupation of every family member, and report "How many academic years in college or graduate school can you finance?" "What is the source of your financial support in college?" and "What do you estimate the total yearly income of your immediate family to be?" Without permission being asked, the "confidential" medical questionnaire was used for statistical research on the correlates between family background and academic performance; the research took place years before the introduction of federal guidelines on research involving human subjects.[102]

The doctor would begin the psychical exam with a checklist on a medical form where the posture photograph would be attached. The third question on the doctor's protocol was on posture, the fourth question was on rating "MASCULINE COMPONENT: strong/medium/weak/very weak." Whether "masculine component" meant muscle definition, extent of body hair, genital size, or some combination of features is not spelled out in the guidelines on the form.

Then, the doctor had to fill in a "personality appraisal" of the student that involved assigning a grade from a four-letter scale, ranking the student "A" to "E" on nine separate areas of self presentation: Appearance and Manner, Speech, Social Relations, Athletic Interests and Participation, Practical Motivations and Life Attitudes, Aesthetic and Cultural Motivations and Life Attitudes, Basic Personality Integration, War Service Adjustment, and College Adjustment. On "Appearance and Manner" an "A" rating was circled if the physician thought the youth "creates excellent impression. Attractive, mature for age, relaxed in posture and movement, a firm handclasp, normal moisture." An "E" rating was given if the youth was "unattractive, very tense, fidgety or have extremely unpleasant mannerisms, or very weak moist handclasp, or be very immature." The guidelines obliged doctors at Harvard in the 1950s to invest a youth's handshake with medical significance. Shy or lone-wolf individuals would get low marks for "Social Relations." On "Athletic Interests," real men played ball, being a mere spectator got one a "D" grade, and the youth who "doesn't even care to watch sports" was rock bottom with an "E" grade. On "Practical Motivations and Life Attitudes," one had to be perceived to be "extraordinarily practical, realistic, and efficient and accomplishes what he sets out to do" to get an "A." Some credit was allowed eggheads on "Aesthetic and Cultural Motivations." If one had only a "casual and occasional interest" or was "completely uninterested in things cultural, aesthetic or ideational," one got a "D" or "E." The category "Basic Personality Integration" was a summary of all that came before. An "A" rating was given for being perceived to be "exceedingly stable, well integrated and feels secure within himself. Unusually very adaptable." To assign an "A" grade to a youth, the doctor was asked to agree with the crystal-ball prediction that the student "may have many achievements and satisfactions" in his lifetime. "D"s were given if there was "lack of good personality integration. Erratic, mildly neurotic, rigid or unstable enough to curtail productiveness and happiness in life." And the "E" grade was assigned if the youth seemed "quite definitely neurotic. . . . May have many failures in his life. Possible mental illness."

In the 1950s, veterans of the Second World War or the Korean War were attending college, and questions were included about their military service. Joseph Heller's Yossarian character from his novel *Catch-22*[103] would have gotten a "D" score as someone who "constantly wanted to get out of service." To get an "A" one should have "liked service so much may have considered becoming a 'regular.'" And combat experience was a good thing; it made grade "A" men. The guidelines for deserving an "A" rating included the statement, "may have had much combat duty," whereas an "E" evaluation went along with the comment, "rarely saw combat."

The final category on adjusting to college life applied to everyone. The lowest grades were particularly relevant to admissions evaluations. On College Adjustment, a "D" was someone about whom the doctor had doubts as to his "college survival." And an "E" meant the youth "probably should never have been admitted to college in the first place."[104]

The posture photos and personality profiles of freshman were retrospective attempts to classify the male undergraduate population in relation to particular normative masculine attributes. The "medical" process influenced the thoughts of both administrators and youths. The idea that the Ivy League gave one a score on one's manliness was not exactly a family secret. "To Be a Man" was the title of one of the most popular films shown by Yale alumni clubs across the nation.[105] It was also a topic, sometimes a sore one, of undergraduate conversation, as President George W. Bush's comments when he was given an honorary degree in 2001 indicated. Self-deprecating jokes aside, Bush said somberly, "In my time, they spoke of the 'Yale man.' I was really never sure what that was."[106]

It is not possible to see in the Yale archive the use Harvard may have made of this information for admissions. At Yale, however, the same logic of physical and personality evaluation displayed in the Harvard medical forms was applied to the process of selecting whom to admit from the applicant pool. Youths were required to attach a photograph to their Yale application, and the task of evaluating personal character was accomplished during an admissions interview with the doctor's role played by alumni. To place the diagnostic effort on as sophisticated a footing as possible, the admissions office in the 1950s organized an elaborate infrastructure of correspondence, visitations, conferences, interviews, handbooks, evaluation forms, and ratings systems that involved alumni and school staff.

Alumni Evaluations of Character

From the 1950s forward, the admissions office wanted every young man (and after Yale College admitted them in 1969, every young woman) applying to receive an interview. Before the 1970s, when applications at Yale averaged five thousand per year[107] for approximately one thousand freshman places, it was standard practice for Yale to interview more than 80 percent of its applicants. In a record year, when 88 percent of applicants were interviewed, the admissions office pushed for more.[108] By the 1970s, there was some falloff in the percentage of applicants receiving interviews, but still from 1971 to 2001, on average, very nearly 70 percent of all applicants, male and female, received a personal interview.[109]

Candidates for Yale were sometimes interviewed by full-time admissions officers, but mostly they spoke with volunteer members of the local Alumni Schools Committee (ASC). On average, alumni conducted 90 percent of the annual interviews.[110] Alumni were the talent scouts of the system. The admissions office had a full-time coordinator to communicate with, for example in 1969, the "approximately 1,900 Alumni . . . active in 260 different [Alumni Schools] Committees throughout the country."[111] Each time an ASC member would interview a prospective youth, he would write up a one- or two-page "Yale Alumni Interview Report," complete with a nine-point ranking scale. The New Haven coordinator would advise ASC members on what to look for and how to write candid evaluations. Examples of informative field reports would be reproduced and mailed to each local committee.

Before the infrastructure of the system is displayed, it is worth asking how important alumni interviews were to the final decision. The OIR repeatedly investigated the value of each item of information in the applicant's file. In a memorandum from Robert Sternberg of the OIR to Henry Chauncey, Jr., Director, University Admissions and Financial Aid Policy, dated April 1972, Sternberg summarized findings that were typical for the decades under review here: "Of the approximately twenty-five ratings and scores on each candidate received by the admissions office, the alumni rating has been shown by statistical analysis to be the most heavily weighted factor used in deciding whether or not to admit candidates to Yale. Thus the importance of the ASC interview report can scarcely be minimized."[112] The alumni interview rating predicted the final action on admissions better than anything else, including high-school grades, SAT scores, and school counselor's letters of evaluation. The admissions office in New Haven trusted its alumni agents in the field. They had been trained very well.

The preparation of alumni for admissions' work began in a sense before they arrived in New Haven as freshmen. But one need not speculate on the broad effects of social-class backgrounds on cognitive frameworks when the record on formal organizational factors is so rich. Each part of the alumni's role in admissions was scripted and coached. Alumni would volunteer or be recruited for admissions work in one of the approximately 260 local ASCs. Each local committee would have a chairman whose responsibility it was to educate new members to the nature of their task. Each would be given an admissions handbook. The 1959 Handbook, for example, under the subheading, "The Interview" stated,

> Shortly after an application . . . is received . . . , the applicant is requested to make an appointment with a designated Alumni Representative in his community. At the same time the Representative is advised that the candidate has been referred to him, ... An objective evaluation of a candidate's promise as a student can be made from school grades and College Board test scores. . . . However, the interview is still the most widely used method of personal assessment and the impressions obtained by an Alumni Representative in this manner, and through conversation with others who know a candidate, can be most useful. . . . [113]

Under the next subheading, "Interview Reports" the manual continued to elaborate: "Reports of interviews and the interviewer's recommendations should be submitted on *Personal Interview Record and Rating Sheets.* . . . In general, an interview report should include: (1) a brief summary of the candidate's background; (2) a concise description of the candidate; (3) the comments of others who know him; (4) a summary of his significant interests and activities; and (5) the conclusions and recommendation of the interviewer. A specimen report is submitted as Exhibit A."[114]

The specimen report, as well as the official page filled in by the alumni interviewer, was titled, "Personal Interview Record and Rating Sheet." It began with a checklist of characteristics and activities that were very similar to those specified on the Harvard medical questionnaire. The alumni interviewer would "Check Items Which Best Describe Applicant" at the top. The list had twenty attributes: "alert—lively; argumentative; attractive; awkward; cocky; dull; effeminate; flabby—soft; forceful; good looking; sense of humor; immature; inarticulate; neat—well groomed; mature; poised; shy—reserved; sloppy—untidy; unattractive." Next came five categories to be checked off of "areas in which you think applicant may have sufficient ability or talent to make significant contributions at Yale." And those were, in the order they appeared on the form: "athletics; debating; dramatics; music; and publications." Then space was provided for comments by the interviewer(s), with the summary recommendation at the bottom. The recommendation was on a nine-point scale, with "'Tops' No Reservations" above the numbers 1 and 2; "Recommend with confidence," above 3 and 4; "Recommend as acceptable," above 5 and 6; "Recommend doubtfully" over 7 and 8; and finally, "Do not recommend" over number 9.

To standardize as much as possible the application of national guidelines for ranking applicants, the chairmen of local committees would attend alumni convocations in New Haven every four years. In 1957, the event drew 220 local alumni chairs to New Haven.[115] At the convocation, they would hear speeches from, and participate in question and answer exchanges with various officers of Yale University including the President and the admissions dean. Frequently, those speeches were given over lunch in Donaldson Commons, an appropriate venue for evoking Yale's compact with its sons. The Commons is in a neoclassical building, behind a fluted Corinthian colonnade, holding up an entablature with a list of the major battles of the First World War. Ordinarily, the Commons is entered under a cupola where a roll call of Yale's war dead from three centuries is cut in stone.

The multiday convocation would train alumni chairs in the logic of admissions by dividing them into groups of about eighteen men with a New Haven facilitator; then they would hold workshop meetings on candidates. Each group would be given real files on approximately fourteen applicants from a recent year; their names, and some details, would be modified to safeguard against identification or embarrassments. Not many of the particulars could be altered, however, without the pedagogical value of the exercise getting lost. Each member of the make-believe admissions committee would read all of the files and make his own judgment rating the academic promise, and the personal promise, of the candidate on a nine-point scale. Then the committee would come together to discuss the pros and cons of each candidate before voting a final-action decision. After the decisions had all been made, the alumni would be given a confidential report on the real-life outcomes for each of the fourteen candidates. They would be told Yale's actual decision on admission as well as updated on the youth's experience over the course of that academic year, regardless of what he ended up doing.

One can understand how the exercise worked by looking at some of the files of the youths, their ratings, and the committee's vote, and then at the follow-up on how things unfolded over the next year. Two examples, one positive, and one negative, should suffice to give a flavor of the experience.[116]

Of the fourteen case files used in the workshop, the youth with the highest combined SAT score, a score between 1,400 and 1,500, was called, "Horace Haddock." Horace was from a town in the northeast where he lived on a farm with many siblings; he attended the local public school. His father had a college degree from a state university and worked in engineering; his mother's college degree was from the same state university, and she was a housewife. The "personal interview record and rating sheet" checked off "good looking" and "shy—reserved." He had nothing checked from the list of five activities that the candidate might do to make significant contributions to Yale. The interview report said, "He had no extra-curricular activities other than Future Farmers of America." At the bottom of the interview sheet, the summary recommendation was a number 6, a low "Recommend as acceptable." (In all of these cases, a "1" was the best score; a "9" was the worst.)

For comparison, we can look at the case of "Truxton Cod, III." His father was a Yale alumnus, employed as a bank officer in a major city. His mother graduated from a Seven Sisters college, and was a housewife. His brother went to Yale. Truxton attended a private boarding school. In the personal description categories, he was listed as "attractive," with the comments, "Athletic looking boy. Very attractive personally and in appearance." At his prep school, he was the president of the Art Society, and vice president of a service club. Regarding activity areas to excel at in New Haven, notes were made about "art" and "student government." The report revealed that Truxton's father was very active in local alumni affairs. Truxton took the SAT more than once. All of his scores were significantly behind Horace's. Despite his privileged family background, Truxton never managed to break the 500-point level on the verbal SAT. There was no disguising that he was academically weak. The prep school's headmaster rated Truxton a 6 out of 9 for his promise as a student, but a 2 for his promise as a person.

The particular alumni group whose records for that year are in the Yale archive voted to reject both Horace Haddock and Truxton Cod III; then they were given the facts on the actual outcomes for the two youths. The Yale official informed the alumni that the admissions office had rejected Horace, with the highest SAT in the bunch, but admitted Truxton, the son of a prominent alumnus. The update explained how Horace had been a bad fit for Yale. It reported, "Horace is now at a state university doing very well in the agriculture program. . . . [H]e is now happy where he should be, studying agriculture."[117] In contrast, on Truxton's first year at Yale the alumni were told that,

> His Freshman counselor describes him as 'very well adjusted,' and comments as follows: "Coming from a Yale family, Truxton found himself very much at home at Yale. Having overcome some initial problems . . . he is now striving towards solid standing in academics. At the same time he has been very active and devoted to the . . . [sports team]. He will be an all-round attractive young Yale gentleman.[118]

One can safely assume that the point of the practice exercise was not lost on the alumni assembled in New Haven. Under the guidance of a Yale authority, alumni leaders had learned a lesson on how meritocracy worked at Yale. Test scores alone would not get one in, and bad scores would take a back seat to family line and personal qualities.

Summing Up

We can end this chapter with some provisional conclusions on what was right or wrong about our three views (the optimistic, cautious, and critical) on meritocracy. The optimistic and cautious meritocratic narratives all presume a shift from "character to intellect." They all view the 1950s as the pivotal decade, moving elite-college admissions away from social connections to intellectual abilities, with the result being a dethroning of the WASP upper-class and the rise of a meritocratic open elite. We now know that this narrative is, at best, a half-truth; there was a dramatic increase in the 1950s in the size and quality of the applicant group that had the effect of driving up test scores in each entering class. But the meritocratic tale on the brains/ character dichotomy, and when character was dominant over the other, is completely wrong. The SAT was intended to assist with social selection. And in the bad-old days of the WASP supremacy, when Jews were being kept under a quota, and women were completely excluded, academic performance still mattered. For Protestant men, from the 1920s to the 1950s, "intellect" trumped "character" when there were conflicts between the two. One had to be above the line, no matter who was one's father. After the late 1940s, the two were joined in a patriarchal marriage with character holding the dominant masculine position. Character was never more important to admissions than after the Second World War. Admissions innovations in the post–war period were not about fine tuning how to measure academic potential—that problem had been settled back in the 1930s; their energies were spent cultivating the art and science of predicting which seventeen-year-old youths had the personal promise to be among America's future leaders. And the most important people in the whole admissions process were alumni; old boys were picking tomorrow's winners.

Meritocracy's optimistic and cautious defenders were wrong about how little intellect mattered in the bad-old days, and how much it mattered in the post-1950s world. For Yale, intellectual selection and social selection went together as institutional policies in both time periods. The machinery of intellectual evaluation was created in the 1920 and 1930s, not the 1960s, and techniques to evaluate and reward character were pursued vigorously in the 1950s and 1960s, not in the pre–Second World War past. In comparison, the critical view of meritocracy, Bourdieu's view, scores well.

Maintaining Yale's distance from public schools and the lower social classes was an overriding priority that determined entry tests and external relations. Even after Yale knew that the SAT was inadequate at predicting college grades, and that secondary school transcripts were more reliable, it would not change course. High-school certificates and subject tests were rejected; the SAT as a type of IQ test replete with social bias was embraced. To take care of its own, the practice of legacy perks was introduced. And when average SAT scores went on the rise, Yale brought into play face-to-face interviews with alumni to discern personal promise to be a Yale man. Yale's position in the symbolic field of cultural excellence was sustained.

Our outstanding questions to be pursued in the rest of this book are these: What impact, if any, did these changes have on the social composition of Yale? Were WASPs driven away, Jews and lower-class youths let in? Did admissions subversives get into control, and with what effects, during President Kingman Brewster's administration? And what lasting effects has this had on the elements of opportunity or privilege at elite colleges today? How much cooperation is there now between colleges and privileged social groups in the intergenerational reproduction of their status?

CHAPTER THREE

Social-Class Diversity at Yale after 1950?

Social-class judgments always played a role in admissions, and it would be an intellectual slight to the people responsible to suggest that they did not appreciate the organic connection between family qualities and the attributes of a youth most deserving of Yale's liberal arts education. Social class was not being "misrecognized" as much as it was being acknowledged as the proper prerequisite for youths to benefit from Yale as a training ground for tomorrow's leaders. Throughout the period covered by the meritocratic narratives, there was at Yale a clearly understood nexus between a family's social class and Yale's liberal arts education.

As admissions dean, Arthur Howe, Jr., repeatedly explained in speeches to, and publications read by, alumni, that Yale was an upper-class liberal-arts college for the education of future leaders. Admissions decisions at Yale had to take its social composition and special mission into account. Howe made this case often, and in detail, so it is worth quoting his words about the nexus of class and education at length. Here we have Howe providing a hypothetical case study contrasting two youths and their suitability for admission at a place like Yale. He wrote,

> Selective colleges are already heavily oversubscribed with qualified candidates, [so] let us turn to the subtleties of interpretation and policy which more often than not determine the outcome of applications.
>
> First, there are certain qualities that make one person intrinsically more deserving of admission than another. . . . The notion that one candidate is more deserving than another is illustrated by [hypothetical] College X's admissions decisions on Bill and John. Both are of good character, both are "B" students. But Bill, who was rejected, had to work hard for his secondary grades, earning them primarily through rote memorization. Though an agreeable, wholesome person, he had neither the time nor the inclination for things, books, or people beyond his required course of study. His lower-class family's aspirations for upward social and economic mobility via a prestige college kept his eyes focused on the one thing he believed would pay off: good grades.
>
> On the other hand, John, who was accepted, mastered his school work with only a reasonable degree of industry. His interests and sensitivities are broad, he has a rewarding social life with his friends, and he reads widely beyond the confines of *Time* magazine and the books required in school. Finally, he comes from a middle-class family that can afford to pay his college bills.
>
> John was judged inherently more deserving of admission than Bill. . . . The decisive factor was that John seemed to have a greater capacity for growth toward intellectually and socially significant objectives. The college was recording its preference for critical thinking over a stuffed brain.
>
> Certainly Bill deserved an opportunity for further education, but there is some question whether he would benefit from the philosophical and theoretical orientation of a liberal arts and science curriculum as much as from a vocational program.[1]

In the 1960s, the logic of exclusion had moved on from "racial" anti-Semitism to social class. The negative image of the Jewish grind of the 1920s evolved into a 1960s portrait of the lower-class ambitious scrambler, sweating to stuff his overheated brain with technical details. The upwardly mobile were suitable for vocational subjects at state universities, after which they could be technicians or accountants, but America's future leaders should be culturally prepped in privileged families if they were to properly benefit from the stock of wisdom available in a liberal-arts residential college.

Howe thought long and hard about the question of Yale's relation to social class. After the Second World War, he even studied social mobility and education one term at the University of London under the direction of a famous visiting Oxford don and intellectual guide to the Labour Party, G. D. H. Cole.[2] Howe was fully aware that a college like Yale was looked to by families in the upper-class for social reproduction, and by ambitious members of the lower classes as a ladder for social mobility. In an alumni convocation speech Howe explained,

> To those who have enjoyed the privileges of cultural opportunities, wealth, and social standing, there is no stronger desire than to preserve the same for their children, and admission to Yale is one of the best ways to do it. To those less privileged, identification with a prestige-laden institution is probably the most effective vehicle for upward mobility. But those who are experiencing such mobility should, we are constantly reminded, have unusual reserves of intelligence and stamina to overcome the frequently painful, disturbing aspects of the process. Most of us have a natural, genuine sympathy for the underdog, and yet it is when sympathy rules reason that we make our worst admissions errors. There is a very thin line indeed, between creating opportunity and causing injury.[3]

The last note struck in this passage, about causing injury to upwardly mobile young men, was a concern expressed by Howe on more than one occasion. In 1961, Harvard experimented with a type of social-class affirmative action known as the "gamble project"; it was reported to the country in the July issue of *McCall's*, in an article on "The Secret of Getting into Harvard." As a result of the article, Howe and five other representatives of New England colleges were invited to publish comments on the program in the pages of a magazine for educators, *New England Association Review*. The gamble project was funded by one individual's gift of fifty thousand dollars. The money would support nineteen boys from poor, uneducated families, selected across the nation as being particularly promising despite modest SAT scores, averaging "75 to 100 points below their classmates."[4]

Howe began his reflections on the project with the statement, "Beneath its veneer of sensationalism [*McCall's* pinpoints] the fundamental issues of collegiate talent-searching amongst underprivileged." For Ivy League colleges, this is a very difficult problem. Howe explained,

> For, the hard economic reality facing Harvard and many others is that 60%

of their undergraduate matriculants must come from families which can from their own resources meet the . . . annual budget which attendance requires. My own estimate is that between three and five per cent of American families can handle such an annual expense, and that therefore the majority of students attending even the best endowed private institutions must be recruited from a narrow segment of the population. This majority inevitably represents wealth and social as well as intellectual sophistication, both of which are reflected in campus values and mores.

The ability of the uninitiated to adjust to such an environment as is suggested above without loss of the vigor and purpose which initially qualified them for a place in the institution, . . . are matters for careful scrutiny. All too many students from underprivileged situations have adjusted to university life by involving themselves in only the worst things that the new community offered.[5]

Howe seemed to fear that the upwardly mobile at a place like Yale would fall in with a fast, hard-drinking set, to the detriment of their studies and meager bank account. Although he wanted to keep the "pipelines" open for new blood, "admissions officers . . . carry a heavy responsibility in locating talented youngsters in limited circumstances, deciding which can stand the gaff of successful adjustment."[6] "Gaff" was not a misprint. Howe meant that Ivy colleges as a tool of upward mobility were like a sharp hook that harms as it hoists the underprivileged.

Howe's conclusions drew on external social science as well as the work of Yale's Office of Educational Research (the predecessor of the Office of Institutional Research). When Howe wrote the gaff comment, Yale's research office had a new assistant director, Robert Ramsey, Jr., recruited from Harvard, where he received a doctorate in education for his 1959 thesis, "A Study of Cultural Influence on Academic Performance in College and Law School."[7] Ramsey was, like Howe, mindful of finding the right social and cultural fit between a youth and college.

Ramsey's dissertation argued that previous research had pretty much exhausted what academic measures of ability could statistically explain about college outcomes; their value to admissions decisions had reached its limit. "Early studies of academic performance in college and professional school" he wrote, "focused almost exclusively on so-called 'intellectual' ability factors."[8] Consistent with Yale's previous findings on the weak predictive value of the SAT, Ramsey reported that research showed grades predicted college performance best, "scores on . . . achievement or content (subject matter) tests have been a close second to high school grade record," and "scholastic aptitude or intelligence tests . . . [fall] somewhat lower," in last place.[9] In combination, previous grades and test scores could account for 50 percent of "the variability of [college and] law school performance. . . . [T]he most serious gap in our knowledge to date continues to be the assessment of . . . nonintellectual influences."[10] It was time, he proposed, for us to rigorously investigate the effects of family social class and culture on academic outcomes. Ramsey called his theory "a sociocultural approach." Its "major hypothesis . . . was that individual differences in cultural background are, on the whole, reflected in differences in academic performance in college and law school."[11]

Ramsey was an Ivy League pioneer of family cultural-strata research that bore striking similarities to the new ideas of the French sociologist Pierre Bourdieu. Bourdieu's work on his theory of "*habitus*," which attempts to explain the generative effects of a family's cultural environment on the behavior of individuals, was begun around the same time, but published in French and English after Ramsey's initial work.[12] Ramsey, however, did not concern himself with Bourdieu's fundamental question on the role of family culture in reproducing social inequalities; rather, he researched sociocultural distinctions within the middle and upper classes. If any social group could claim Ramsey's sympathy, it seemed to be the upper class whose culture caused it to be academic underachievers. He saw studies of college performance where success was measured as test scores and grades to having a "middle class bias."[13] By "assuming that all students, regardless of cultural background, are motivated toward some definite standard of excellence in academic behavior, . . . [is to be] biased in favor of those [middle class] groups."[14] Upper-class youths would be more attuned to "quality" and less driven to perform than middle-class youths; Ramsey mused, "perhaps the 'gentleman's C' is not under-achievement for the 'St. Grottlesex' boy."[15] Ramsey was a sort of proto-Bourdieu for the bourgeoisie.

Ramsey published an article in the *Journal of Legal Education* summarizing his dissertation's theory and research findings.[16] He offered evidence of a social-class-home-environment cognitive split that neatly mapped onto Howe's social class divide on liberal arts versus vocational subjects, although where Howe had written "middle class" and "lower class," Ramsey would substitute "upper class" and "middle class." According to Ramsey, upper-class families provided a home "typically characterized by a cultural and intellectual atmosphere in which the emphasis is on flexible manipulation of ideas (or learning for its own sake) . . . [while middle classes were] focused on the external symbols of success (grades) without commensurate attention to the more important underlying processes."[17] The variables that best predicted this cultural orientation for a youth were religion, parents' occupation, family income, and type of high school attended. His work "indicates that products of different cultural orientations perceive their academic roles differently."[18] It was essential, if admissions were to be based on science, for colleges to study the non-intellectual variables that predict outcomes. Knowledge of social and cultural factors would help selective colleges pick youths who were right for them. "Only [then] . . . will we extricate ourselves from the quick-sands of [admissions] hunch and approach the foundations of science. In the meantime, we must live enviously with that rare and inexplicable creature, the admissions artist, whose persistent insights dazzle us all, himself included."[19] Howe's staff and alumni interviewers tried to be "admissions artists," but they also supported attempts by Yale's research office to identify the social and cultural attributes that could scientifically explain success in college.

The Office of Educational Research kept precise data on applicants' and matriculants' family backgrounds. All of Ramsey's variables (parents' religion, income, occupation, and education) were whenever possible recorded and monitored. It would, however, take a decade before Yale would fund major empirical studies into alternative definitions of college success other than first-year student grades. In the meanwhile, the admissions artists on staff in New Haven or in the field in Alumni Schools Committees (ASC) were doing the evaluating and selecting for personal promise.

Regardless of Ramsey's empathy for the upper class, Howe's views on the relation of the top 5 percent to Yale were not an unqualified celebration of social Darwinism. Howe understood the dilemma facing elite private colleges in America: they are too expensive for most, and they cannot stop being expensive without ceasing to be elite. The state-sponsored alternative of remaining elite and becoming inexpensive through government nationalization, such as occurred in England to Oxford and Cambridge during this same period, was never considered an option by administrators at Yale.[20]

Howe knew better than most how socially exclusive Yale, Harvard, and other elite colleges in the private sector were, and he found it regrettable but inevitable that tuition fees and room and board expenses made them so. In 1958, for example, tuition alone at Harvard was $1,056, at Princeton $1,200, and at Yale $1,100, whereas flagship public universities such as Berkeley, Michigan, and Wisconsin charged residents $106, $250, and $200, respectively.[21] In an interview with the *Herald Tribune Magazine*, Howe detailed the total package. For Yale and its fraternal colleges, Howe said, "A realistic budget covering all of a student's expenses for one academic year will often amount to $2,500. (This divides roughly into $1,100 for tuition, $900 for room and board, and $500 for clothes, travel, and other living expenses. . . .) These costs are disturbing," Howe pointed out, " . . . when compared with the median annual income of American families, which is now approximately $4,500."[22] In 1957, Yale cost 55 percent of the median family income in the United States. Over the decades Yale's relative price has gotten worse; in 1989, it cost 62 percent of the median family income, and in 1999 it was even higher, up to 73 percent.[23] By 2004, Yale's tuition was $29,820, room and board were $9,030, and if we conservatively calculate expenses somewhat under Howe's estimate, as one-half of room and board, then adding $4,515 gives us a total of $43,365 as Yale's average cost. In 2004, the expense of keeping a youth at Yale was equal to 75 percent of the median family income of $57,500.

The standard defense for the expensiveness of elite private colleges involves two complementary lines of argument.[24] First, it is a necessary price for academic freedom, and second, it is essential for a top-quality education. Like many other academics, Howe believed that universities could best advance learning and science by being masters of their own fate.[25] Academic freedom required financial self-sufficiency; purse strings were an effective means of imposing external controls. Leaders at Yale thought that the whole of higher education in the United States benefited by having some of its most prestigious institutions in the financially independent private sector. Berkeley enjoyed as much autonomy as it had, Howe and others would assert, largely because the self-governance of elite private universities in America. They believed that politicians would hesitate to micromanage state universities when those institutions had to compete with autonomous private ones.[26]

The academic freedom argument was matched with the best quality education argument. Expensive private institutions put more resources into the education of their students than did inexpensive state ones.[27] Relative to the total real bill for physical plant, faculty quality, small classes, libraries, and instructional materials, Yale subsidizes a very substantial portion of the educational expenditures for every one of its undergraduates. In 1957, a press release from the President's Office put the deficit between what undergraduates pay and what Yale spends on each at $1,247.[28] Yale supplied from its endowment and gift income 37 percent of the real cost of educating its undergraduates in 1957. The ratio of what a student pays to what the institution contributes to the true cost of his or her education has improved to the student's advantage over the years in the private sector; calculations for the academic year 1994 to 1995, put the percentage of total costs subsidized by elite private colleges at 61 percent, nearly double what Yale reported in 1957.[29] Paradoxically, students pay the most at elite colleges, and still end up contributing "the smallest share of their educational costs" in comparison with state institutions.[30]

For Yale and other elite colleges to remain fiscally solvent, Howe estimated that 60 percent of undergraduates had to pay full fees. The rest could receive various levels of financial assistance, but 60 percent of undergraduates should come from rich families. These were, Howe believed, the inescapable underpinnings of academic freedom and excellence, and they forced Yale into an embrace with the upper class.

Howe was troubled, nonetheless, by Yale's drift in the 1950s toward becoming more and more socially exclusive. Howe's 60 percent upper-class quota was being exceeded with no limits to its growth in sight. Each year brought a small decline in the number of applicants requesting financial aid and a large increase in applicants without any financial needs. Howe explained to the alumni,

> Since World War II, . . . though there has been a vast growth of alumni and corporation sponsored [aid] awards, the percentage of Yale undergraduates receiving financial aid has declined approximately 5%, . . . Furthermore, if we compare Yale applicants of 1952 with those of 1957, we find a slight decline in the number of scholarship candidates, whereas the paying applicants have increased by approximately 700.[31]

Yale was attracting fewer and fewer applications from boys in families unable to pay Yale's full sticker price. In other words, a larger number and a higher relative percentage of boys from wealthy families were applying to Yale than ever before. The post-war upsurge in applications reflected rising participation rates for the affluent; whereas in the past only a minority of wealthy offspring bothered with college, now it was becoming the norm for high-income families to send all of their children to college.

Being knowledgeable about the social geography of wealth in America, Howe worried that if Yale lost its 60/40 balance and became exclusively upper class, it would cease to be a national institution. Yale's scholarship policies and its financial aid programs were recruitment tools to assist Yale's efforts to broaden its geographic reach. Howe explained, "I would state without reservation that Yale College does have an abiding interest in preserving a strong undergraduate scholarship program. We must, as a significant national institution, cater to more than the top 5% of the nation's income group."[32] If Yale had the special mission of selecting and educating leaders, it should do so for the whole country.

In addition to Yale's interest in geographic distribution, Howe thought Yale's dedication to selecting tomorrow's leaders meant it should not entirely restrict itself to the very rich. He believed that America's leadership talent was not monopolized by the top 5 percent. Yale should keep open some opportunities for aspiring leaders to emerge out of the middle class. Harvard's gamble project was designed for the lower class; Howe was less worried about their representation at Yale than he was concerned about Yale becoming an exclusive club for the ultra rich. He wanted to use financial aid as a means of holding onto Yale's middle class.

Financial Aid as a Means of Managing Social Composition

Yale had decades of experience using financial assistance as a way to include or exclude particular social categories of candidates. There were always scholarships at Yale for "deserving" but needy boys. After the vast fortunes donated by three families (Sterling, Harkness, and Whitney) in the 1920s, worth then $74 million dollars (estimated by Yale's OIR to be equivalent in 1999 dollars to $790 million), Yale had sufficient endowment to assist approximately one-third of each class.[33]

If a boy requested assistance, he would have to explain the financial assets and debts of his family. Yale could admit and grant or deny aid as it saw fit. In the 1930s, for example, refusing aid was a way to restrict the number of Jewish youths matriculating, although appearing to be fair about academic standards. The admissions dean in 1932, Robert N. Corwin, wrote to Yale's president, James Rowland Angell, on the offers being made that year. Corwin scribbled in long hand next to some statistics, "The [Jewish] racial quota among the provisionally accepted is somewhat larger than is usual or desirable—I trust that it will be reduced by the conditions imposed in the letters sent to those requesting aid."[34] It was a calculated risk to admit a Jewish boy with a demonstrated need, and then refuse any aid in the hope that it would be the last time they would communicate with him; they hoped he would not, as Howe put it, "pull a rich grandmother from the closet."[35] It was a bet Yale repeatedly made and won.

In Howe's time in office, there were social-class benefits to be collected by wealthy applicants in the admissions game. Being able to pay one's own way increased one's odds of admission. And not being self-supporting could leave one vulnerable to the scholarship whims of local alumni committees. Even if the office in New Haven wanted to admit a boy and give him financial aid, the alumni committee from his local area could have already rejected him as an aid recipient for alumni funds, and the alumni action could preempt any money offer.

In a memo to Yale's leaders in preparation for a vote on aid policy by the highest governing power of the university, the Yale Corporation, Howe elaborated on the realities of how financial assistance was allocated in the past. He wrote,

> For many years it has been our avowed policy to reach admissions decisions without reference to whether candidates requested financial assistance, and then separately to make a decision whether to offer aid to those requiring it. It must be acknowledged, however, that the Admissions Committee has not fully observed its avowed policy. Among the reasons for the discrepancy between policy and procedure are:
>
> a. Occasionally we sense that we must choose between two candidates of approximately equal strength in all respects. If we are satisfied that there is no basis on which to distinguish between them, we may rationalize that one is free, and the other would require substantial scholarship, and that we should therefore favor the former for admission as he will not cost us anything.

b. On other occasions we compromise our policy in order to handle difficult relationships with alumni associations possessing their own scholarship
funds. . . . [W]e tend to put admissible candidates who have not been approved for aid [by the alumni association] on the Reserve List for admission,
solely as a device to insure that we stay within our budget. . . . Though our
decision may be expedient, it clearly breaches our policy of not considering
financial circumstances in reaching admissions decisions.[36]

The Yale Corporation, which holds powers of final say on anything it
cares to rule on, always kept tight control over financial aid. The Corporation legally owns and controls Yale; it has ten self-perpetuating trustees
and six elected alumni members, with Yale's president and the governor and
lieutenant governor of Connecticut serving *ex officio*.[37] The Corporation received detailed reports on and voted on exactly how many could receive
aid, how much of that aid should be in the form of grants from restricted
or unrestricted funds, how much should be work-study employment, and
how much in loans. The policy from 1953 to 1963 was, Howe explained, to
restrict the use of university funds for aid. Howe reported,

> A Corporation Committee headed by Mr. Hadley recommended and the
> Corporation voted in 1953 that not more than 25% of entering freshmen
> should be assisted from University funds. In recent years we have been able
> to provide the help needed by approximately 35% of entering classes only
> because we annually receive considerable support from Alumni Associations
> and other outside sources.[38]

The Corporation imposed a cap of 25 percent in 1953 because in previous years Yale was assisting more students, and at a greater cost to its bank
account, than either Harvard or Princeton. In 1952, when Yale was helping
43 percent of its undergraduates, its two closest rivals were providing aid to
33 percent.[39] And even more important than the percentage benefiting from
tuition sticker-price discounts and housing grants, Yale was spending too
much of its unrestricted income on aid. The Corporation report stated,

> The degree of student aid drain on general funds at Yale represents one of
> the University's most serious budgetary problems. . . . Princeton's entire aid
> program . . . is supported without resorting to general funds. In 1948–49,
> 26% of Harvard student aid was financed from general funds ($342,000) as
> against 44% the same year for Yale ($526,000).[40]

The Hadley Committee's solution was to limit those in each class year receiving aid to 25 percent, to shift the aid package away from grants toward loans, and to raise more endowed scholarship funds.[41] As we saw with Howe's comments on admissions practices, a social-class bias against very needy boys was put into effect. If one were without any means of contributing to the costs of a Yale education, then one would face the prospect of not receiving any financial award whatsoever. The report proposed, "Through prior agreement with the alumni committees, reduce the proportion of awards to Freshmen who have virtually no resources of their own."[42] If you got admitted despite financial need, the Corporation wanted to reduce your odds of matriculating by offering help to fewer truly needy boys than before. The Hadley Report estimated that these proposed measures would save Yale $100,000 in 1953 to 1954 alone, and after four years, over $400,000 per year.[43]

Although the Corporation set financial policy, Yale coordinated its aid program with the rest of the Ivy League, and from 1958, Yale also worked with MIT, the University of Chicago, and Stanford University. Financial officers from all those institutions would meet as the "Ivy Group," sometimes twice a year, to "compare and negotiate awards to joint scholarship candidates . . . [and ensure] progress towards the standardization of awards" and tuition increases.[44] For these colleges, competitive markets may be fine for many things, but not for setting student financial aid costs for universities.

The Ivy Group was the first version of the name "Ivy League," and it dates to an agreement signed by presidents of the eight colleges on athletics in 1945.[45] The group wanted to prevent scholarship candidates from bidding one college against another, and that was also the motive for the "ninety-five mostly northeastern private colleges and universities" who used the College Board (CB) to launch the College Scholarship Service in 1954.[46] Just as the College Board set up the Educational Testing Service (ETS) to promote the private sector's preference for SAT tests over school grades in college admission, the board created the College Scholarship Service to formalize and legitimate the private sector's guidelines for awarding "needs-based" financial aid. The Ivy Group worked in tandem with the College Scholarship Service.

It was convenient that the private sector's championing of scholarships for needy youths boosted its reputation for equal opportunity as well as for meritocracy. The private sector could say it had the best of both by claiming to admit based on merit, and assist based on need, and that helped improve its public image. The "dramatic increase in College Board membership after 1960 [is attributed] to the attraction of this stance to a growing body of colleges and universities."[47]

The Top Five Percent of Family Income

The Ivy Group's and the College Scholarship Service's policies for awarding financial aid were very generous from the start. But their guidelines were designed less with an eye for promoting equal opportunity than with a focus on keeping the middle classes in private elite colleges. Their policies fit perfectly with Howe's calculations on quotas for income groups at private colleges. Everyone below the top 5 percent of the income pyramid would receive some support. For example, in 1958 the median family income was $5,100, yet one's family had to earn over $12,000 to be disqualified for financial aid.

To illustrate with specific reference to Harvard's policies in 1958, which were typical of the whole Ivy Group, if a candidate was from a poor family in the bottom quartile earning approximately $3,000 per year, and he had two siblings, his family would be expected to contribute $250 or 8 percent of its annual income toward tuition and expenses, and that 8 percent would cover only 8 percent of the estimated total student budget of $2,818. If a student came from a family in the top income quartile, making $8,000 (which put one at the lower boundary of the top quartile), and had two siblings, his parents would have to contribute $850 or 11 percent of their income; that $850 would cover 30 percent of his total expenses. One's family could be in the top 10 percent of the income pyramid, earning $12,000, and if one had two siblings, one's parents would kick in $1,550 or 13 percent of their income, and that would pay for 55 percent of one's student budget.[48]

On face value, it would seem like quite a gamble to offer some assistance to every one not coming from the very rich, but Ivy Group institutions knew their applicant pool. They knew that self-selection was giving them more self-supporting applicants each year, and that their admissions practices of selecting for leaders from among those with high academic records would keep the social composition of undergraduates overwhelmingly upper class. Administrators could honestly say it was not their fault if most applicants with good grades, high SAT scores, and credentials as school leaders were from privileged families. Those who did the calculations knew that officially generous financial aid programs were not going to bust their budgets.

If the idea was to have a trickle of students from low-income families, and a giant river of youths from high-income families, it worked. Hard numbers on income percentiles and matriculations in the Ivy League are difficult for scholars and the public to come by, though they are known by each college's office of institutional research. To illustrate again with Harvard, and working with years for which we have reliable data, one can be confident that undergraduates from the bottom-income quartile were no more than 8 percent of the student body in 1935, 5 percent in 1986, and according to numbers released by Harvard's president's office, 7 percent in 1999.[49] When President Lawrence Summers issued a call, late in the day but not necessarily hypocritical, for greater access by the economically underprivileged to "highly selective colleges"[50] he gave out the statistics on income quartiles and selective institutions referenced in our introduction.[51] Summers did not, however, break things down within quartiles so one could see the percentage of undergraduates at Harvard who came from the top 5 percent. Was Howe's advice on needing 60 percent of one's undergraduates from the top 5 percent being followed?

We can get a useful approximation of the size of the top 5 percent in any given year at Harvard, Yale, or any of the colleges in the Ivy Group, by looking at the percentage of undergraduates who do not receive any needs-based financial aid whatsoever. If one uses financial aid policies that provide some assistance to everyone except the top 5 percent, then those without aid may be reasonably assumed to derive from that category. There are, no doubt, exceptions; there are middle class families too proud and self-reliant to request assistance. But over the years, especially with the type of family that sends its children to Ivy League colleges, one may assume that most knew and took full advantage of how the system worked. Those without any need-based aid may be viewed as a proxy for membership in Howe's top 5 percent.

From Table 3.1, we can see that at Yale the percentage receiving financial aid from 1952 to 2002 has gravitated around 40. If one takes just those years for which we have continuous data for Yale, from 1981 to 1998, the average for all undergraduates on financial aid has been exactly 40 percent (with a low of 37 percent and a high of 44 percent, and the most frequent percentage being 38). Howe's 60 percent enrollment target from the top 5 percent of America's families appears to have been successfully implemented for half a century, without any public outrage about class privilege. And it is equally obvious that Yale's decision in 1963 to do admissions "needs blind," which has been highly praised as a victory for meritocracy, made no impact on Howe's basic 60/40 formula.

TABLE 3.1

Percent of Entering Undergraduates Receiving Financial Aid at Yale, 1952–2002.

Year	Percent in Entering Class with Aid	Year	Percent in Entering Class with Aid
1952	43	1986	38
1958	34	1987	38
1960	29	1988	38
1961	36	1989	38
1962	37	1990	38
1963	38	1991	41
1964	40	1992	43
1965	39	1993	44
1966	49	1994	44
1971	44	1995	44
1981	37	1996	42
1982	39	1997	41
1983	39	1998	41
1984	38	2002	37
1985	38		

SOURCES: Office of the President, *Griswold Papers*, Box 6, Folder 45, "Report of the Committee on Scholarship Aid," 1952–3; Office of the President, Griswold Papers, Box 6, Folder 43, "Statistics on Admissions 1958"; Office of the President, *Brewster Papers*, Box 3, Folder 7, "Statistics on Admissions and Financial Aid," 1960-1966"; Office of the President, Brewster Papers, Box 4, Folder 4, "Profile of the Yale Class of 1975," for 1971;Office of Institutional Research, "Percentage of Students Receiving Financial Aid, 1981-1998," Table L-3, Yale University; *U.S. News and World Report, America's Best Colleges* 2003, On-Line Premium Edition, *Yale University Profile, for* 2002.

Needs-Blind Admissions

When Yale went "needs blind," evaluating applicants without any reference to their ability to pay, Howe was admissions dean; he was among those who labored for over six months drafting a report to present to the Yale Corporation explaining how "needs blind" could work. The working group on this included Kingman Brewster, Jr., provost of Yale; Charles S. Gage, the University treasurer; John Perry Miller, dean of the Graduate School, and Admissions Dean Howe.[52] During this project, Howe wrote to Gage, "We have adequate financial aid to provide what help is needed by approximately one-third of each entering class, and presumably will continue to be able to do so even if costs go up. What concerns me is that the remaining two-thirds of each class must be recruited from approximately the upper 5 per cent of American families in terms of income distribution. This inherently restricts the range of our selection."[53] In a memo providing background for the proposal to the Corporation, he drew attention again to the top 5 percent with these words, "I would remind the Governing Board that approximately 95% of the families in the United States are not capable of meeting our present charges to undergraduates."[54]

The sixteen members of the Corporation met in April 1963 in their special room in Woodbridge Hall, with each member sitting in a tall leather chair displaying his name in brass, and voted in favor of the new policy. The social logic and statistics backing the policy may be a stunning confirmation of Yale's analytical capacities. We cannot know for certain, however, because Yale's administration refuses to release the report for scholarly evaluation.[55]

When the needs-blind policy was announced at a press conference on May 28, 1963, Yale's statement reported, "At the present time, approximately 35 per cent of the 1,025 students who enter each year in the Freshman Class receive financial aid. Dean Howe estimates that in 1964 under the new program, the number receiving aid will increase to at least 40 per cent."[56]

As a scientific hypothesis in 1963, Howe's 40 percent prediction was extraordinarily accurate, if one believes that Yale has not fudged the matter. Systematic manipulation, however, probably has not been necessary. The 40 percent formula represents what Yale could reasonably expect, given its applicant pool, its selectivity standards, and the well-known (inside and outside Yale) correlation between high socioeconomic status and high academic grades and test scores. The role of SAT scores in all of this is particularly ironic because the combination of needs-blind and high SAT scores was taken as evidence of Yale's meritocracy, when the opposite was closer to the truth. Researchers at Yale knew that high SAT scores correlated well with high family income, and badly with first-year college grades. So if one was going to practice "needs-blind," what better way to screen out most charity cases in advance than to insist on high average SAT scores? The higher the average scores publicly reported for last year's entering class, the more elevated will be the social composition of next year's self-selected applicant pool. And candidates with leadership promise would also, like high SAT scores, tend to come from privileged social-class backgrounds. Yale was not risking a financial crisis by the "needs-blind" policy. Besides, if the admissions office made a mess of it, such as appears to have been the case at Princeton and MIT in the late 1960s when those two institutions reversed course for budgetary reasons, the policy could always be changed.

The real social policy behind needs-blind was to hold onto some middle-class students, as the financial aid director's report submitted under R. Inslee Clark's administration as admissions dean made clear in 1969. When the policy of meeting the full needs of all of those admitted was brought into question because other members of the Ivy Group were retreating from it, the aid director, Ralph Burr, explained Yale wanted it to hold onto the middle class. Burr wrote, "The question naturally arises whether we can hold to our current policy. . . . M.I.T. and Princeton have withdrawn from similar policies, and at present Yale would appear to be the only major private university making this kind of commitment. . . . The real danger of a retreat from our present policy would seem to lie in the possible creation of a 'very rich—very poor' split in the undergraduate body. The middle economic range is apt to be squeezed out."[57] Yale had room for 40 percent of its students to come from relatively affluent yet below the top-5-percent-income bracket, and needs-blind was a way of getting them.

The needs-blind admissions policy was also, ironically, the perfect way to flatter children of privilege. Beginning in 1963, and ever since, each youth enrolled at Yale could claim, no matter how wealthy his parents, to have been admitted based on his merits and not on his family's bank account. What better way to affirm a class myth of superiority than to be able to say to them collectively, "We pick you because you are the best, not because you are rich." Yale's President Brewster understood perfectly well the value of that conceit. He wrote, once "the pocket book was no longer relevant to admission, the privileged took pride in the feeling that [they] had made it on the merits rather than on the basis of something ambiguously called 'background.'"[58] When the bottom half of the family income scale provides not more than 10 percent of one's undergraduates, and the top quarter provides nearly 80 percent, the impact of needs-blind is more symbolic than material. Perversely, it comforts a larger number of privileged than underprivileged youths.

Needs-blind was a brilliant policy that promised something for every social class. It held out a hope of upward mobility for the bottom, a means to stay in the game for the middle, and confirmation of individual merit for the top.

Wrapping up the 1950s

Before we turn to the Brewster years at Yale, we can see from this chapter that the nexus between upper-class families and Yale's liberal arts culture was clearly understood and cultivated under President A. Whitney Griswold and Admissions Dean Howe throughout the 1950s and early 1960s. A young man from a privileged family had, Yale's administration thought, the right sensibilities to benefit from residence at Yale; youths from lower social classes, Jewish or not, would not be well matched to the college culture. They would be grinds when Yale wanted gifted and subtle thinkers. Yale's office of admissions explored, with the assistance of Ramsey, a "sociocultural" model to predict whether a youth had the right sensibilities for an elite liberal arts education. They did not call it "cultural capital," but in effect, they were looking at the same qualities that interested Pierre Bourdieu.

Separate from family culture, admissions staff, administrators, and alumni intensified their hunt for personal character. Every technique available was used to search for physical and psychological signs of a youth's personal promise to be a leader of tomorrow. Whether as pre-admissions alumni interview or post-admissions nude posture photo, the machinery of evaluation in the 1950s was calibrated to identify the Yale man.

Under Howe's direction, Yale aimed at and succeeded in getting 60 percent of its youths from families able to pay the full costs of tuition and residence. Howe may have been wrong that only the top 5 percent of families ranked by income could afford a Yale education, but he could not have been off by much. Families had to be very well off not to qualify for Yale's generous aid arrangements. Measured by Yale's financial schemes, the economic composition of its undergraduates remained constantly privileged.

CHAPTER FOUR

The Brewster Years, Meritocracy in Power?

The New Administration in 1964: Kingman Brewster and Inslee Clark

Did Yale abandon its leadership-class mission shortly after A. Whitney Griswold's death in 1963 and Arthur Howe's resignation in 1964? In Nicholas Lemann's book,[1] the new administration of President Kingman Brewster and Admissions Dean R. Inslee Clark, Jr., waged war against legacies and WASPs to usher the new meritocratic elite into Yale. Many things did change at Yale during Brewster's years in office, but not Yale's sense of mission, its loyalty to legacies, or its embrace of wealthy families.

Kingman Brewster, Jr. (1919–88), president of Yale from 1964 to 1977, features prominently in all of the meritocratic accounts of the decline of privilege on the Long Island Sound. According to the authoritative dissertation on Brewster written by Geoffrey Kabaservice, Brewster was a meritocratic modernizer with many impressive accomplishments.[2] During his administration Jews, Blacks, and women gained acceptance at Yale College; the neglected natural sciences were transformed with federal funds; an incestuous and underachieving faculty were supplanted by aggressive external talent searches and new professional standards; graduate programs and professional schools flourished. And, most important of all, Kabaservice's text presents Brewster as the man who oversaw the meritocratization of Yale's admissions; in parallel, he advocated placing talented newcomers in positions of leadership across the range of American institutions, from government and the professions to corporations and universities. Brewster championed, in Kabaservice's narrative, an open and meritocratic elite.

Kabaservice describes Brewster's approach to meritocracy as being "subjective" to distinguish it from an "objective" form of meritocracy that relies on standardized measures of ability, such as test scores. As Kabaservice states, "The 'subjective' version of meritocracy . . . attempts to judge fairly between candidates, but based on personal judgments of quality, character and ability rather than numerical measures alone."[3] Whether or not "subjective meritocracy" is a fudge that inflates personal chemistry over competence, Kabaservice is onto something important about Brewster's life and about his approach to administration and admissions at Yale. Brewster was a talented member of the upper class who thought he could recognize similar qualities in others; after all, his distinguished mentors in life had recognized those qualities in him. "Subjective meritocracy" is one way to describe Brewster's recurrent experience of being elevated by an older mentor into a new career position. And, in turn, the concept of subjective meritocracy captures how Brewster trusted more in personal face-to-face evaluations than in paper files, whether that judgment was for a position in the administration or a place in an undergraduate class.

Brewster's style of subjective meritocracy is shown in his anointing of a leadership team for Yale. His inner circle was composed of young and relatively untested men. As Kabaservice points out, Henry "Sam" Chauncey, Jr., was aged 28 when appointed special assistant to Brewster. Sam was from a very old Yale family, and his father worked as a scholastic talent scout at Harvard before founding the Educational Testing Service (ETS). R. Inslee "Inky" Clark was 29 when Brewster made him admissions dean; Clark was a graduate of Yale College, and his only accomplishment away from Yale was employment as a teacher at a private boarding school. Charles "Charlie" Taylor was "a little-known, thirty-five year-old associate professor of English and an assistant dean in the Graduate School" when Brewster made him Yale's Provost.[4]

Brewster, as Kabaservice's narrative makes abundantly clear, was as much of a blue blood as any American could get.[5] With Mayflower lineage on his father's side, wealth and culture on his mother's, Brewster was nourished and networked by generations of the New England establishment. His father had a Harvard law degree, his mother a BA from Wellesley. Although his parents divorced when he was 4, his mother's family fortune was more than adequate to cushion against social ostracism. From age 7 to 11, he lived in the maternal family's mansion with a full staff of servants, an English governess, and a chauffeur to drive him to school. Upon his maternal grandfather's death in 1930, his mother took her share of a four and one-half million dollar inheritance and moved her children to an affluent neighborhood adjacent to Harvard. She married a Harvard music professor, Edward Ballantine. Edward's father was president of Oberlin College, and his brother was "undersecretary of the Treasury under Hoover and Roosevelt."[6] Brewster went to the local school for Harvard's faculty children, the Belmont Hill School. As a youth at home in Cambridge, and during summers spent on Martha's Vineyard, Brewster met many prominent figures in the worlds of music, politics, law, and academia. The list included Dean Acheson, Roger Baldwin, Felix Frankfurter, Whitney Griswold, Rudolph Serkin, and Igor Stravinsky. While at school, Brewster's debating team "defeated a Groton . . . team that included Franklin Roosevelt, Jr., and William and McGeorge Bundy."[7] As a youth, Brewster loved sailboats and competed hard in regattas against, among others, the Kennedy brothers. Twice Brewster won the highest possible prize for a teenage sailor, the Prince of Wales Cup.[8] After two European tours and an extended stay in England, Brewster entered Yale College in 1937, a member of the class of 1941.

In those post-Depression, pre-war days, Yale was an oasis of upper-class comfort. It had maids to clean the undergraduates' rooms. Young men wore jackets and ties to dinner, and sometimes to class. Brewster was in Timothy Dwight, one of the residential colleges at Yale. Like the others, its "dinning hall featured white linen tablecloths, silverware and china bearing the college's insignia, fresh flowers in place settings, printed menus, and waitress service."[9] Harvard and Princeton were at the time similarly privileged upper-class clubs. There were 858 in Brewster's class, maybe 10 percent were Jewish, but not one Black; 30 percent were legacies; and 74 percent were from private schools.[10]

Brewster worked on the student newspaper, was president of a student club, and "helped found the America First Committee (AFC) which became the most prominent organization leading the struggle to keep America out of the European war."[11] The AFC campaign was not Brewster's best moment as a member of the leadership class. He refused to join a secret society, but he was popular, well known as an intelligent critic of many established practices, and he gave the oration on Class Day in June 1941.[12]

After graduation, he took a job in Washington, D.C., working for Nelson Rockefeller. The Pearl Harbor attack propelled Brewster into the Navy to fly anti-submarine planes. During the war, he married his Vassar sweetheart, and failed, to his regret, to see any enemy action.[13] When the war was over, he went to Harvard Law School; in doing so, "Brewster was following a well-trodden establishment path."[14] He made Law Review, and most importantly, formed a student-to-mentor relation with Professor Milton Katz. When Katz was made general counsel to the central office of the Marshall Plan in Paris, he took Brewster along. After a year in Paris helping process billions of dollars of U.S. aid, MIT beckoned Brewster back to Cambridge for a research position in the economics department. Before the end of his first academic year at MIT, Brewster was offered (again through the personal intervention of his Harvard mentor, Katz), and accepted, an assistant professorship at Harvard's law school.[15] Three years later, at the age of 34 and with one published article to his credit, Brewster was made a full, tenured professor. Kabaservice interviewed Brewster's step-nephew, Harvard Law Professor Duncan Kennedy, who explained Brewster's tenure as, once again, largely because of his mentor, Katz. Kennedy said, "It was a lifetime job based on your mentor saying to [the Law School Dean] . . . , 'This guy would be good.'"[16]

Brewster taught law at Harvard for nine years when, sailing one day off Martha's Vineyard with "his longtime friend and teacher, Yale's president Whit Griswold," he was offered the provost's job at Yale.[17] Brewster accepted; he was not exactly having a brilliant career at Harvard. As Kabaservice reports, "Brewster brought with him no great reputation from Harvard, . . . The Yale Law School faculty grumbled at giving him tenure upon his appointment [as provost], . . . because, as Law Professor Leon Lipson says bluntly, 'We had the impression of Brewster as a straight-shooting mediocrity.'"[18]

Brewster arrived in New Haven for the fall of 1960 coinciding, sadly, with Griswold's cancer diagnosis. Griswold's illness compelled Brewster to assume some presidential responsibilities. Griswold's death was, at the end, "an ordeal for Brewster"[19]; they were products of the same social milieu and very old friends. Griswold died in April 1963; Brewster was announced to the world as Yale's new president that October.

Brewster, the offspring of economic and cultural privilege, was no doubt brilliant and charming. It was, nonetheless, his connections to older mentors that opened the doors to his positions at Harvard and Yale.

Brewster and Admissions' Controversies

Less than one year after Brewster's spectacular coronation-like inauguration as president, he addressed alumni representatives on the issue of admissions. There were in the 1960s, as in the 1930s, alumni complaints that sons with good character were being passed over for test-score-wiz kids. After lunch in Yale's Commons dining hall, Brewster was introduced by William Rockefeller, Yale Class of 1940, to the Alumni Convocation on Saturday, February 20, 1965. Brewster remarked on the mythical controversies clouding the air over Yale's admissions' policies. He said,

> The first issue . . . overdrawn to the point of being misleading is in the area of admissions policy. The caricature would portray a tug of war between an allegedly anti-intellectual, well rounded alumnus on the one hand, and a purblind intellectualized faculty member on the other. Each is portrayed as determined to see Yale perpetuate his own kind to the exclusion of all else. . . . But now, just as the admissions problem is made to seem dramatic by the appalling avalanche of applications, this caricature is perhaps less valid than ever.[20]

Brewster sought to assure alumni that, like Howe, he wanted to keep a balance between brains and character. He was not trying to elevate one criterion over the other. And like Howe, Brewster could point to "the appalling avalanche of applications" as the reason why Yale could have it both ways.

Alumni in the field were not alone in expressing concerns in the first year of Brewster's administration about admissions. Some feathers were ruffled on the sixteen members of Yale's all-powerful Corporation by reports that Clark was not being obsequious at trips to boarding schools, that he was visiting public high schools in New York, and admitting too many Jews. When Clark went, as was customary for the admission dean, to one of Yale's top 'feeder' schools, Andover, he put his foot in it. "Meritocratic" Harvard had the week before promised to be kind to the bottom of Andover's graduating class; when Clark was asked about underachievers, he said Yale was looking only for the best.[21] Many of Yale's Andover alumni were appalled. What is the value of the Yale/Andover nexus if, after a father invests in his son's school, Yale draws the line above the heads of Andover's bottom quartile? Clark's naïf affront to privilege was matched by an unusual trip to some hitherto off-limits high schools in New York. Before Clark, the admissions office ignored requests from New York's three specialized public schools (Stuyvesant, Bronx Science, and Brooklyn Technical) to attend college nights, mostly because of the presence there of Jewish boys.[22] When word of those steps reached some members of the Yale Corporation, they thought Clark was searching in the wrong places for talent.

There was broad agreement at Yale on the desirability of educating leaders. Clark wanted to admit young men who would become tomorrow's leaders just as much as any member of the Corporation. As Clark explained about his admissions practices to Kabaservice many years later, "Yale was not for a minute changing its elitist approach to its role in world leadership."[23] There were, however, differences on where one should look for them. Clark was not limiting Jews to 10 percent of each class, and he was not, despite his own background, giving private schools preference over public schools. At a Corporation meeting the year of Brewster's alumni speech, Clark was brought up short by a blunt-speaking upper-class and Protestant member of the Corporation. The Corporation Fellow said, "You're talking about Jews and public school graduates as leaders. Look around you at this table. These are America's leaders. There are no Jews here. There are no public school graduates here."[24] No less than the anti-Semitic member of the Corporation, Clark and Brewster both wanted to be able to say at its meetings that here sits a representative slice of America's leaders, but they wanted non-WASPs at the table as well.

Outside Woodbridge Hall where Corporations meetings are held, its members need not fear public ostracism for their views. They are the highest power at a prestigious university that is a non-profit, private foundation. Their meetings are confidential, and their records are sealed for 75 years after the resignation of the Yale president in office at the time. In the case of this particular Corporation member, any evidence of his comments in the Corporation's minutes of 1965 will not come to light until the year 2052. We know about this only because Clark offered his version of the exchange to Kabaservice's oral-history project in 1993.[25]

Anti-Semitism and Brewster's Administration

Brewster tiptoed around the anti-Semitism of Corporation members and prominent alumni. No evidence has come to light suggesting that he objected at the Corporation meeting to the comments on Jews. And when a similarly anti-Semitic view was articulated by a major alumni contributor, Brewster ignored the rhetoric to mollify the outraged old blue. The occasion of Brewster's diplomacy was presented by a report in the press. In 1967, the *New York Times* published an article claiming, "Yale has almost completely abandoned the goal of geographical distribution, . . . the move . . . is cited as a possible reason why Jewish enrollment [from New York] . . . has increased sharply. At Yale, more than 20 per cent of the freshmen this year are Jewish. Ten years ago the figure was 10 per cent."[26] Apparently, Yale's forty-year-old 10 percent Jewish quota had been dropped.

Ten days later, a prominent alumnus banker from Manhattan wrote Brewster,

> The NYT News Service . . . discloses some very radical changes and some
> of these disturb me very much. The article quotes Mr. Clark, the Dean of
> Admissions at Yale, as saying that Yale has completely abandoned the goal
> of geographic distribution. . . . The second thing which gives me concern
> is the change in the policy with respect to the admission of Jews. I am not
> anti-Jewish and I have some very close personal friends who are Jewish.
> However, I feel it would be a great mistake for Yale to admit 20% to 25%
> Jews. Many of these are bound to come from NYC. While I have great
> respect for the brilliant minds of many Jewish men who have been leaders
> in science and industry, I feel that Jews as a class are clannish, self-centered,
> rather selfish and do not rank high in public service. If our total Jewish
> population is 5.6 million . . . I can see no reason why Yale should be much
> above that percentage in its admission of Jews. Certainly, 25%, which is
> four times the National percentage, is far too much.[27]

The alumnus implicitly favored a 6 percent ceiling for Jews (possibly a miss estimation because it is actually larger than their national percentage) and warned that if Yale's Jewish population reached the same proportion as Columbia University's or the University of Pennsylvania's, then "I think many gentiles might well hesitate to enroll."[28] Brewster was quite familiar with the idea of a quota for Jews that would keep their presence at Yale roughly proportionate to their size in the U.S. population. He was the one who cut any reference to that idea out of a confidential admissions policy statement drafted under Griswold's presidency.

When Yale felt under legal threat for its treatment of Jews from the State of Connecticut, it wrote an admissions policy statement as a defensive measure, possibly with an eye toward producing it in court. Drafts of the statement were treated as top secret; in at least one instance the current version was taken from Griswold's office, transported and delivered to Howe by a campus policeman. Yale's lawyers and Brewster, as provost and someone with legal training, were party to eleven drafts that stretched from February to May in 1962 before Griswold settled on a final version. The complications in the correspondence, draft revisions, and hand-written notes all turn on the issue of Jewish admissions.

One draft version raised the idea of a proportional quota in these words:

> As a national university with a Protestant tradition, committed to the nation-wide recruitment of its students and to a student body representative of American society in the large, the relative proportions of the various religious and racial groups in the nation may be of significance to their proportions at Yale.[29]

Brewster's handwritten instruction, next to the draft section just quoted, was "omit."[30] (As an aside, it is worth noting that in all of this discussion of Yale undergraduates representing the composition of the nation, no one raised the issue of including women.) Brewster also convinced Griswold to cut the following affirmation of Yale's undergraduates' Protestant identity. Draft number eight said, "Just as educational institutions founded in other religious traditions will appeal to practitioners of their respective faiths, so Yale will appeal to students of Protestant background or affiliation."[31] Brewster penciled a note about how this was a historical statement, and the troublesome sentence was cut. Whether or not Brewster knew that Yale's administration in the 1920s and 1930s wrote about having a "racial quota" for Jews, he knew that the current administration saw Yale as a Protestant institution with legitimate interests in keeping the size of its Jewish enrollments down. Brewster may not have agreed with discrimination, but he certainly had an idea it had been practiced by his college.

In 1967, Brewster's response to the alumnus' letter of complaint on the *New York Times* article came more than a month later. In his correspondence to the alumnus, Brewster claimed the delay was because of his end-of-semester workload, but he did find the time to respond to others on this topic first, as we shall see below. It is probable that the discomfort created by the need to deal diplomatically with a prominent alumnus' anti-Semitism caused the tardy response. In any case, Brewster wrote on June 9,

> Dear Mr. . . . :
> I am sorry to have been so slow to answer your thoughtful expression of concern about Yale admissions.
> First, let me say that I too resent the implications of the NYT article on Ivy League admissions, particularly its emphasis on the racial aspect. Everyone here tried to talk the reporter out of this pitch. . . . Second, as far as the facts are concerned, we do not have quotas or built-in discriminations. . . .
> As always I am grateful for the concern which prompts your letters, . . . Your loyalty means a great deal to everyone here who knows how much you have done for Yale.[32]

Brewster sent a copy of the letter to his assistant, Charles M. O'Hearn, who had a personal relation to the complaining banker.

O'Hearn addressed the alumnus by his Christian name and conveniently blamed his anti-Semitic distress on the provocative and unprofessional behavior of the journalist working at the *New York Times*. On June 15, 1967, O'Hearn wrote,

> Dear . . . :
> Kingman sent me a copy of his letter to you of June 9 on the subject of admissions, along with a copy of your letter to him—provoked (and that is a good word) by the New York Times article. I have grown accustomed to bad reporting by the editors of the Yale Daily News, but it seems inexcusable when a staff reporter for one of the best newspapers in the country can write an article as poor as this one was.
> One would think, for example, that Yale was abandoning its position as a

national institution and was concentrating its attention upon the big metropolitan area schools. . . .

I am [also] sending . . . news that I know will please you. . . . Yale did quite well at Andover this year. . . .

With every good wish, I am

Cordially.[33]

Brewster was not so diplomatic when the alumnus was insufficiently "prominent." When an alumnus in secondary education wrote about the same *New York Times* article, objecting as the New York banker had to any drop of Yale's national representation and to any turn away from private schools to public ones, Brewster sarcastically dressed him down. Writing about two weeks before his letter to the New York banker, Brewster said to the educator in New York,

Dear Mr. . . . :

Your right to dissent is, of course, acknowledged.

I suppose you also have the right to impute facts and to jump to wholly unwarranted conclusions, but it disturbs me that you should. . . .

It amazes me that a member of our profession should be so ready to attribute a reporter's remarks . . . to the University.[34]

Sarcasm and accommodations to anti-Semitic alumni aside, it is clear that Brewster put the last nail in the coffin of Yale's infamous discrimination against Jews in admissions. In the Brewster section of the Yale archive, one does not uncover anti-Semitic documents as one does for the Griswold era. Under Griswold, one still finds boys excluded by the admissions committee because of the anti-Semitic prejudice that Jews were incapable of becoming good community citizens and future leaders. For example, a faculty member serving on the admissions committee, Basil Henning, wrote a letter to Howe in July 1955, asking if Yale could do a study proving that Jewish boys made worse "citizens" than Protestants. He was troubled by the impressive academic credentials of Jewish youths who were being rejected in the last round by Howe or Donald Walker because of the assumption that they were poor contributors to the community. The euphemism used for Jewish youths is "Brooklyn boys." Henning wrote to Howe,

Dear Art:

I am . . . a little concerned about the boys with high [academic] predictions whom we reject. I realize that in most cases you and Don are right in bopping these predominantly Brooklyn boys, but I still feel a little uneasy. Would it be possible to make a survey of the ones we do accept to see what kind of citizens they really turn out to be?[35]

One does not find this sort of thing under Brewster's leadership. On admissions, Brewster's administration looks free of anti-Semitism. He did, however, present a legalistic cover-up of Yale's history of discrimination.

Brewster repeatedly said that Yale never had a quota, which of course legalistically depends on how one defines the word *quota*. For example, in 1963, Brewster received a letter asking, "I've been told by someone who has the opportunity of knowing that Yale has definite restrictive quota systems in operation against Jews, Negroes, and other minority groups and also restrictive quotas in reference to the area from which the applicants come from." To which shortly after taking on the office of Yale's presidency, Brewster replied, "I can advise you without qualification that Yale has no quotas. . . . To the best of my knowledge, Yale has at no time in its history had such restrictions as you mention."[36] Brewster was not in this letter or other places being entirely forthright about what he knew.

Brewster and Yale's Mission to Select Future Leaders

Brewster and Clark dropped the restrictive Jewish quota, but not Yale's commitment to the leadership class. Brewster's admissions policies were intended to capture America's future leaders. As he said at an alumni convocation 1966, "I think we are making a conscious effort to be sure of the fact that we are a national institution whose ambition is nothing less than to try to frame a leadership for the nation in the years ahead."[37] Yale's leadership mission was constant throughout his administration.

Brewster knew first hand world-class statesmen, academics, and musicians. When he spoke of selecting young men for Yale based on their potential to become tomorrow's leaders, he had a very clear idea of what he was talking about. He was more interested in future statesmen than in local businessmen, and that desire was not new with his administration. The previous president, Griswold, and admissions dean, Howe, were equally of like mind in wanting to recruit boys who might become major figures on the national or even international stage in their respective fields of endeavor.

The search, whether as art or science, could not be always, or even often, on target. In a report to the Corporation, Howe expressed some frustration with an admissions process that all too often mistook high-school distinctions as reliable signs of future promise. Howe wrote,

> We also identify, too frequently I fear, the dull conformity of a less gifted matriculant who was admitted primarily for his high personal qualities (senior class president at high school!), but who now emerges as an undistinguished individual destined to sell insurance in the Chicago area and use his status as an alumnus to protest the college's athletic losses.[38]

Under Brewster, Yale hosted more than one major alumni event on the theme of leadership. In one particular case, the leadership conference contrasted dramatically with what was going on in the world outside New Haven. In November of 1968, the same year that witnessed the shockingly successful Viet Cong Tet offensive in the Vietnam war, the assassinations of Martin Luther King, Jr., and Robert F. Kennedy, the May–June student-trade union general strike in France, a police riot at the Democratic Party's national convention in Chicago, and student-police campus confrontations at Columbia and Harvard, Yale hosted in its gothic quads an alumni convocation with the theme "Training for Leadership."[39] It was a celebration of Yale's role in producing past leaders, and an assertion of its enhanced value to leaders of today and tomorrow.

Every alumnus attending was given a two-by-two-inch pocket booklet with the title "Yale's Role in the Education of American Leaders" written by Yale's historian, George Pierson. The booklet provides a summary of how Yale men had dominated politics, industry, commerce, and the professions over the years. Statistics were marshaled showing how in every category of leadership, Yale was number one, or when number two, then just behind Harvard. This was intended to reassure the alumni that Yale was pursuing its traditional social mission. The last page stated, "The percentage of future leaders among these [current] Yale men might prove to be even higher than in previous generations. For while in the past it has been possible for 'self-made' men to rise to the top in certain fields, today every segment of society looks for leadership to those with the best formal education."[40] Yale's position as a gatekeeper to the leadership class should be even greater today and tomorrow than in the past.

Critical Issues: Athletes

Both Brewster's administration and its critics accepted "leadership" as the grounds on which to argue about admissions policies. The three overlapping and most vocal critical cliques were provided by athletic advocates, alumni fathers with rejected sons, and families with private-school connections. Each would claim that their constituency provided Yale with its best source of potential leaders and that their own were being denigrated and discriminated against by an admissions committee's obsession with brains and brains alone.

Athletes had a champion in Chester "Chet" LaRoche, Class of 1918, a former Yale football player, chairman of the alumni association's information committee, and chairman of the National Football Foundation (NFF).[41] LaRoche attended Yale University as a Sheffield Science School student, so his proper class designation was "1918s." Sheffield was a technical-science school that stood separate from, and in a second-class relation to, Yale College from 1862 to 1945. It was a fruit of the Land-Grant Act of 1862 that Yale successfully snatched for itself away from the public sector. Sheffield had its own faculty, curriculum, and physical plant. Until 1919, Sheffield students did not even have a common freshman year experience with the rest of Yale College.[42] In comparison with the college, Sheffield boys were stigmatized as lower-class engineering grinds, relegated to the periphery of an affluent liberal arts community.[43] It took the Second World War before Yale would fully absorb Sheffield and technological science into the college. Playing football enabled LaRoche to bridge the two milieus. Whether or not any negative stigma affected his undergraduate experience, in adulthood he was bluer than Rockefeller (blue being the color of Yale College).

Lest anyone find the argument that athleticism builds character antiquarian, one has only to look at George W. Bush's White House. As the *Economist* pointed out, Bush had a reputation as "the jock-in-chief" because of his resurrection of the Victorian belief "that a combination of sport and religion could develop the all-important quality of 'character.'"[44] Faith in the moral character building qualities of sports originated in nineteenth-century England as a way to tame unruly middle-class boys in private boarding "public schools"; the practice, in combination with compulsory chapel attendance, became known as muscular Christianity. If any particular public school headmaster was responsible for the innovation, more credit should go to Harrow's Charles Vaughan than to Rugby's Thomas Arnold.[45] Games became the grounds for turning boys into the men who would spread cricket and British imperialism wherever the sun was not setting. The sports-character cult did not die with empire. Brown-tinted photographs of Yale's athletic teams, from LaRoche's days and earlier, casually posed in emulation of Harrow's eleven, its cricket team, line the hallways of the Yale Club in New York to this day. And more importantly, the sports ethos carried on by contributing to the governing tone, if not the policy substance, of Bush's administration.

As the *Economist* noted, "Bush's well-known enthusiasm for God goes hand-in-hand with an equally well-marked enthusiasm for muscularity." He not only is "surrounded by fellow jocks" in his cabinet and entourage but when he introduced his candidate for the Supreme Court to the nation, he "highlighted the fact that [John Roberts] . . . had been captain of his high-school football team." The *Economist* sees a zeal for muscles rippling through the Republican Party's ranks. Unlike Democrats, for whom "the main qualification for a top job is 'intelligence' . . . for Republicans the most important qualification is 'character'—by which they mean an ability to hit balls and bang heads."[46] Even today, character, as a mixture of religion and athleticism, continues to be seen by some as a vital qualification for America's leaders. The early 1960s' conflict at Yale between jocks with character and scholars with brains remains relevant to contemporary American leaders and politics.

LaRoche's first pronouncement on admissions came in 1957 when *Sports Illustrated* printed his comments objecting to the idea that women should be admitted to Yale College. LaRoche said, "Coeds at Yale? Never! Football greats like Walter Camp . . . would turn over in their graves. What's the world coming to? Women are even trying to crash the Naval Academy and West Point."[47]

In 1967, LaRoche pursued a campaign to reverse Yale's allegedly new admissions policy. LaRoche wanted to restore character, as he saw it, to its rightful position above academic evaluations. Real men of character were found on the playing fields, that is where leadership is learned, not in the classroom. Athletics should count as an academic subject, and boys with top character should be admitted to Yale even if they were low achievers academically. At an Executive Committee meeting of the Alumni Association in January 1967 in St. Louis, LaRoche delivered a report and a memorandum presenting his case. Its impact was sufficient to elicit in response a special discussion in the Corporation's room at Yale that February 15, 1967. As his memo put it, LaRoche wanted "a study of the problems of leadership; . . . How this problem relates to our admissions policies and Alumni Schools Committee."[48] This was necessary because "far too high a percentage of influential alumni are not only sullen—but are in revolt . . . against present-day Yale policies, which, right or wrong, they blame on Inslee Clark."[49] Leaders were being lost, LaRoche believed, because Clark wanted to reward only test scores and grades. LaRoche wanted "a C+ or a B- student, but with an A+ in character; leadership; directed energy; high moral purpose, [to] be given preference over the many brilliant 'specialists.'"[50] And, he thought forming a "Stag Legion" to foster leadership and pro-business attitudes on campus would be a good idea. Yale should

> organize a "Stag Legion" that would be composed of major sport managers and major sport captains, together with the heads of Yale News, Political Union, etc. Such a group would automatically be self-perpetuating. It would bring to the campus monthly business leaders not to talk about their own businesses, but rather the place of the American corporation as our greatest social instrument, its relation to government and to the people.[51]

In November 1967, LaRoche challenged Brewster at the alumni convocation in New Haven with the same arguments. The meeting was held in the oldest building on campus, Connecticut Hall, where Nathan Hale roomed during his Yale days before his execution as a spy during the Revolutionary War. During a question and answer session with Brewster, LaRoche said,

> I think we are all proud of the fact that Yale has developed more leaders, proportionately, than any other college in the country. We developed those leaders under an admission policy that I think most of us understood. We have announced, as I understand it, what amounts to a new admissions policy, . . .
>
> Now . . . we measure men by marks. I doubt whether you can measure men by marks. . . . Now I question whether or not it wouldn't be better if we selected men on the basis, not of marks or brains, but character. If we did that, then there would be a place for the B-minus man or C-minus man who is an A-plus man in character. To me, that is the man that probably would be the leader as against the specialist.[52]

LaRoche urged Yale to find those men with golden characters and weak academic records and admit them as having the metal to become American leaders.

Brewster's off-the-cuff comments in response to LaRoche are worth reproducing because he hit upon many essential points about Yale's admissions policy. Brewster said, given the high

> demand for entrance to places like Yale . . . we haven't found it necessary to submerge the level of intellectual capacity or brains, to reward character. Now the real question is, by what evidence? There, I think that Inky Clark has done more . . . to go behind the test scoring, behind the grades in order to rely on personal judgment of the people who knew the boy, . . . Yale is not known among the competition for automatic response to the testable record as against the subjective record. . . . I would have to say that the [admissions] policy has not changed. The circumstances in which we operate have changed. . . . I don't think you can say there is any proven correlation between mediocre academic performance and outstanding leadership capacity.[53]

Yale's admissions policy of placing more weight on subjective reports of an applicant's character than academic records remained the same during Brewster's administration as under Griswold and Howe. Given the 'avalanche of applications,' why not go for both character and brains? Would anyone seriously claim that one had to be intellectually dim to have a sterling character? LaRoche did not offer himself, or fellow alumni, as evidence of the combination.

When asked a similar question in a letter from an alumnus about leaders with stronger character than brains, Brewster replied, "I am convinced that our people are looking for the right boys and are choosing by the right standards. . . . [W]hile the academic threshold is higher than ever, we have more extracurricular achievers in [the class of] 1970 than we did in 1967; far more in the class of '67 than in 1952. So the canard that we have shifted to a 'brains only' myopia is not borne out by the record."[54]

Brewster was referring to some hard evidence compiled by the Alumni Board of Yale's success in selecting leaders. Brewster could compare youths matriculated in 1948 (total entering were 1,178) with 1966 (total entering were 1,021), the Yale classes of 1952 and 1970. Although school presidents or student council heads were only 5 percent of those entering Yale in 1948, in 1966 they were 22 percent of their class. The same growth was repeated for editors and athletes. Editors of school papers or yearbooks were 3 percent of freshmen in 1948; in 1966 they were 29 percent. Matriculating youths with varsity letters were 21 percent in 1948, and 39 percent in 1966. And varsity captains were 3 percent in 1948, and 10 percent in 1966.[55] If LaRoche was in effect urging more space for athletes, Brewster and Clark had already filled that request.

The rate of improvement in matriculating leaders for the 1966 cohort over 1948 was approximately a 400 percent jump in class presidents or student council heads, a 900 percent leap in student editors, a 200 percent swell in varsity letters, and a 300 percent enlargement in the number of sports captains. The distance between the two classes was greatest for editors, and least for varsity letters. There was under Brewster and Clark, in comparison to Griswold and Howe, spectacular progress in Yale's ability to recognize and reward leadership promise. Although average combined SAT scores went up significantly during those 18 years from approximately 1,200 in 1948 to about 1,400 in 1966,[56] the relative rate of academic upgrade was moderate in comparison with Yale's new record in matriculating leaders.

Critical Issues: Legacies

If the fears articulated by LaRoche and other advocates for more athletic boys with leadership qualities were groundless, what about the complaints of alumni with sons rejected by Yale? To evaluate Brewster's record on legacies we must look at administrative policy as well as objective performance. Did Brewster or any of his admissions deans consciously attempt to reduce the percentage of legacies at Yale? And regardless of intent, what happened to legacy enrollments under Brewster?

Brewster was president of Yale effectively from the fall of 1963 to May 1977 when he left to serve as ambassador to the United Kingdom. He had three different admissions deans under him, first and very briefly Howe, held over from Griswold's administration, then the controversial Clark from February 1965 to the spring of 1971. Clark's first official class entered in September 1965, and his final one began in the fall of 1971. And, last, there was Clark's uncontroversial successor as dean, Worth David.

Sharp declines in the relative percentage of legacies at Harvard, Yale, and Princeton were, one should recall, an important claim in the meritocratic narratives reviewed in the first chapter. What were the objective records of those three universities during the key "transition" years? Harvard's, Princeton's, and Yale's records on legacies from 1950 to 1965 can be seen in Table 4.1.

If we judge the meritocratic narrative of Richard J. Herrnstein and Charles Murray's *Bell Curve* with the years they specify, their argument falls down.[57] If one uses Herrnstein and Murray's years for Harvard, 1950 to 1962, the percentage of legacies goes up slightly. The same is true at Princeton. Only Yale experiences any decline during those years of 3.8 percentage points. For the years given by Herrnstein and Murray, there were no significant signs of legacy displacement.

Lemann was even more specific than Herrnstein and Murray on the subversive effects on legacies of Brewster's admissions dean, Inslee Clark. If Clark's office was driving any change, we should be able to evaluate that by contrasting his record with Howe's on the percentage of legacies enrolled in each class. And we can see if Clark did a personnel house cleaning by checking on how much overlap there was in committee membership between Howe's and Clark's administrations.

Lemann claims that in 1965 Clark cut the number of legacies entering Yale by 40 percent, reducing their relative weight in the freshman class from 20 to 12 percent.[58] The authority he cites for this statistic is an unpublished interview with Clark. Assuming Lemann got Clark's numbers and the year right, then Clark's memory was faulty; however, no matter the source of error, Lemann's account is mistaken.

TABLE 4.1

Percent of Legacies in Freshman Class at Harvard, Princeton, and Yale, Selected Years, 1950–1965.

September Entry Year	Harvard % Legacies	Princeton % Legacies	Yale % Legacies
1950	17.6	16.4	24.0
1962	18.7	17.5	20.2
1965	20.1	20.1	18.2

SOURCES: *Griswold Papers* (Yale Archive, Box 5, Folder 32), October 17, 1950; *Brewster Papers* (Yale Archive, Box 2, Folder 10), October 6, 1966.

Howe resigned as dean of admissions in October 1964, and Clark was announced to the press as the new dean of admissions in February 1965.[59] There was, however, a long overlap between Howe and Clark. Since 1961, Clark had been working as the assistant director of admissions under Howe. In spring 1963, Howe was deeply affected by the death of his close friend and superior, President Griswold; consequently, beginning in May of 1963, Clark was effectively functioning as head of admissions.[60] Officially, Howe's last class was selected in the spring of 1964, entering in September 1964; it was the class graduating in 1968. The percentage of legacies entering in September 1964 were 19.6; George W. Bush, with an unimpressive 566 verbal SAT score, was one of them.[61] Bush's score put him in the bottom 10 percent of his class, and below the line for what the *Bell Curve* authors saw as the average in the bad-old days of social selection.[62]

Clark's first class may be calculated, as Lemann does, as the one selected in the late winter and early spring of 1965. Unfortunately, the numbers of legacies in Clark's first class do not sustain his recollection as reported by Lemann. The percentage of legacies entering in the fall of 1965 was 18.2, which is a drop of merely 1.4 points from Howe's last class.[63] As actual numbers, rather than percentages, in 1964, Howe's office offered admission to 214 legacies; in 1965 Clark's invited 211 to attend Yale.[64]

Lemann's particulars are wrong; yet even if counterfactually all of Lemann's historical details were right, would that still add up to an internal subversion of Yale's admissions system, replacing it hence forward with a meritocratic one? Clark held the office of admissions dean from 1965 to spring 1971, and as of 1967, John Muyskens, Jr., was the new director of admissions, orchestrating the process. Lemann sees Muyskens's appointment as a retreat from Clark's policies to appease the alumni.[65] If Clark did all that Lemann claims, would those measures over the course of two or, at most, six years push Yale over some critical tipping point placing meritocracy irreversibly in power?

If one examines Yale's record from 1920 to 2000, there have been sufficient variations over the years to lend some credence to the meritocratic case. If one looks at the 25 years after 1950, there were high and low tides for legacies, with the years 1960 and 1961 as a high water mark, and the years between 1967 and 1972 as the low ebb (see Table 4.2).

TABLE 4.2

Percent of Legacies in the First-Year Class at Yale College,
Entering in September, 1920–2000.

Year	%	Year	%	Year	%	Year	%
1920	13	1940	29	1961	27	1981	22
1921	15	1941	27	1962	20	1982	24
1922	15	1942	27	1963	19	1983	22
1923	14	1943	26	1964	20	1984	21
1924	21	1945	19	1965	18	1985	22
1925	17	1946	24	1966	17	1986	20
1926	19	1947	27	**1967**	**14**	1987	20
1927	21	1948	24	**1968**	**14**	1988	19
1928	22	1949	22	**1969***	**14**	1989	18
1929	21	1950	24	**1970**	**15**	1990	15
1930	24	1951	20	**1971**	**14**	1991	15
1931	27	1952	21	**1972**	**14**	1992	13
1932	30	1953	22	1973	16	1993	11
1933	30	1954	24	1974	20	1994	12
1934	27	1955	22	1975	19	1995	14
1935	26	1956	22	1976	19	1996	13
1936	29	1957	23	1977	20	1997	14
1937	30	1958	24	1978	20	1998	13
1938	31	1959	25	1979	23	1999	14
1939	31	1960	26	1980	24	2000	14

N O T E S : "Limitation of Numbers" discrimination against Jewish applicants became policy in February 1924, for the entering cohort of September 1924. Legacy affirmative action became policy in February 1925 for incoming freshmen in September 1925. To calculate the Yale "Class" year, add four to the year given. The abnormal years during middle of Kingman Brewster's administration are in bold. The eighty-year average was 20 percent.

*Yale College admitted women for the first time in 1969.

s o u r c e s : For 1920 to 1932: President's Office, *James Rowland Angell Papers, 1921–1937* (Yale Archive, Box 1, Yale Sons Tables Folders 11 and 13), "Memorandum for Members of the Board of Admissions: The Admission Requirements as Applied to the Sons of Yale Alumni," 28 September 1929. For 1933 to 1975: George W. Pierson, *A Yale Book of Numbers: Historicla Statistics of the College and University 1701–1976* (New Haven, CT: Yale University 1983), 87–88; Sam Chauncey, "Memo to All Corporation Members," Brewster Papers (Yale Archive, Box 2, Folder 10), October 4, 1966. For 1976 to 2000: Office of Institutional Research, Yale University.

Lemann should have based his case on the dramatic 14-percentage-point drop in legacies between the high in 1961 and the ebb in 1967. In 1961, there were 280 legacies in the class; in 1967, there were 141. Clearly, a 49 percent reduction in the relative size of the legacy contingent provides reliable evidence of a difference between Howe and Clark, and the drop provides an objective basis for a conflict between alumni and the admissions office. Some Yale fathers did have grounds for complaint.

The crucial objection to Lemann's meritocratic thesis, however, is that the substantial reduction of 1967 was only temporary; a legacy restoration in 1974 swung things very nearly back to where they had been before. The shifting legacy fortunes occurred under Clark's boss, Kingman Brewster. There were three stages to the Brewster administration's objective performance on legacy admissions: stasis (1963–66), decline (1967–72), and recovery (1973–77). At the start, from 1963 to 1966, legacy percentages averaged 18.5 percent; then in 1967, the percentage of legacies in each class dropped to 14 percent and stayed there until 1973 when they recovered to 16 percent; and then they went up again in 1974 to 20 percent where they remained on average for more than a decade after the end of Brewster's administration, until 1989.

If we cut up the twentieth century into "pre- and post-meritocratic" time blocks, legacies from 1920 to 1939, as well as during Howe's time in the admissions office, from 1953 to 1964, averaged 23 percent; from Clark's time in office to the recent period, 1965 to 1989, legacies averaged 19 percent.[66] If we take 23 as the pre-meritocratic norm and treat that as worth 100 percent of what legacies as a group could count on as a traditional entitlement, then in 1967 there was a 39 percent fall away from that norm, followed in 1974 by a 26 percent recovery. From 1974 to 1989, legacies occupied 83 percent as much space at Yale as during the "pre-meritocratic" time period, which is considerably more than what one would expect if, as Lemann and others contend, a new meritocratic elite had shoved aside an old-WASP one. By the end of the "transformation" period, legacies retained nearly all of their traditional space within Yale.

Based on these numbers alone, however, one cannot rule out Lemann's claim that for a period under Clark's deanship, meritocratic subversives were in control of the admissions process. One cannot know for certain whether legacy privileges were gutted and character lost out to brains temporarily, even if only from 1967 to 1972, or permanently after 1967, until we evaluate the boost given legacies by the admissions office during and after this time period. We need to see if legacies being admitted in the "post-meritocracy" period were being treated the same as other admitted youths in the applicant pool, or if they were receiving special privileges.

Fortuitously, Yale's Office of Institutional Research did an exhaustive study of the different standards and admission rates being applied to legacies and non-Yale affiliated applicants for Clark's last class, the class of 1975, entering in September of 1971. The study is perfect for our question because the cohort came in the fifth year of the six worst years for legacies since the introduction of the SAT in 1926. If legacies were ever being held to the same standards as ordinary applicants, that should be apparent during those lean years when legacies averaged only 14 percent of each entering class. Conversely, whatever privileges legacies may have enjoyed then would have to be magnified to capture the extent of their relative advantage in the years when legacies averaged 20 percent of each class.

The study was conducted by Robert Sternberg and written up as a report for Sam Chauncey, special assistant to President Brewster; both Chauncey and Brewster were, according to Lemann, subversive agents of meritocracy. The title of the report was, "Comparative Expectancies of Admission for Yale Affiliates and Non-Affiliates." It began, "There is currently a considerable amount of alumni pressure to ease standards of admission for Yale affiliates (those applicants who have or have had a sibling or parent here), . . . It is helpful to know in this respect to what extent standards are already eased for affiliate applicants. This memorandum deals with this question."[67]

Sternberg worked up expectancy tables displaying the admissions probabilities for legacies and non-legacies with every possible combined academic and personal score in the admission ratings. The admissions process would give each candidate four separate ratings, all on a nine-point scale: two academic ratings and two personal ratings. All applicants would have a possible score of eighteen points on the academic scale and eighteen points on the personal scale. Sternberg looked at the ratings for all applicants and then at the actual admissions decisions to quantify "the comparative chances for admission of two applicants of equal merit, one with a Yale affiliation, one without it." He wrote, "It can easily be seen that for almost every combination of ratings, the probability of admission for affiliates is higher than for non-affiliates."[68] To illustrate, Sternberg used the example of an average applicant with scores of five from every reader on every dimension, giving him a total of ten points on the academic scale and ten points on the personal one. Of the example given Sternberg wrote,

> Suppose that Joe Average is not a Yale affiliate. We look at Expectancy Table 2, and . . . find the 10/10 intersection. We find the number 6 written at this intersection. This means that Joe's chances of admissions, given that he is not a Yale affiliate, are 6 out of 100. Were Joe a Yale affiliate, we would have consulted Table 3 instead of Table 2. We would have found at the 10/10 intersection the number 30. Had Joe been a Yale affiliate, his chances of admission would have been 30 out of 100, 5 times as high as if he had not been affiliated.[69]

Sternberg could have illustrated his point with a non-legacy whose scores were a 12 on academics and an 11 on personal promise; his odds of receiving a positive admission decision were 58 out of 100. If, however, that same score was attached to a legacy, his odds were a perfect 100 percent. All legacies with that score got in. The legacy boost during one of their most difficult years in the twentieth century was very substantial. Legacies could win the admissions contest performing half as well, or less, than non-legacies.

Two years later, still under Brewster's administration, Yale's highest governing body, the Corporation, decided that the legacy privileges described by Sternberg were inadequate to ensure sufficient space for Yale's children. The Corporation voted to create a legacy quota or target of 20 percent for each class beginning with freshmen in September 1974; they would be in Yale's Class of 1978. The Office of Institutional Research was given the job of determining how this new policy affected the average performance of legacies in comparison with non-legacies in Yale College. The OIR produced a study in December 1977 "to examine the impact of the 1974 policy change whereby, beginning with the entering Class of 1978, an increased number of Yale affiliates were admitted to Yale College." The report found that "the Corporation's policy directive on the admission of Yale affiliates was implemented, . . . Alumni children now constitute around 20% of each entering Class."[70] With three years of data to work with, the OIR concluded that there was a "relatively consistent tendency for the academic qualifications and performance of Yale affiliates to be lower than that of non-affiliates, . . . In athletics, however, Yale affiliates are better performers, in terms of athletic awards earned. . . . [T]he change in admissions policy has had no discernable effect on the quality or performance of Yale affiliates as a group."[71] Legacies were no worse in the mid-1970s than they had been before, but now there were more of them, thanks to the Corporation's establishment of a 20 percent target. Judged by the actual percentages of legacies admitted after 1973, the quota must have remained in effect until 1990.

Because legacies were not held to the same admissions standards as the rest of Yale's students, and the Corporation set quotas to protect them, one can hardly build an argument about the meritocratic makeover of Yale based on its record with legacies. In light of persisting legacy privileges, Lemann's assertion that Clark swept away all of Howe's old cronies in the admissions office as evidence of a battle to establish meritocracy seems inconsequential.[72] Nonetheless, it is worth noting that the archive shows Lemann's claim to be mistaken. Not counting Howe, his admissions committee in 1963–64 had ten members on it. Of those ten members, six (Carroll, Napier, Taft, Walker, Burr, and Ramsey) were still serving on Clark's committee in 1965–66.[73]

In sum, the accounts given us by meritocratic authors do not match the objective records on legacy enrollments. Can we uncover a different story if we look at intentions and policy? Perhaps Brewster and Clark were meritocratic subversives whose program of reform was derailed by institutional rigidities and stronger external interests?

The spirit behind Brewster's admission policy was to recruit and civilize tomorrow's leadership class. Legacies were an essential part of that as long as they could stay close to the standards set by their peers. In respect to legacies, Brewster's policies were hardly different from Howe's.

Legacy admissions were carefully, even obsessively, monitored. When a 1 percent decline from 1965 occurred in 1966, Brewster's team and the Corporation exhaustively examined the issue. This was Clark's second year as dean, and the Corporation's anxieties were less focused on Jews than on Yale's sons.

In October 1966, Sam Chauncey sent all Corporation members a lengthy memo with statistical information for the last eleven years on legacy admissions, including comparative data on Harvard and Princeton.[74] The contrast between legacies as entering freshmen in 1958 and 1966 showed that Harvard and Princeton were doing better than Yale, and keeping pace with the other two was an overriding priority for Yale. Harvard matriculated 231 legacies in

1958, and 228 in 1966; Princeton had 138 in 1958 and 128 in 1966; Yale had 231 in 1958 and 170 in 1966. Most of the decline took place during Howe's time in office. There were ups and downs under Howe, especially in 1962 when legacies dropped by 83 from the previous year's number. They recovered a bit in 1963 and held on in 1964; then, for the last two years with Clark in office, legacies fell by 17 in 1965 and 22 in 1966. The performance of the last two years, with Yale matriculating 39 fewer legacies than three years before, was enough to set off alarm bells in the Corporation in 1966.

The Corporation and others needed reassurances that the issue of legacies was being addressed, so Brewster and Clark went on an alumni-relations offensive. They used a special issue of the alumni magazine to clarify the issues and to rally alumni talent scouts. Lest anyone find an obsession with admissions unseemly, the magazine underscored its importance by reminding readers, "It is through the people admitted that a college establishes its character, its distinctiveness, and ultimately its future."[75]

Brewster's article, "Admission to Yale: Objectives and Myths,"[76] elaborated on his comments to the alumni convocation previously referenced.[77] Brewster began with such an assertion of grandeur for the role and mission of Yale that were it presented as fact, rather than as a self-professed "claim," his attempt to avoid sounding pretentious would have been a sham. He wrote, "Yale is one of those institutions . . . which claims to be truly an asset to the survival of Western civilization." By serving as a training ground and gatekeeper for leaders, Yale stands out among the "relatively few institutions whose education does conspicuously offer a special career advantage." Yale contributes to "the moral quality of civilization" by cultivating a steady flow of leadership talent. The task cannot be accomplished, however, unless Yale works "to sustain the widespread conviction that . . . success is at best related to effort, . . . and as little as possible rigged by either private status or public favor." Admission to Yale "must be convincingly . . . based on merit." The public's faith in meritocracy and its confidence in Yale's fidelity to those principles are both "fundamental to the survival of our way of life."[78]

With the survival of Western civilization riding on the contest, Brewster then sought to dispel "three persistent myths" about Yale's admissions. "The first myth is that Yale has an admissions process that is faculty dominated and interested in brains only. . . . The second myth is that we are against athletes. . . . The third myth is . . . that Yale . . . is somehow rigged against the established independent schools."[79] Brewster did not explicitly mention legacies, but they provided the article's subtext on alumni anxieties. Many alumni were fearful of the faculty's role in admissions, legacies were, relative to non-legacies, better athletes than scholars, and disproportionate numbers of legacies passed through the private sector of secondary education.

The campaign to reassure the alumni did not rest with Brewster's and Clark's magazine articles. To appease critics with a cosmetic change, Brewster brought John Muyskens on board to serve as director of admissions under Clark as admissions dean. They took the occasion of Muyskens' appointment to formulate a policy document for wide distribution. Lemann's meritocratic narrative discusses this move and mistakenly contextualizes Brewster's communiqué to Muyskens as a private letter with an underground circulation.[80] It was the opposite, a product of a collective discussion and multiple drafts between the president, admissions officers, faculty, and the Yale Corporation, that was intended for frequent official distribution. Anyone writing the president's office or the admissions office with questions about Yale's undergraduate selection policies was routinely sent a copy of the "John Muyskens letter," as it was referred to from the beginning. Ready-made cover letters, with spaces for a personal touch, were available for staff distribution. Large passages from it were reprinted in alumni newsletters.[81]

Brewster sent copies of the letter to, as he called them in a note to the Corporation, "some of our friends." Variations of the following, sent by Brewster to an alumnus disgruntled on admissions, reached many in various Yale circles. Brewster wrote, "I think that the Yale Corporation as well as the administration, faculty, and staff are all of one mind about what we are looking for. I tried to set this forth in a letter to our new Director of Admissions, John Muyskens, . . . I have every reason to believe that the standards in the Muyskens letter have in fact been taken as guidelines. From everything I hear . . . the entering class . . . are brighter than ever in terms of academic achievement, they also contain far more class presidents, team captains, publication editors, and lettermen than their predecessors did a decade or more ago. . . . If we can keep this up both the Yale spirit and the Yale leadership should be sustained."[82] Recipients of the memorandum were informed in the cover letter as well as in the text itself that the missive sets "forth the considerations which should guide the admissions selection process. It speaks for the Yale Corporation. It has the complete support of the Admissions Staff and the Faculty Advisory Committee."[83] The letter was unquestionably official policy.

The "Muyskens letter" reaffirmed Yale's mission to select and educate America's leaders. In the first of seven propositions detailed by Brewster in the letter, he stated, "We want Yale men to be leaders in their genera-tion. . . . While we cannot purport to pick seventeen and eighteen year olds in terms of their career aims, we do have to make the hunchy [*sic*.] judgment as to whether or not with Yale's help the candidate is likely to be a leader."[84] And it made explicit Yale's commitment to legacies. Brewster wrote, "The only preference by inheritance which seems to me to deserve recognition is the Yale son. Tradition, loyalty, familiarity deserve to be given weight if—but only if—the candidate has survived initial comparison and appears to be as worthy of the Yale opportunity as any of the others being finally considered."[85] What exactly the odds were of a legacy surviving the first cut were made clear in correspondence, four months after the release of the Muyskens letter, between an assistant to the president, O'Hearn, and a prominent alumnus and senior partner in a law firm.

In 1967, it remained as true under Brewster as it had been in Griswold's days that well over 80 percent of all applicants performed academically at or above Yale's standards. Of those, fully 50 percent "survived [the] initial comparison," and all legacies in that group were admitted. O'Hearn wrote to the alumnus, "My understanding of our present policies is the same as yours . . . of the 6,000+ applicants, approximately 5,000 are capable of doing Yale work, that from this group some 2,500 boys are selected as so-called 'finalists,' and that any Yale son in this latter group is normally admitted. To this extent he is given a preference."[86] O'Hearn knew, but did not comment on, the nuances at play in determining how the records of Yale alumni fac-tored into which legacies made it to the "finalist" list, those 50 percent of all capable boys, who were as legacies usually automatic admits. Even among alumni, not all were equally entitled to the full legacy tip.

O'Hearn was intimately familiar with the unequal reward system for leg-acies because he was one of two persons at Yale responsible for running it. Starting in 1964, the admissions office gave O'Hearn a list of all legacies who applied each year. It was his job to make notes on each one so the admissions committee would "consider the father's whole record of service both to Yale and to American society in determining the degree to which preference should be granted."[87] The admissions committee met with O'Hearn when the policy began in 1964, and "After some rather cold-blooded discussion of the problems inherent in recognizing degrees of Yale son preference, the Committee agreed that this was the only feasible approach." In the discussion, the admissions dean said, "I pointed out that the differential treatment of alumni sons would inevitably cause problems . . . and that once known this policy would raise a cry. All present felt that we had to be prepared to face this. . . . Certainly we shall make no effort to publicize our practices."[88] Brewster signed off on the policy. He wrote back to the admissions dean saying, "It seems to me it is quite right for the Admissions office to obtain factual information from the Alumni and Development offices with respect to the relationship to Yale of an applicant's family. . . . I agree with the standards by which we now discriminate between alumni sons and non-alumni sons."[89] The policies of the Brewster administration were to positively discriminate in favor of legacies and, most especially, in favor of legacies from families of note.

There were some dramatic exceptions to this preferential policy that enabled Yale to draw public attention to its 'meritocratic' standards. For reasons that remain discretely hidden, one of the university's largest benefactors, Paul Mellon, found his stepson turned away from Yale in the mid-1950s. The time period was when social selection was still supposed to matter, according to the meritocratic account. Yet Yale could proudly note that it said no to the stepson of the man who funded its British art museum.[90]

The Muyskens letter offered reassurances for alumni, but it was not universally applauded in every detail. When the Muyskens letter was being circulated for comment to faculty members, Professor D. A. Bromley, a nuclear scientist, noted that scientific aptitude and achievements were not being given any weight. He thought outstanding scientific excellence should be given at least the same recognition as a desirable quality for admission as athletic or artistic accomplishments. Bromley appealed to Brewster, "I would be happier if you would add the words, 'or scientific' following 'artistic.' . . . Outstanding scientific achievement is now more frequently demonstrated by students in many high schools than was true in the past and I would like to see it included with other areas of possible excellence."[91] Bromley's concerns were not addressed in any draft of the Muyskens letter. Kind words about the arts, drama, music, journalism, athletic, and organized extracurricular activities were offered, but even the terms "natural science" are absent from the policy statement. The point was raised again, a few months later, after wide circulation of the Muyskens letter, by a Yale physicist, Charles Bockelman. He explained at an Alumni Convocation, "We simply do not have enough undergraduate science majors at Yale. Why is this? Well, I think part of it may have been related to the Admissions Policy. . . . The prospective science student may not often have the image that one likes to think of for the Yale man. He may very much be an introverted person. He may not have been a leader in the school. He may not have participated heavily in extra curricular activities."[92] Selecting for extroverted youths with demonstrated leadership ability did have, in the opinion of some Yale scientists, the unintended effect of selecting against many youths with a talent and temperament for natural science. It was also not coincidental that technical and science subjects were historically associated more with the public than the private sector of higher education, and that many working-class youths excelled better at them than in the liberal arts. Selecting for leaders had multiple layers of social-class bias built into it.

Although scientists worried about prospective students, at least one prominent member of the Alumni Board saw proposition number six in Brewster's letter as making too much of "equality of opportunity." Brewster's letter spoke of the issue in two respects: the external world should feel convinced that Yale supports through equality of opportunity an "open society," in other words, a meritocratic society. The emphasis was placed on "convincing" people of Yale's fairness, rather than on the thorny issue of how one should evaluate equal opportunity. The second respect in which the issue mattered was, again, to leadership recruitment. Equal opportunity was "the only way to assure that we are drawing to us the people who give the most promise of being leaders in their time."[93] Objecting to the implications of Brewster's points, the Alumni Board member wrote, "There has been a fear expressed, however, that in the quest to find worthy underprivileged boys, the proof of ability to do Yale work may be compromised, with the end result an unhappy boy in over his head. . . . I have begun to develop a feeling that the really 'disadvantaged' candidates are the academically qualified, privileged boys who have all the potential for leadership in later life, but have not, at age 17, been motivated to the same extent as a less fortunate applicant."[94]

Setting aside for the moment the issue of the "disadvantages" facing privileged boys, which have not reduced the proportion of youths from top-income families at Yale over the years, all of these correspondents on the Muyskens letter understood its fundamental message on admissions. In sum, academic record took a back seat to demonstrated leadership. Grades and test scores would not carry one as far as being a class president, school newspaper editor, or athletic captain. The only exception was, of course, legacy status. Being a legacy, as the 1971 OIR report documented, improved one's odds regardless of leadership or academic performance. And even then, not all legacies were born equal; family contributions mattered.

Written when the United States was embroiled in Vietnam, the "Muyskens letter" has helped to guide admissions at Yale for nearly four decades. During those years, it has been reprinted in the *Yale Alumni Schools Committee Handbook* prepping alumni admission's interviewers in the field. In 1996, the director of admissions stated in the alumni magazine, "From time to time, Yale Presidents have tried to update or rewrite that letter, but it remains the most eloquent expression of our ideal."[95] It continues to inform admissions even today.

Regarding our question on whether Brewster intended to reduce or eliminate legacy privileges, materials in the archive show conclusively that he did not. Objectively, legacy numbers were below average for six years, but there are no reasons to think that Brewster saw that decline as a desirable or inescapable effect of his policies. Indeed, Brewster oversaw one of the greatest changes in the composition of Yale's undergraduates with the hope of recapturing those boys, legacies and non-legacies, admitted by Yale who chose to go instead elsewhere, and in particular to Harvard. The change was Yale's decisions to admit women starting in the fall of 1969.

Women Join Yale College

Bringing women into Yale College would, in time, transform gender relations at the institution just as it would contribute to reducing the barriers to professional careers for women in society at large. The meritocratic authors, however, do not address how the end of Yale's mono-sexual status would or would not matter to its alleged shift from social to academic selection. Lemann's book, where one would expect to find a chapter on the "revolutionary change," deals with women at Yale in one sentence.[96] Although introducing women to Yale would not automatically alter the college's social-class composition, it could affect admissions standards. And regardless, the end of Yale as a masculine club is a very significant change that requires separate analysis.

Yale College was an all-male institution from its founding to 1969 when the first undergraduate females breeched its defenses. Women had been allowed into Yale's graduate art school for a bit of cultural polish since the late nineteenth century, but in the undergraduate domain, the only women in New Haven were visiting relatives, girl friends, prostitutes, or strippers. It was an adolescent boy's world with more than its share of ugly episodes. One of the worst was "the gang rape of a prostitute . . . in 1940 that was a running public joke during Brewster's undergraduate years."[97]

Masculine exclusivity was part of the college experience that carried over after graduation, acting as a bond pulling alumni back to New Haven. Class reunions were stag affairs. After all, who could recapture the feel of his undergraduate days with a wife along or offspring under foot? Until 1970, women and children were cleverly kept out of the way during reunions, which happen for each class every five years. At reunions, men could stay in college rooms, but wives were forbidden. A letter sent the first semester of coeducation for a meeting of the alumni fund was typical of all that came before it. The alumni fund's secretary wrote, "You (and your spouse) are cordially invited to . . . New Haven. . . . Although rooms in the University will be provided for men not accompanied by their wives, unfortunately no on-campus accommodations are available for our women guests. So we have reserved a limited number of rooms for you to take at your own expense in nearby hotels."[98] Bring your wife if you want to pay for the privilege of staying with her, away from the other old boys.

All class reunions were climaxed at a formal dinner, sometimes in silly costumes, where last-minute contributions to Yale's endowment were flushed out with the aid of nostalgia, clouds of cigar smoke, and copious amounts of alcohol. In 1970, reunion costs for rooms, bedding, and meals averaged $27.40 per man for the event, and that year the Classes of 1950 and 1940 spent on alcohol, and mostly on liquor, a total of $3,232 between them.[99] Those two classes sipped away in a few days booze worth more than one-third of the U.S. annual median family income for the year.

Brewster would make the rounds, moving from one reunion venue to another, socializing and offering, near the end of his visit, comments on how much money had been raised. Being scheduled at half-hour or hour intervals to make "informal" appearances at fourteen class reunion events, cocktail in hand, in a forty-eight-hour period was not unusual for the president.[100] Social stamina and high alcohol tolerance appear to have been requirements for the job. Given that all reunions since 1939 had established "new records" of gift giving, Yale had a form sheet made out that would be updated as the weekend progressed, and used by Brewster to spur them on to even higher levels of giving. The sheet was a text with blanks for actual amounts to be filled in by hand at the time it was handed to Brewster for his informal comments to the celebrating alumni. The text would say, in part, "Although Alumni Fund efforts are still continuing and will until June 30th, I am happy to announce that the following reunion classes have already broken the records for their respective reunions."[101]

It was not unusual for the final reunion dinner to have entertainment. In 1965, William F. Buckley's class of 1950 had strippers. Buckley was famous in Yale circles as a conservative opponent of Brewster's administration and the liberal culture in America's universities. His *God and Man at Yale,* published in 1951, was an indictment of Marxist academics and moral corruption in the university. It stirred up a heated debate the likes of which were not seen again until Alan Bloom's attack in 1987 on the soul crushing failures of higher education in his *The Closing of America's Mind.*[102] It is not clear how common strippers were at reunions, but its timing, which coincided with a public discussion of coeducation at Yale, left Buckley discomforted by its incongruity. Brewster was not in attendance, but the provost of the university, Charles Taylor, was there. Buckley wrote in an alumni newsletter about the event,

> I sat after dinner at the courtyard of Branford College, next to Charlie Taylor who was next to Van Galbraith. Suddenly, . . . we found ourselves looking at first one, then a second strip-tease, . . . after the girls had withdrawn, the cheers of the class of 1950 ringing in their ears, Van Galbraith turned and said, "Charlie, what is Official Yale's position toward this?" Charlie removed the pipe from his mouth, looked sternly in the direction of the now empty stage, and replied, "Yale's official position is that the Second One is better than the First One."[103]

Going coeducational ended the most blatant manifestations of Yale's masculine culture, both in college and at alumni events.

Brewster's administration, however, did not approach coeducation with an eye toward reforming the culture of masculinity or even toward equalizing educational and career opportunities between the genders. The initial impetus came entirely from the desire to recapture young men admitted to Yale who refused and went elsewhere. Legacies were not the only ones; nonlegacies with high abilities were slightly more likely than legacies to turn Yale down. The Yale administration was very conscious of the desirability of going coed to attract what Brewster called, "the best men." Continuing his comments, Brewster said, "the main reason for first suggesting the admission of women . . . was that not admitting women was a great handicap for the recruitment of men."[104]

Annual meetings in the 1960s of the Alumni Board on more than one occasion involved exchanges on the topic of why so many legacies admitted by Yale chose to go elsewhere. In 1968, for example, when the matter came up, a verbatim transcript of the meeting shows,

> Mr. . . . '36: My name is . . . Has anybody tried to study the agonizing and frustrating thing we run into, . . . a guy is promoted by us, . . . and . . . he is also accepted at Harvard. All too many times he elects to go to Harvard . . .
>
> Mr. Cook (Alumni Board Officer): I hear your concern. . . . Perhaps to answer that question, . . . is a survey of Yale sons who are accepted here and choose not to go to Yale. We found that 80 percent of them show up at Harvard. We ask why the switch, and the most popular reply is the atmosphere of Boston and the presence of Radcliffe and Wellesley. So sex rears its head.
>
> Mr. . . . '36: That is a pretty tough argument.[105]

Again, later in that same year, at a meeting of the Alumni Executive Committee:

> Mr. . . . asked why so many of these [legacies] who are admitted do not matriculate and Mr. Cook responded that the two principal reasons . . . seem to be the lack of women at Yale and the more urban environment provided by Harvard.[106]

It was becoming apparent that for Yale to compete with its nemesis, it had to have a Radcliffe in town.

The idea had been kicked around for years. The first proposal put to the faculty to include women in the university was made by Admissions Dean Howe in 1956. Howe argued at the faculty senate, which agreed, "Sexual separation of academic and social life was no longer the norm in American society."[107] Howe wanted an Oxford University type solution, with women in their own separate colleges, yet that avoided Oxford's mistake of putting women's colleges on the geographic periphery of town.[108] Griswold, Yale's president, had discussed with Howe the idea of buying Albertus Magnus, a Catholic women's college in New Haven on Prospect Street at some distance from the center of Yale's campus. Howe thought that was a bad idea for being too far away; Griswold, disagreeing, thought having women close by was a terrible idea. In 1956, Griswold shot down Howe's proposal, to the delight of LaRoche and others who warned of the "emasculation" of the college.[109] The idea of coeducation was raised again, in 1962, by a Yale committee's report on reforming the freshman year that deliberately tossed it out as a false hare to distract controversy from its central concern.[110] Coeducation was not seriously entertained as a practical proposal for Yale until Brewster's presidency.

Brewster did not want Yale to loose the "best men" by being out of step with the competition. Harvard had Radcliffe, Brown had Pembroke, Columbia had Barnard, Brewster wanted Vassar. It was, Brewster thought, the only Seven Sisters college without "a natural dancing partner in its own neighborhood,"[111] but Yale was not too far away for relations. When Brewster found his future bride, she was at Vassar, although their marriage put an end to her degree work. After some preliminary courting, Brewster and the president of Vassar agreed on the desirability of exploring options on some sort of a collegiate marriage. In 1966, the Corporation authorized a joint study with Vassar to examine every conceivable cost and benefit for each institution of establishing an association of one type or another, including the idea of relocating Vassar to New Haven where it would be merged with Yale as a college in the university.[112] It took Vassar's Trustees eleven months to decide against it. The presidents of Vassar and Yale held simultaneous press conferences in Poughkeepsie and New Haven on November 20, 1967, declaring the prenuptial conversation at an end. Brewster, disappointed, told reporters, "In view of Vassar's decision . . . Yale will proceed to explore the possibility of founding an independent women's college in New Haven."[113]

The reporters knew that Brewster favored not only a separate women's college within the university, but also a separate educational experience for women at the university. He was asked, "You indicate that you think that girls need a different sort of education from boys. Can you briefly say why . . . ?" Brewster replied, "I think that of the things that's now lacking particularly in the Harvard-Radcliffe situation, . . . is an opportunity in the context of a major university to devote resources to what might be the priorities for the education of women to the extent that they might in particular feel different from the priorities for the education of men." When pressed to clarify what he meant, Brewster said,

> I think that inevitably at a first-rate university-college, most of the men students are under considerable pressure to prepare themselves for advanced education. . . . I think the majority of women do not plan to go on to advanced education immediately after receiving a baccalaureate, and therefore it's quite possible that a less departmentalized curriculum, . . . would be appropriate for the majority of undergraduate women when they might not be appropriate for the majority of undergraduate men.

The difference appears here to be driven by occupational destinations, women will be housewives, not lawyers, so men and women should have separate experiences through the curriculum. Brewster's sense of sexual difference, however, went beyond those drawn by social roles; he also believed in the notion that women have a separate sensibility, vision, and voice from men. Brewster said, "I think that the attitude and values and point of view of women students would add an additional dimension . . . particularly in those fields that deal with human values, philosophical values, esthetic values." Lastly, Brewster hoped the presence of women at Yale would civilize the men and make for more moral relations between the sexes than had been the case in the past. Brewster mused, "of course there is . . . the relationship between the sexes in the social sense. . . . [Coeducation] would offer infinitely better, more natural, more normal, and I would say more moral life for the Yale community." A reporter asked, "Can you explain that 'more moral'?" Brewster's response, "Sure, I think that the concern which anyone feels about relationships with other human beings is definitely more moral if they are all part of the same community instead of . . . if you have your relationship with people solely on a transient or visiting basis."[114] In sum, Brewster saw women "as wives and mothers" with more refined cultural sensibilities than men.[115] Yale's men needed them, but in separate facilities and with an unprofessional curriculum. Women at Yale were there to civilize the boys, not to compete with them.[116]

Separate and unequal was the conventional wisdom on the sexes at Harvard, Yale, and Princeton until the late 1960s. Of the Big Three, Harvard alone had a women's college, and Radcliffe women could not share a classroom with Harvard men until 1943, or study law at Harvard until 1950.[117] Princeton and Yale had been complete holdouts; "no women please, we are educating future leaders here, thank you" was the official line.

Within Yale, there was opposition to Brewster's separate gender spheres approach. Students favoring a fully coeducational Yale spoke up. They organized as a type of protest a teach-in "Coeducation Week," to transport in women from other campuses for an experience with mixed-sex classes and coed campus life. Brewster deftly absorbed "Coeducation Week," turning it into an official activity, which may have helped to build the momentum for change. It brought "750 women from 22 schools to the campus for a week."[118] And provided the context for the "Coed Steering Committee and Coed Action Group," a student organization opposed to Brewster's coordinate college plan and in favor of gender equality, to issue a statement. The steering committee declared,

> The administration is not talking about co-education among equals, . . . Yale will remain a MALE institution, with a decorative coterie of females. . . . Yale . . . is one of the last education bastions of this system of supremacy, . . . it serves to propagate the distorted notion that males have the right and duty to rule. By now we are familiar with President Brewster's argument against complete co-education. Yale, he insists, has as its mission the production of 1000 leaders a year . . . and, of course, these leaders must be men. This seems to us to be a rather narrow view of both education and leadership. . . . And if Yale is to produce leaders, let us produce leaders, male and female, who will not accept a distorted society based on male domination.[119]

Outside events overtook Yale more quickly than the Coed Action Group or Brewster anticipated. Princeton decided to admit 1,000 women without a coordinate college, and that would leave Yale alone as the only Ivy without both sexes. The Yale Corporation, in a rare display of reformist initiative, pushed Brewster to act. As long as Yale did not reduce its ranks of 1,000 male leaders in each class, 500 women should be admitted.[120]

In the first academic year of coeducation, 1969–70, there were 1,025 men, and 588 women. The "freshman" class had 230 women, but 358 transferring women moved into the sophomore, junior, and senior classes to spread women around, helping to set a new tone on campus. The Seven Sisters colleges, close to Yale in social composition and geography, provided more than their share. Of the transferring females, fully 124 were from just three of them: Wellesley, Smith, and Vassar.[121] The 500-target quota on women lasted from 1969 to 1972, and during that time period women were admitted according to different standards from the men.[122]

Female applicants posed a challenge to many different levels of Yale's admissions system. Yale's alumni and admissions staff were ill prepared to interview female candidates, and they were clueless about how to conceive of seventeen year-old girls as "leaders." In central New Jersey, where many Yale men came from and returned to, the alumni interview committee found it wise to call on six of their wives with college degrees from Seven Sisters colleges (Barnard, Mount Holyoke, and Smith in particular) to participate in the interviews. The "ladies auxiliary" with one Yale man in attendance interviewed all of the best 35 female applicants, whereas "only men interviewed the [130] male candidates."[123] The author of the report offered advice to the admissions office in New Haven on how to select women for this inaugural experiment. He wrote,

> Becoming a female member of Yale's first coeducational class involves great risks for both the University and the young women involved. . . . [I]n the absence of any better standard, Yale will be well-advised to select a substantial number of women from fairly proximate places—proximate by geographical locations and proximate in terms of family environment. . . . I think that a good case can be made for taking a substantial number, if not a majority . . . from geographical locations that are within no more than 250 to 300 miles from New Haven and from the qualified daughters of Yale graduates. Next in line, I would choose women who had some other connection, including brothers, uncle, or male friend who had them become familiar with Yale even before it had become coed.[124]

His advice to play it safe by sticking close to home was not followed. Legacy females received no discernable boost 1969; their admit rate was exactly the same as non-legacy males, a modest 18 percent success rate.[125]

In Yale's second year of female admissions, the separate standards facing women and men was a subject of intense criticism by a faculty member of the admissions committee. Paula Johnson, an instructor in the English department, after one season on the admissions committee, wrote to Brewster complaining,

> I would like to communicate my dismay. . . . In your letter . . . to John Muyskens . . . and in your address to this year's committee you have advised that we should take into account the varieties of excellence. For male candidates this is done; for female candidates by and large it cannot be done. . . . [T]here is not room for women whose undeniable distinction is not fully represented by class rank and test scores; but beyond that, there is not even room for all those women whose academic excellence is demonstrable in numbers. The guidelines for admission are rendered invalid for women, solely because not enough places for women have been made available.[126]

Initially, women were admitted to Yale based almost exclusively on their academic records. Ironically, there was not room physically in Yale College, or in the minds of most administrators, for women whose abilities went beyond academic grades. For women during the years when their numbers at Yale were restricted, the meritocratic story was the reality. And that contributed to making 1970 the peak year for Yale's entering students' SAT scores (see Table 4.3).

Just as at other elite universities during the same time, such as Oxford University in England, the admission of women had the immediate effect of raising academic standards.[127]

Women were put at a disadvantage in comparison with men because they were mostly judged in academic terms. The feminine handicap can be illustrated with an account of how the admission system awarded points. There were two stages to the assignment of numerical ratings to a candidate's file: first, two readers of the file would give each applicant a personal promise score and an academic promise score on a nine-point scale. Then, with those scores on hand, the penultimate evaluation would be assigned by an admissions committee member on a four-point scale, with a "1" being an automatic admit, and a "4" being a no need to consider further. Apparently, the committee did not see women as worthy of a "1" score. Even in the third year of admitting females, there was not one woman who received a "1" classification. In the summer of 1971, Robert Sternberg of the OIR wrote a memo in which he noted that even though 18 percent of male applicants

TABLE 4.3

Matriculants by SAT Verbal Scores, Yale College 1958–1992.

Admit Year	Score for Bottom 10th Percentile of Matriculating Class	Score for Lower 25th Percentile of Matriculating Class	Score for Median of Matriculating Class	Score for Top 75th Percentile of Matriculating Class	Score for Top 90th Percentile of Matriculating Class
1958	534	581	634	680	717
1962	563	609	656	700	740
1970*	**570**	**635**	**699**	**751**	**782**
1973**	520	595	645	695	725
1982	540	600	660	710	740
1992	540	600	660	700	740
34 Year Averages	**551**	**610**	**666**	**711**	**744**

NOTES: * 1970 was the highest year. It was also the second year women were admitted to Yale College.
   ** 1972 Data for men and women combined was unavailable, so 1973 was substituted.
SOURCE: "CEEB Test Data for Yale Matriculants," *Brewster Papers* (Yale Archive, Box 2, Folder 10); George W. Pierson, *A Yale Book of Numbers* (New Haven, CT: Yale University Press, 1983), 102; "SAT Scores for Freshman Matriculants, 1975–1999," *Office of Institutional Research* (New Haven, CT: Yale University, 1 November 2000), Table D-8.

received a top rating, there were no women in that group.[128] Sternberg acknowledged the gender gap in the system of personal and academic ratings, and mused, "It could be due to a tacit (or not tacit) double standard, in which everyone knows that [on a nine-point scale] a 5 for girls is really higher than a 5 for boys."[129] Regardless of the reasons, female applicants received lower final ratings, even though their grades and test scores were on average higher than men's.

Sternberg followed up this memo with a report near the summer's end that touched on the disparity in admissions standards for women and men. He was looking at the points awarded to applicants by the two readers of each admissions folder to see if there was a cut off at which every applicant at or above that score was a "guaranteed admit." It would save time and labor if the admissions office could automatically assign a "1" score based on the combined points given in the previous step. Because each reader gave the file a personal and academic score on a one-to-nine-point scale, each candidate could earn a combined total of 36 points. He found the score that would guarantee men admission was lower than the score required of women. He wrote, "The subset of [male] applicants whose combined Reader 1 and Reader 2 academic and personal ratings total at least 24 points" were virtually assured admission. Of the 675 men who received a score of 24 or higher, only two were rejected. On women Sternberg wrote,

> Because of the extreme selectivity involved in the admission of female appli- cants, it is much more difficult to create an acceptance rule for women than it is for men. . . . Female applicants were rejected with double accept ratings from readers and as many as 27 points in '75 and as many as 28 points in '74! . . . [I]t is difficult to believe that a woman with ratings this high could be rejected. If we use an acceptance rule for women at all, the suggested cutoff is 27 points.[130]

To achieve an automatic admit coding, women would have to receive three more points than men.

In sum, undergraduate women for a brief period were the only ones at Yale to experience an admissions regime based primarily on academic per- formance. Their short-term impact on admissions statistics was to raise aca- demic scores between 1969 and 1972 while Yale grappled with how to apply the criteria for "personal promise" to young women. Because girls were not viewed in 1969 as candidates for leading positions in society, Yale at first relied mostly on grades, class ranks, and test scores in admitting females. By 1973, women were being evaluated in similar terms to men, albeit with lower expectations of a record of leadership. With the restriction on fe- male numbers dropped, and women's relative weight in the undergraduate population going up, women's academic standards went down. Once women achieved relative parity with men, they were no longer being admitted ex- clusively because of their brains. Yale's experience with pure academic meri- tocracy in admissions for women was over.

By the end of the 1970s, female undergraduates in Yale College achieved numerical parity with men. Although the culture of the institution changed, not everyone, including alumni, celebrated. Alumni class reunions on oc- casion would poll their members on whether or not coeducation had been a good idea. As late as the 1990s, reunion classes from the 1940s still had upwards of 24 percent who thought it had been a mistake that should be re- versed.[131] To their voices was added that of George W. Bush, who "told an in- terviewer in 1994 that Yale 'went downhill since they admitted women.'"[132]

What difference did the admission of women make to the gender composition of the faculty? In 1970, there were three women with tenure in the whole of Yale; overall women were just 6 percent of the faculty in Yale College and Graduate School of Arts and Sciences.[133] Thirty years later, in June 2000, 25 percent of faculty were female. The breakdown between tenured and non-tenured or "term" faculty was lopsided; although just 16 percent of the tenured faculty were women, 34 percent of the "term" faculty were females.[134]

Blacks Join Yale College

The other important change in the composition of Yale College in the Brewster years was the enrollment of approximately 90 Black undergraduates in each class. Minority recruitment at Yale began under President Griswold, largely because of the efforts of the admissions dean, Arthur Howe. Howe's family line included abolitionists, one of whom helped to found in 1868 the Hampton Normal and Agricultural Institute, a historically Black college in Virginia that by 1984 grew into Hampton University. The family kept ties to Hampton. Howe's father served as president, and Arthur lived on campus for a while. Later in life, Arthur served on Hampton's Board of Trustees.[135] Howe began recruiting Black students cautiously, in very small numbers. Howe recalled, "When I arrived at Yale you might have one or two Blacks per class. I started using my connections through Black schools and colleges to recruit, 4 or 5, 8 or 10, we crept up slowly."[136] Then, after Brewster arrived in New Haven as provost, President John F. Kennedy held a meeting in Washington with a handful of leaders of elite universities urging them to "make a difference" by recruiting minorities.[137] Howe said that Brewster returned "with fire in his eyes to get a program that would help step up Yale's recruitment of Blacks. My first thing was to contact a number of traditionally Black schools and colleges. And I got a grant from the Carnegie foundation for the Yale summer high school."[138] The summer program was intended to prep promising Black high-school youths for possible admission to Yale or other elite colleges. When Brewster became president and Howe resigned, recruitment efforts were greatly increased. The new dean, Clark, reached out and enrolled in 1969 a total of twenty-six

Black undergraduates.[139] Aggressive efforts to enroll Black students were put in place, including trips funded by the president's office by undergraduate members of Yale's Black Student Alliance around the country to solicit applications from promising candidates.[140] By 1975, eighty-six undergraduate Blacks entered Yale. The average between 1975 and 1997 was ninety-one per year or approximately 7 percent of each undergraduate class.[141] Yale's admissions policy for Black students was to deemphasize test scores in the search for youths with the potential to become leaders of Black America. As Kabaservice reports, Brewster was known to say, "Yale wants to . . . turn out the black leaders of the future. The Martin Luther Kings."[142] Although falling considerably short of the immodest presumption that tomorrow's Martin Luther Kings would find all that Yale's gothic campus represents irresistible, it does have the former Baltimore Mayor Kurt Schmoke and Harvard's Henry Louis Gates as Black alumni of distinction.[143]

When, by 1969, Black undergraduates became more than a trivial few at Yale, the atmosphere on campus remained even less hospitable to them than to females. Yale was as white as elephant ivory. Racist drawings adorned the inner walls of Payne Whitney Gym, and the college named after the radical slave master John C. Calhoun, had Confederate battle flags and bull whips outside its dinning room. Brewster had the offending items removed.[144] But there were no Black faculty role models in town, only an abundance of Black janitors. The Black Student Alliance confronted the ever-charming Brewster with demands for African-American Studies and Black faculty, which Brewster happily embraced.[145] Progress, however, has been snail-like. Even five years after Brewster left office, only 2 percent of Yale's faculty, ten tenured, and twenty-six untenured, were Black. By 2000, Black faculty representation had only inched up to being 3 percent at Yale, with eighteen tenured and twenty-eight untenured members.[146] Blacks, however, continue to be overrepresented in maintenance positions. In 2002, Blacks were nearly 44 percent of Yale's blue-collar workers.[147]

Regarding the questions posed by the meritocratic narratives, the admission of Blacks to Yale did not raise SAT averages as had been the case with female admissions. Black youths then, as now, on average fall below Whites on the SAT. Yale's recruits were not exceptions to that trend. What the admission of Blacks did change slightly was the geographic distribution and social-class composition of the Yale undergraduate population. The geographic hegemony of New England at Yale was modestly eroded by Black recruitment. Also, unlike the admission of females, which would not necessarily alter the class composition of Yale, Black admissions brought youths to New Haven from low-income families. Since the late 1960s, social-class diversity at elite colleges has been tied to their race sensitive admissions policies.[148] This diversity, however, involves only 7 percent of undergraduates. Even though Yale is now, without doubt, more diverse in gender, race, and religion than ever before, the preponderance of wealthy, White families has not changed from 1952 to the present.

Policy Changes on Cultural Capital

Under Brewster, the admissions machinery was upgraded. Between 1967 and 1971, Yale revised two distinguishing features of its admissions process and began a search to quantify the personal qualities that would predict college success. As a selectivity paradigm, the physiognomy of leadership was being replaced by the social psychology of leadership. The intermediate step came in the form of a new emphasis on culture.

In 1967, Brewster and Clark dropped Howe's personal evaluation categories and photos. The eugenicist search for bodies on which a leadership script could be discerned had petered out. Women were being considered for a coordinate college, and Jews were not being excluded, so the time seemed right to discontinue the photo in the application packet and the Ivy nude measurement ritual for entering first-year students. The effort to classify and predict personal qualities and leadership potential had not been abandoned, but its technology was being re-tooled.

The alumni board and the admissions office sent out a mailing in October 1967 with copies of the new forms and advice about how to write up comments on future interviews. There was plenty of continuity in the areas of emphasis: leaders and athletes remained top concerns. But there was a modest shift toward more explicitly cultural criteria than before. Applicants with talents in the fine arts, especially the performing arts, such as violin players, were being courted. And those with what Pierre Bourdieu identified as the "embodied" form of "cultural capital" were being singled out.[149] Those with poise, cosmopolitan seasoning, and highbrow sensibilities were being noticed.

Bourdieu found that cultural capital was a resource, passed down within privileged families, of "shared, high status cultural signals (attitudes, preferences, formal knowledge, behaviors, goals, and credentials) used for social and cultural exclusion."[150] Privileged offspring have a homegrown "natural ease" with those signals that are rewarded over time by "key gatekeepers," such as interviewers for college or employment.[151]

There were signs of Brewster's team taking a more favorable attitude toward highbrow pursuits than had been the case in the past. It is possible to see this as reflecting a conflict within upper-class circles between old-school businessmen and new-school professionals, with the former valuing business acumen and the latter putting more stock in culture. This reading is offered by Kabaservice's dissertation. Kabaservice sees Brewster's administration engaged in an "intra-class struggle within the establishment . . . between traditionalists (many of them business-oriented) . . . and progressives (mostly aspiring professionals) . . . [and that] helped tilt the balance toward cultural and intellectual rather than economic" skills.[152] The contrast may be overdrawn; the importance of the fine arts to Yale was not new to Brewster. Griswold was a champion of the highbrow. Yet the new interview forms did draw attention to arty abilities and habits.

The six model evaluations sent out when the interview forms changed in 1967, for example, all featured comments on the fine arts, and some on highbrow magazines. For example, on one candidate, "his academic interests seem to center around Music (he has studied piano for nine years), Fine Arts and Language." On another, his "extra-curricular activities include: (1) membership in the Thespians, a dramatic club." On yet another candidate, his "interests are, I should think, largely literary. . . . He has written short stories and, as I remember it, a play . . . he likes dramatics." Cultural capital magazines were mentioned in a context of praise. One interviewer wrote, "he . . . has a broader perspective . . . it shows in what he reads (*The New Yorker* magazine . . . and he discovered a 'great new magazine, maybe you heard of it: *Atlantic Monthly*')."[153]

The biases of high culture, which overlapped with Yale's liberal arts culture, were visible in the comments written on undesirable candidates. One interviewer noted on an applicant, "Grades are so important to him that he is not able to recognize the validity of pride in the mere fact of accomplishment, or in the world of ideas, or in learning for its own sake."[154] On another candidate the alumni interviewer wrote, "I suggested that college in general might provide an opportunity to develop the breadth of interest in culture, politics, society . . . that the path [candidate's name] was following might be a bit narrow; that perhaps he should consider [instead of Yale] those colleges that would give him this breadth as well as the highly technical vocational training he is expecting. There was no response."[155] In these exemplary reports written by alumni and sent to the rest of the national interview network, college is envisioned as the playful pursuit of culture as an end in itself, and not anything as vulgar as a race for grades or vocational qualifications.

There are other materials in addition to the written interview reports in the archive displaying the use of cultural capital as an undergraduate screening device. News clippings on alumni interviews, such as those given by the chairman of the Alumni Schools Committee for Central New Jersey, Robert U. Redpath, were circulated to other ASC members. Redpath commuted from his home in South Orange, New Jersey, to his office on Madison Avenue, New York city. In the *Newark Sunday News* of January 15, 1967, there was a featured article on Yale's recruitment activities with a large photograph of Mr. Redpath interviewing two youths. Redpath's idea of an icebreaker was to pose questions about his household's art objects. He started interviews by sitting the candidates down at a dining room table with a sculpture on it, and then, as the reporter noted, "He asked the youths what they thought the work meant."[156] The newspaper's photo shows Redpath leaning back comfortably in his chair, both hands flat on the table, with one other member of the ASC next to him and two youths sitting opposite. Redpath is White, balding, overweight, carrying a second chin, wearing a conservative dark suit, white shirt, a proper tie, and thick eyeglasses. The two youths, one White and one Black, are both wearing dark jackets, white shirts, and ties. The White youth is gazing at the sculpture, gathering his thoughts, and the Black candidate is looking earnestly at Redpath. The other Yale interviewer, Mr. Seabrook, White, perhaps in his late thirties or early forties, is sitting almost reverently, with his head tilted forward, eyes down, and hands clasped together prayer-like in front of him on the table. At such an encounter, the odds were that a youth raised in a family with cultural capital would be more at ease, and have more to say, than one who was not.

One should not imagine that each ASC had a Madison Avenue cultural cognoscenti like Redpath chairing it, so the question arises why culture would be a natural sales pitch for alumni across the nation? The answer lies with the residential college system at Yale. Since the 1930s, Yale men have lived in small residential colleges based explicitly on the Oxford and Cambridge model.[157] Small colleges have been an essential part of the socialization and networking experience at Yale. In both theory and practice, the colleges were venues for official undergraduate cultural activities, almost exclusive of the highbrow sort.

On the theory or policy side, the administration was conscious that cultural education was a primary justification for the expensive residential colleges. The president of Yale from 1950 to 1963, A. Whitney Griswold,[158] known for promoting the natural alliance between the highbrow arts and universities in the *Atlantic Monthly*, wrote a confidential memo to the admissions staff on the importance of picking undergraduates with an eye for their potential contributions to the cultural and social life of Yale's residential colleges. Griswold, in a "Confidential: Undergraduate Admissions Policy" statement stressed that a goal of undergraduate selection was "to serve—and further—the interests of the residential principle, especially the residential college system, which emphasizes the education of undergraduates by one another outside the classroom as important as their formal education in the classroom."[159] One needs dramatists, musicians, lovers of the fine arts, and athletes for each of Yale's twelve residential colleges because the extracurricular is as vital as the curriculum. In the 1960s, the president of Yale, Kingman Brewster, commissioned and received reports on "the cultural and educational activities that are now carried on in the colleges."[160] As Brewster said in his remarks to the Alumni Convocation of 1967, Yale is "above all a place where a person becomes civilized," and the civilizing process is the work of the colleges.[161] Whether Yale made a person civilized or just added a bit of polish on top of what a boy brought from his cultured family was not commented on.

Not only in theory, but also in practice, the fine arts were paramount at Yale's residential colleges during the period under consideration here, the 1960s and 1970s.[162] Each year, the residential colleges wrote annual reports on their activities for the president's office. The records of Ezra Stiles College, one of Yale's twelve, were typical. In 1968–69, the college held fourteen classical musical concerts; it sponsored nine plays, mostly but not entirely highbrow stuff, there were modernist works by Gertrude Stein and Wallace

Stevens; and there was a visual and performing arts festival in the spring that lasted one week.[163] The only organized activities in college that rivaled or surpassed the arts were athletics. Yale's residential colleges would play football and lacrosse against each other, while putting on concerts and dramas for themselves.

Every member of an Alumni Schools Committee doing interviews knew that the dozen residential colleges back in New Haven needed "arty" types as well as "jocks." If, improbable or not, a candidate combined athletic skills and musical ability, he would be a great catch. As the secretary for the Yale Class of 1924 put it in his annual newsletter for 1966, "If you have a burly tackle maybe he could learn to play the flute?"[164] Other criteria in addition to cultural capital came into play, but culture was a regular and highly profiled aspect of the interviews conducted by the admissions office and the Alumni Association in the late 1960s.

Wrapping Up

Brewster and Clark introduced diversity, but they were not subversives. They wanted a modernized but masculine leadership class, not an academic meritocracy. They undermined Yale's provincial ways, but not its relation to legacies or athletes. And they updated Yale's compact with America's cosmopolitan upper class of wealth and culture.

CHAPTER FIVE

The Old Machinery of Meritocracy Is Discarded

No More Predicting Grades, No More Verbal Analogies

The basic machinery Yale used to evaluate the academic performance of prospective students broke down in two widely separate stages. First, Yale retired its predicted grade algorithm in 1972, and then, because of events in California, verbal analogies were eliminated from the Scholastic Assessment Test (SAT) effective in 2005. When Yale discontinued its effort to predict first-year grades, it became more simplistic in its estimate of what constituted academic preparation while it stepped up efforts to be more subtle in its assessment of personal qualities. After 1972, Yale focused its energies on the search for personal qualities that could predict leaders and successful performers later in life, and it abandoned any research into better measures of academic ability. Yet how would it make Yale more academically meritocratic to replace predicting grades with predicting personal success? And why did it stand aside from the national debate, started in California at the turn of the twenty-first century, regarding the academic legitimacy of the SAT?

The Retirement of the Predicted Grade Algorithm

After the introduction of the new interview forms featuring leadership and cultural capital, the next innovation was to discontinue Yale's "predicted grade" formula, used since 1930 in admissions to estimate first-year grades. This radical departure from Yale's tradition of measuring academic ability could be seen as yet another move away from objective measures of brains toward subjective selection based on character, except there was no intent to abandon quantifiable indicators. The report that proposed to end it suggested, as a partial replacement, to conduct research on reliable measures of personality.

In March 1971, staff members in the Office of Institutional Research (OIR) proposed to the Educational Policy Committee of the Yale Corporation that its "predicted grade" be retired. There were problems with the formula from both ends: the OIR was having difficulties estimating a school grade adjusted (SGA) for all of the schools with applicants for Yale. When an application came from a youth at a school without a proven track record with Yale, it required a guess to assign a scaled value to its grade point average (GPA). And, more importantly, inside Yale there was too much grade inflation for the system to continue working. The report diplomatically put it as there being "very wide departmental and course variations in grading."[1] The predictions were not correlating at the .70 level any longer because grade inflation and variability in high-school transcripts made precision impossible.

Grade inflation hit Yale between 1968 and 1973, during the height of the Vietnam War. In 1968, 28 percent of the graduating class received honors; in 1973 fully 57 percent did so.[2] Harvard's experience was similar, but starting from a higher threshold. In 1966, nearly 65 percent of Harvard's graduating class received honors; in 1976 it was up to approximately 84 percent.[3] The last class at Yale to receive honors under an unregulated grade-inflated system, with 58 percent of them doing so, was the Class of 1991. For the Class of 1992, and all of those following it, a ceiling of 30 percent was enforced. The limit was deemed necessary by the administration because approximately 80 percent of the grades in Yale College were from a "B+" to an "A"; the faculty could not be relied on to exercise restraint in the award of honors.[4]

If Yale's faculty awarded high grades without much variation between them, the SAT scores of applicants did not provide for much differentiation either. For a predicted grade algorithm to work, one must have variation in the input and output. On the input side, high-school grades and SAT scores of applicants must be distributed in something close to a bell curve, and Yale College grades must also be spread out along a range, for statistical analysis to work. If everyone comes in with similar records, or receives similar grades, there is nothing for the algorithm to predict.

On the SAT, the OIR report noted that most of Yale's candidates were from the top end of the scale, which reduced the variability in applicants and made first-year grade predictions futile. But it did not conclude from the difficulties with the SAT that alternative measures, such as relying more on high-school GPA or subject specific tests, such as the SAT-II, should be pursued. Since 1930, admissions researchers at Yale had known that the SAT was a weak predictor of first-year grades. And now, with first-year grades losing their meaning, the OIR proposed to drop the old remedy for an inadequate SAT, the "predictive grades" formula, but not the SAT itself. The SAT would continue to be used in admissions, and the author of the report must have felt no need to make any case for that decision. Yale's history with the SAT, its convenience as a screen selecting for family income, must have made abandonment of it inconceivable.

The Search to Quantify Personal Qualities

The OIR report, which appears under the name of its director, John H. Hoskins, is fascinating as an overview of admissions and as the first document identifying the need to formalize Yale's search for the personal characteristics that could predict college success better than academic measures alone. High-school GPA and SAT scores had been milked for all their worth; now it was time to quantify the personal qualities that predicted college success.

The report divided the admissions process into five parts: "A. Cognitive or intellectual. B. Personality. C. Sociological (socioeconomic). D. Process. E. Policy."[5] In the cognitive category, the report began by commenting on its gendered and social-class components: "Three factors are generally considered basic correlates of academic performance—cognitive ability, sex and socioeconomic factors (SES): High Cognitive Ability—Higher Performance; Women—Higher Performance; Higher SES—Higher Performance."[6] Then the author went on to describe high-school grades and College Board (CB) tests as the best available academic measures of cognitive performance, but ones of limited use in predicting first-year grades at Yale.

Under personality, the report noted, "The question of what may be referred to as expressive characteristics of the person—his values, motives, skills in social perception, motivation for achievement—is handled in the admissions process by successive subjective evaluation of interviews and written evaluations." And those ratings "are highly correlated with admissions selection."[7] Personal promise, subjectively measured, remained central to admissions, but the OIR hoped that more rigorous methods of measuring it than alumni interviews and letters of recommendation could be found.

The report attempted to summarize some cutting-edge research on personal characteristics. It reproduced in full a list "of 27 personality variables which are associated with higher levels of academic performance."[8] This line of research inspired Hoskins to raise the idea of finding alternative measures of personality beyond what gets recorded in interviews. Hoskins wrote, "It does seem proper to suggest the usefulness of investigating whether other methods than scored interviews and teacher's reports are available to aid in personal evaluations, and whether it is useful to construct an account of Yale's requirements to which applicants are matched."[9] Hoskins wanted Yale to clarify what it wanted to see in a candidate's "expressive personality," and he thought Yale should use that knowledge to construct a means to evaluate those qualities in applicants.

Under category C, the sociological one, Hoskins wrote, the "plain fact is that background factors like sex, social origin, and ethnic derivation are associated with such large differences in the yield of academically talented persons that they can be used to improve talent identification."[10] Obviously, Robert Ramsey's sociocultural model for calculating academic ability had not been forgotten. The D category, process, was about the size, organization, and turnover rate of the admissions staff. And the E category on policy required no comment from the OIR staff because such matters as the "admissions treatment of alumni sons, geographical distribution, public-private school mix and sex ratio . . . seem clearly in the province of the Educational

Policy Committee of the Corporation."[11] The Corporation sets policy, as it had recently with the 20 percent legacy quota.

The problems identified in the Hoskins report and his suggestions on the need to reevaluate personal promise were acted on quickly. A standing Undergraduate Admissions Research Committee looked into Hoskins' concerns. In May 1971, the committee, composed of John Hoskins, Judith Hackman, D. L. Hamilton, E. A. Petrovick, P. T. Seely, Robert J. Sternberg, and E. M. Thomas, presented Henry "Sam" Chauncey, Jr., with a follow-up report.

The second report began ambitiously by asking Yale to reflect on its educational mission. There was considerably more to a Yale College experience than grades. Yale saw a successful undergraduate experience as something much broader than classroom performance. Grades were becoming less meaningful not only as something worth predicting but also as the appropriate way to evaluate success in college. The committee went in search of the views of members of the Yale community on what constituted a worthwhile undergraduate experience. They reported that their

> committee has observed that among the faculty, the participants in the admissions process, the students, and the alumni, there is lacking both clarity and agreement about what defines a "successful" student. . . . We became aware of Yale's concern with leadership, and of the difficulties in predicting leadership capacity, . . . We discussed the very clear awareness among participants in the admissions process, both staff and faculty, that some "signals" of high performance and leadership—presidencies, editorships, and the like—are easier to discover in an application than others.[12]

Yale needed to articulate its vision or visions, if more than one was required, of what characterized a successful college student and her or his relation to its traditional emphasis on selecting and training leaders. And Yale should see how that information could play a role in admissions.

In just over one month, on June 18, 1971, a program for action was presented under the names of John H. Hoskins and Henry Chauncey, Jr., speaking for the Undergraduate Admissions Research Committee, the Office of Institutional Research, and the Office of Undergraduate Admissions and Financial Aid Policy. The long awkward title summed up the research agenda, "A Proposal to Study Measures of Selection for Yale College, and to Study Criteria of Success in Yale College and Performance of Undergraduates, Compared to the Measures by Which Undergraduates Are Selected."[13]

The proposal was framed by the same considerations that contextualized every admissions study since Arthur Howe's deanship. It said,

> Yale College is one of a small number of undergraduate schools highly selective in admitting students. Selectivity here has a particular meaning: it means that numerous applicants (between four and seven in Yale's recent history) for each undergraduate place are able to meet the minimum academic requirements for admission to work in the College, and that the Office of Undergraduate Admissions must consider other personal qualities and qualifications in order to select between many academically qualified applicants.[14]

Ever since the Second World War, Yale could select from an abundance of academically acceptable candidates those who looked most like being tomorrow's leaders, but now Yale wanted to quantify personal promise and possibly broaden that criteria beyond leaders. The proposal was funded and treated as a pilot study on personal qualities in college admissions and college success.

Results from the initial foray into the field were encouraging. In the following year, a second proposal was presented for a large-scale two-year multiple-site study. The principle investigators were an assistant professor of administrative science, Thomas Taber, and an Associate in the OIR, Judith Hackman.[15] Their effort was endorsed by Henry Chauncey, Jr., secretary of Yale University; John H. Hoskins, acting director, OIR; and Joseph S. Warner, director of Grant and Contract Administration. The plan was ambitious; it would take two years (1973–75) and involve nine colleges at an estimated cost of $134,991.[16] Yale's administration signed off on the study.

The Taber and Hackman effort would be Yale's last major research project, to date, on admissions criteria. Nothing else since the 1970s of this scope on the topic of admissions has been attempted. These studies represent Yale's last word, to date, on how to fine-tune the admissions process.

Yale's admissions selection process was driven by non-academic considerations, so it would help if the non-academic correlates of a successful student could be identified. At Yale, "the serious work in admissions is to choose wisely among the many academically qualified candidates on other than academic grounds—usually some combination of demographic factors, personality assessments, special group memberships, and special skills and talents."[17] The non-academic grounds could be legacy or minority status, or some skill, such as flute playing or football throwing.

For most students, however, who did not fall into any of those categories, how should Yale assess their personal suitability for its college experience? Because the "prediction . . . of academic criteria is at a plateau,"[18] non-academic criteria would have to do, and it was time to refine that procedure.

The logic of the researchers was simple and compelling. If one could identify criteria of college success in terms that go beyond academic grades, then one could turn around and apply those criteria to the selection of applicants. Fortuitously, Taber and Hackman could write, "College faculty, college officials, students and educational researchers believe that there are many more ways to 'succeed' in college than by demonstrating exceptional academic proficiency through conventional attainment measures."[19] Even the Educational Testing Service (ETS) had done work on this nearly a decade prior. The report noted, "ETS undertook a major study under the direction of J. A. Davis in the early 1960s, aimed at determining valued personal qualities beyond those reflected in the grade point average. The study was an effort to arrive at a broader definition of college criteria, in particular to assist the college admissions process."[20] This new research would pick up where Davis left off.

Taber and Hackman wanted one- to two-hour semi-structured interviews with 480 randomly selected members of the whole Yale community, from students to faculty, to extract and distill behavioral criteria on what characterizes a successful student. They would ask each interview participant to "name three Yale students from the classes of 1963–76 whom he considers most successful and three whom he considers least successful."[21] The interviewers would probe for behavioral descriptions of the three successful and unsuccessful students. Taber and Hackman emphasized, "*To Be Generally Meaningful Criteria Must Be Defined in Terms of Actual Student Behavior. This is the cornerstone of the study.*"[22] Those accounts would be analyzed exhaustively to pin down quantifiable characteristics for each type. From the full list of reported student behaviors, researchers would use factor analysis to isolate the most salient attributes that underlie all of the hundreds of descriptions of success and failure. Once those factors were identified and verified through validity tests, those attributes could become part of a personal assessment profile for admissions.

One should be mindful that the student population being tapped for exemplars of success and failure was not Yale's most diverse ever. Most members of the classes of 1963–76 were neither female nor racial minorities. In 1973, when the Yale part of the study would be completed, female enrollments had not achieved parity with men's, and minority students were at best 6 percent of the student body. The social-class backgrounds of undergraduates were skewed toward the top of the income pyramid. All of the undergraduates at Yale in 1973 had been admitted under Brewster's admissions regime with its stress on leadership.

Even with the unexamined biases introduced into the study by the privileged social-class composition of the student body, and the leadership admissions culture of the postwar years, the Taber and Hackman study was path breaking. They showed that one could objectively describe and measure student behaviors that hitherto had escaped quantification. And they identified fourteen factors common to successful students and eleven factors common to unsuccessful ones.

They immediately set about translating those factors into behavioral types. In a follow-up study, Taber and Hackman reanalyzed the same data and came up with seven types of successful students and five types of unsuccessful students. The seven were artists, athletes, careerists, grinds, leaders, scholars, and socializers. The five failures were alienated, directionless, disliked, extreme grinds, and unqualified. Behavioral indices for each type were specified. They offered the administration a codebook with seventy-three separate measures for all twelve types.

The OIR, with Hackman always as the first author, in two years turned out five reports on the topic. Their titles suggest something of the range and rigor of the findings: *Dimensions of student performance in Yale College: A first report of the college criteria study*, November 1974; *Patterns of successful performance in Yale college: A second report of the college criteria study*, August 1975; *Relationship of success types to quantified admissions variables: Addendum to the second report of the college criteria study*, August 1975; *Relationship of the 7 success types with additional admission and background variables*, November 1975; *Patterns of unsuccessful performance in Yale College: A third report of the college criteria study*, December 1975.[23]

Although at no point did any of these studies challenge the social-class underpinnings of the student body or reexamine the role of the SAT, they did broaden the criteria of selection. Here was a way to re-tool admissions that looked beyond SAT scores and that cared about something other than whether or not the youth was a high-school class president. The overidentification of leadership with official titles from high-school organizations was balanced here by an emphasis on a variety of types, from artists to grinds, the latter being previously only a pejorative label.

These studies of personal qualities gave the admissions committee more things to look for than just leaders, and that represented a type of diversification. Social-class diversity, however, was not part of the plan. The privileged social-class composition of the applicant pool was ensured, ironically, by the academic side of the admissions package. Youths applying to Yale with the right sort of high-school transcript, with difficult or advanced placement courses prominently displayed, with strengths in foreign languages, and most importantly, with high SAT scores would continue to come overwhelmingly from families in the upper-income quartile.

Yale could cherry-pick from among privileged and prepared youths the most promising artists, athletes, careerists, grinds, leaders, scholars, and socializers, while reserving room for legacy and racial targets. Most of those admitted, non-legacies and non-minorities, would ultimately be selected not for their academic qualities, but for their personal qualities. Brains alone or test scores alone were still not ruling the admissions game in the post-1960s "meritocratic" world.

External studies by researchers employed by the College Board confirmed that colleges like Yale in the late 1970s based more of their admissions decisions on "personal qualities" than on academic qualities. In 1979, Warren Willingham and Hunter Breland conducted a study of five thousand entering undergraduates in nine colleges, ranging in academic selectivity from Williams College at the top end to Ohio Wesleyan University at the bottom of this group. The researchers' goal was to empirically investigate the weight of personal qualities in college admissions at fairly selective liberal arts colleges. They found, "The particular personal qualities of the freshmen who enroll at these institutions are determined to a considerable extent by the self-selection process that creates the original applicant pool." In turn, self-selection reflects "stratification on academic achievement."[24] The marker of academic achievement that determined who applied was the SAT. Given that SAT scores sort out who puts themselves into the applicant pool, the research question was what differences personal qualities make to who is selected from that pool by the college? Their findings were paradoxical, and yet they were exactly what one would expect from Yale's record. The less "academically selective" the college, the more likely the institution was to base its admissions decision on academic criteria; the more "academically selective," the more likely the college was to count personal qualities over academic ones. The low to medium "academically selective" colleges weighed academic factors as counting from 75 percent to 100 percent of their admissions criteria; the highest "academically selective" colleges weighted personal qualities as worth more than 50 percent of their admissions criteria. In other words, the higher the average entering SAT score was at a private liberal arts college, the more likely the admissions decision was driven by non-academic personal qualities.

The attempt to appraise character evolved into the sophisticated form of "personal qualities" ratings that count for between 30 percent to more than 50 percent of one's admission's odds at most "very academically selective" institutions today, those that are listed in Barron's top tier.[25] Currently, there is a search for an updated personal-characteristics diagnostic tool for college admissions regardless of tier, which is being funded by a very large grant from the College Board. The principal researcher is the Yale psychologist, and former OIR staff member, Robert Sternberg.[26]

At the highest end of the college prestige scale, occupied by the Ivy League and kindred private liberal arts colleges, the reality during the last three decades was that test scores and grades could disqualify one, but they would not get one in. Academic record was a useful but insufficient condition of selection; admission required a combination of intellect and personal characteristics, with personal qualities being what put an applicant above the line. The balance between intellect and personal qualities was not fixed; it could depend on whether one was an athlete, legacy, or a racial minority. Personal qualities were often displayed through extracurricular activities, but merely being a volunteer to feed the poor would not matter as much as displaying creative social-entrepreneurial skills. If one was neither a legacy nor a minority, then one had to be an artist, an athlete, a fast-track careerist, a leader, a scholar, or a charming socialite to be noticed. Otherwise, one would do best to apply to a state university where academic brilliance mattered most, such as Berkeley or Michigan.

Does Selecting for Personal Qualities Work to
Identify High-Performance Individuals?

If it has succeeded in its program, Yale has a meritocracy of talented individuals, selected from the top end of the SES and SAT scale, who go on to make extraordinary contributions in a variety of fields. But how do we know the system works? How could one evaluate the effectiveness of Yale's personal-ability admissions scheme? On the in-flow side we know it works to capture approximately 75 percent of its students from the top income quartile, and about half from the top 10 percent of SAT scores; but on the out-flow side, how well does it work as a talent-scout system to identify future high-performance individuals? In A. Whitney Griswold's and Kingman Brewster's day, counts of *Who's Who* or tables compiled by Yale's historian, George Pierson, would suffice to satisfy doubters that Yale was contributing a significant number of American leaders. But how should we evaluate the effectiveness of its talent selectivity today? There is a debate among economists that sheds light on this issue. The debate turns on the question of whether degrees from top-tier colleges matter more or less than being a top-performance individual to lifetime income. Do top colleges have a value-added "school-effect," or do they mostly select high performers who would do as well regardless of where they went to college?

There is a widespread belief that graduates from top-tier colleges do better on the job market and at earning a high income than graduates from no-tier colleges; a degree from Yale is supposed to carry one further than one from Northeastern. It would not be much of a stretch to say that most upper-middle-class and upper-class parents believe that particular schools matter, all the way from kindergarten to college. And at least by the time of high school, youths join in the parental obsession over the search for the perfect college. Their mental turmoil is stirred or calmed by the ratings industry, from *Barron's* to the *U.S. News and World Report*, and by high-school counselors, college administrators, admissions staff, and alumni interviewers who try to sell applicants on the merits of a college. Parents and youths act as though particular schools matter, not just to one's educational experience, but to one's future life chances. Not all social scientists, however, share the public's confidence in "school effects."

Recently, U.S. economists have given new life to the controversy about whether there are "school effects" with research on how college tier matters to the lifetime earnings of graduates. As previewed in this book's first chapter, the current scholarly consensus is that there are income differences between college graduates in the United States that correspond to their colleges' tier.[27] Graduates from higher-tier colleges earn more money than graduates from lower-tier ones. Most participants in this controversy think of college tiers as corresponding, more or less, to the categories displayed in *Barron's Profiles of American Colleges* that cluster colleges into six tiers ranging from most competitive to non-competitive. *Barron's* began publication in 1964; its six tiers were in play by 1966, and then carried forward, annually or bi-annually, ever since.[28]

The crux of the debate about whether tiers really matter turns on the issue of causal mechanism. If college-tier income disparities are real, what causes them? Is there something about top-tier colleges (their resources, external social networks, and social prestige) that matters to the lifetime earnings of their graduates? Or, are top-tier colleges simply better than their rivals at capturing the best talent in the applicant pool? Plainly put, does a person of high ability have to attend Princeton to be a top-income earner, or would that person do just as well with a degree from Rutgers? Ironically, if Yale's admissions system works as intended that would undermine any claim by it to add substantial value to the earnings potential of its graduates. For then it would not be Yale College, but its selection of high-performance individuals that explained income premiums for its graduates.

The most persuasive evidence yet that income advantages are conferred by top-tier institutions in the United States comes from books and articles written by former Ivy League presidents, Harvard and Cornell economists, and their colleagues at the National Bureau of Economic Research.[29] All of these authors draw substantively the same lines between top-, middle-, and bottom-ranked colleges.

William Bowen, past president of Princeton and current president of the Andrew W. Mellon Foundation, and Derek Bok, a former president and interim president of Harvard, offer a preliminary cut into the issue of graduates' earnings disparities. Using the Mellon Foundation's College and Beyond (C&B) data, they worked with 1995 income data on undergraduates who enrolled in 1976 at thirty-four very selective colleges. They compared those very selective college youths with a national control group surveyed in

1996 of individuals who were eighteen years old in 1976. They found that all of their selective college members (regardless of race, gender, or academic ability) from the 1976 cohort earned in 1995 on average $98,200, in contrast to White-male graduates with all "A" grades from the national sample, who were making on average $71,400 in 1996. Bowen and Bok conclude from this, "Even after controlling for ability as best one can, . . . [t]here is, indeed, a real wage premium associated with enrollment at an academically selective institution."[30] Other economists working with more precise comparisons than Bowen and Bok have uncovered similar disparities favoring first-tier institutions in contrast to colleges lower down the scale.

Dominic Brewer of the Rand Corporation, Eric Eide of Brigham Young University's economics department, and Ronald Ehrenberg, the director of Cornell University's Higher Education Research Institute, used two national longitudinal surveys, *National Educational Longitudinal Survey of the High School Class of* 1972 (NELS) and the *High School and Beyond*, to estimate the effects of college tier (defined with reference to *Barron's* classifications) on graduates' income, holding constant both student academic ability and decisions on which educational investments were worth making. They found "there is a large premium to attending an elite private institution, and a smaller premium to attending a middle-rated private institution, relative to a bottom-rated public school. There is weaker evidence of a return to attending an elite public university."[31]

The most extensive case for tier-dependent income inequalities has been presented by Caroline Hoxby, professor of economics at Harvard University. She took the *Barron's* selectivity index for 1980 (while noting that it has changed so little from the 1960s to the 1990s that any year would produce the same statistical results), and classified all "selective" higher education institutions into eight tiers. Using data from three national surveys, covering first-year students in the United States in 1960, 1972, and 1982, she estimated lifetime career incomes. Working with a sample restricted to males and using controls for academic ability, Hoxby found, "Since 1972, the returns to attending a more selective college have been rising over time. For students with the aptitude to attend a [tier] rank 1 or rank 2 college, the returns to attending a more selective college have [been] rising over the *entire* period since 1960."[32] Hoxby showed that, other things being equal, a graduate from a tier-one college would earn during a lifetime approximately

$300,000 more than a tier-four college graduate, and $1,200,000 more than a tier-six graduate.[33]

In additional work on the topic, Hoxby and Bridget Terry, both in Harvard's economics department, published a National Bureau of Economic Research paper that calculates for college graduates the percentage of "wage inequality [that] is associated with aptitude or college rank."[34] They estimate that college tier, by itself, "accounts for about 32% of total increase in the variance of income" between 1972 and 1995 for college graduates.[35]

Bowen, Bok, Brewer, Eide, Ehrenberg, Hoxby, and Terry all argue that income disparities among college graduates are not merely "selection effects," which is to say, the result of applicant self-selection or institutional selection of individuals with particular abilities and ambitions. Rather, even when holding individual abilities constant, there remain measurable "treatment effects" of attending different types of institutions—even if that effect is to carry a label that signals one's ability to employers. For these researchers, there appears to be little doubt that receiving a degree from a top-ranked institution gives one a comparative income advantage over others with BAs from lowly ranked colleges.

The counterargument that "selection effects" matter more than college tier "treatment effects" comes from an associate of Bowen's at the Mellon Foundation, Stacy Berg Dale, and her coauthor Alan B. Krueger, a Princeton economist. Dale and Krueger concede that if one works only with observable indicators of academic ability, such as SAT scores and grade point average, then one finds strong tier effects on income. Controlling for academic track record, as the others have sought to do, one finds income differences between individuals with the same academic abilities if they graduate from colleges located in different tiers of the system. College tiers apparently transmit income premiums and penalties.

What if, Dale and Krueger argue, academic performance is not all that matters to one's income earning abilities? What if unmeasured personality attributes are also relevant to one's career success? It is uncontroversial to point out that high-test score achieving youths do not automatically make the best entrepreneurs or corporate executives. And top-tier colleges, such as Yale, do not select just for academic characteristics; they look at personal qualities, such as drive or leadership, and those characteristics may be "positively correlated with wages."[36]

How might non-academic, yet high-performance personal qualities weigh more on the income scales than tier effects? Dale and Krueger believe that elite colleges have admissions professionals who have perfected the art of selecting candidates for personal characteristics that go beyond SAT scores. Qualities of persons, unavailable from college transcripts for social scientific scrutiny, are what admissions committees at top-tier colleges pick up on during applicants' interviews and while reading essays and letters of recommendation.[37] Selecting for personal characteristics is why it does not bother Harvard, Yale, and Princeton admissions' officers that Berkeley, Michigan, and Wisconsin all have more "super students"[38] with ultra-high SAT scores than any of them. Although top state universities have to accept everyone who applies with ultra-high SAT scores, the Ivy League does not want to. If top-tier colleges excel at admitting and matriculating high-performance individuals whose outstanding personal abilities fall outside the observable academic record, then tier effects could be spurious. College tier disparities in earnings for graduates may be due more to the non-academic abilities of the talent stream than to the qualities of the college.

Dale and Krueger devised an elegant analytic strategy to test whether personal character explains tier effects. Assuming that personal characteristics are what elite college admissions committees earn their pay recognizing, they argue that individuals with comparable personal promise and academic records will be similarly accepted or rejected by comparable colleges. Data on personal characteristics "can be inferred from the outcomes of independent admission decisions by the schools the student applied to."[39] Social scientists can control for personal ability effects on incomes by matching individuals with the same patterns of college applications, acceptances, and rejections who then attend colleges in different tiers. If those matched individuals go on to earn roughly the same income later in life, then tier effects are spurious, but if there is an income disparity between those matched individuals that corresponds to college tier, then we know tier-treatment effects are real.

In sum, Dale and Krueger control, as described later, for the academic and personal abilities of graduates from a 1976 C&B cohort and a NELS 1972 cohort. Then they rank colleges three ways: by selectivity measured as average SAT score, as location within one of *Barron's* six tiers, and by average tuition costs. And, for outcomes, Dale and Krueger model income for the C&B cohort for 1995, and for the NELS cohort for 1985.

Their findings are mixed. If one measures college selectivity as average SAT score, then, once personal abilities are controlled, "students who attended more selective colleges do not earn more than other students who were accepted and rejected by comparable schools but attended less selective colleges."[40] An alternative way of ranking colleges, *Barron's* tiers, also does not display significant effects, once personal qualities are factored in. Consequently, SAT selectivity and tier income premiums appear to be spurious selection effects, rather than a treatment effect; top-tier college graduates make more money than graduates from low-tier colleges because of their superior personal capabilities. Dale and Krueger conclude, "Students who attend the more selective schools may have higher unobserved [personal] ability."[41]

The question is not settled yet because if one ranks colleges differently, by tuition costs, then personal ability controls do not remove the disparities in income effects. It is possible that colleges with higher tuition rates provide more human capital, economically relevant skills, to their graduates; "these results suggest that tuition matters because higher cost schools devote more resources to student instruction." In addition, the income payoffs of attending a high-tuition college "are greatest for students from more disadvantaged backgrounds."[42] For one's earning capacity, the more expensive one's college the better, especially for the upwardly mobile. Dale and Krueger do not rule out the possibility that something about the institution one attends matters to one's life chances.

On balance, however, Dale and Krueger's findings are consistent with the hypothesis that Yale's admissions system works as intended and that selection for personal qualities is a more reliable method for selecting high-performance individuals than are academic measures alone. The number of institutions in Dale and Krueger's data suggest that Yale's methods are common to top-tier institutions. Although the public and many scholars argue about academic qualifications in the narrow sense of grades and test scores, top-tier admissions offices left that issue behind decades ago. Though test scores alone earn one a place in the second rank or lower, personal ability gets one to the top.

The practical impact of the income debate is certain to be marginal. Even if Dale and Krueger were right on the effects of tier on income being spurious, high-performance individuals cluster there to such an extent that it makes it risky for a youth given options between first- and second-tier institutions to matriculate at the lower-tier one. Why should a youth forgo the possible positive benefits of peer group while in college and social networks once out, and of signaling to employers her or his top-tier abilities? Youths with options will find it unreasonable to swim against the stream just because two economists found that tiers are not the causal mechanism responsible for the indisputable correlation of tier with earnings. Although some parents do encourage their offspring to attend a less expensive lower-tier state university, for example, Florida State University instead of an expensive third-tier institution, such as the University of Miami, the evidence suggests that neither parents nor youths are likely to decline an offer from a tier-one college to save money.[43] The prestige of the top tier trumps the rational lessons of social science.

In sum, contrary to conventional meritocratic accounts, from the 1950s to the early 1970s, Yale created new techniques for evaluating personal character, not for measuring intellectual merit. The idea that new methods of identifying and estimating academic performance, understood as ability to do classroom work, were developed and applied is without substance. At Yale and in the top tier, we have a student body drawn from a self-selected wealthy and academically proficient applicant pool, people who are uncommonly capable of personal performance. The top tier selects for young professionals from families in the upper-middle and upper class.

The Fate of the SAT

When Yale dropped its predicted grade algorithm and formalized its use of "personal qualities," it was left with high-school transcripts and SAT scores as its only raw measures of academic ability. High-school grades had always been a more reliable predictor of first-year college grades than SAT scores—Yale has known that since 1930, and the College Board's own researchers confirmed that fact at various points in time, most recently in a 1990 publication covering more than two decades of data kept by the ETS.[44] Without the predicted grade algorithm to correct the statistical weaknesses of the SAT, what was the point of keeping it? To estimate college competence, high-school GPA by itself or in combination with SAT-II subject test scores might do better than either the SAT alone or in combination with GPA. Most of Yale's applicants, from 1926 to the present, took two SAT-II subject tests in addition to the SAT; data on SAT-II subject tests were available for Yale's evaluation. Yet Yale did not take the opportunity of the demise of its predicted grade to reexamine its tools for evaluating academic potential. Rather, Yale relied more than ever before on the value of the SAT for admissions.

Yale publicized its median SAT score for each entering class annually. It did so knowing the SAT's poor capacity to predict first-year college grades, and with an awareness of the linear relationship between SAT scores and a family's SES. In the past, neither Yale nor the College Board has been embarrassed by the correlation of test scores with family SES, measured as income and parent's education. It has been taken for granted that a more resource-rich home environment will produce youths with greater capacities to perform well on standardized tests. Yale, despite its vast resources and commitment to academic excellence, never bothered to research whether the SAT was more contaminated by SES bias than were other available substitutes. Perhaps, the SAT was too convenient to Yale's goal of capturing approximately 60 percent of each undergraduate cohort as full-fee paying clients for the OIR to raise the idea that the SAT's linear relation to SES was anything other than an unfortunate and inescapable reality of educational standards.

Over the years, the SAT, and especially the verbal analogies section, has been criticized for being biased by the SES of the family.[45] There will probably never be a test that can eliminate every disparity in the academic performance of youths that is caused by inequalities in family environments, but that does not excuse researchers from the obligation to search for tests that minimize background effects. Real meritocracy requires as level of a playing field as possible. What Yale never investigated, when it had the data to do so, was whether the verbal and math sections of the regular SAT test were more contaminated by SES, racial, or gender biases than were subject specific tests, such as the SAT-II; that job was done by the University of California (UC).

Nationally, research on how to evaluate academic ability, after 1972, was channeled into the debate on race and academic performance gaps between Blacks and Whites. Political events that grew out of the controversy on affirmative action eventually caused the UC to reconsider the academic validity of the SAT. When the UC completed its investigation, it exposed the poverty of predicting college performance based on SAT scores; the exam that Yale helped create and sustain finally lost its credibility. During the exam's mortal illness, Yale neither attended the patient, nor wrote an obituary. Yale seemed quite content to stay aloof from its demise.

University of California Admissions and the SAT

Founded in 1868, the UC pursued the 1862 land-grant act's mission of being a public university, accessible and relevant to the state's citizens. From the nineteenth century, the university employed the certification system, pioneered by Michigan, in partnership with the state's public high schools. Until 1934, graduation from a certified high school automatically got one into the university; then, starting in 1934, standards were tightened and one had to receive respectable grades in subjects specified by the UC to be eligible for admission.[46] In addition to certification, UC looked into the alternative admission's route of entry tests. When in the 1930s, the SAT became well known as the East coast, private colleges' preferred method of evaluating candidates, the UC's "Academic Senate considered—and rejected—the use of standardized admissions tests."[47] Course grades received in high school were reaffirmed as the appropriate way to qualify for the UC.

After the Second World War, the university again considered using standardized tests for admission. Part of the attraction to leaders of the university came from their sense that all of the most prestigious private universities in the state were using the SAT, apparently to good effect. And some of the interest came from bureaucratic convenience; the test was seen as a way to cope with large numbers of applicants. In 1947, when a temporary bulge in applications threatened, because of the large number of GI Bill veterans looking to enter college, the university requested that each take the SAT.[48] The older candidates were a few years out of high school, and the test might help verify their suitability for college-level work. In practice, the usefulness of the SAT in 1947 was a disappointment, and the university did not require it of future applicants.

The next time the university's leaders reconsidered the SAT it was, again,

because of demographic pressures. The prospect of the baby-boom generation arriving on the university's doorstep caused the regents, the university's
highest governing body who were to the university much like the Corporation was to Yale, to hold an educational policy meeting in November 1956 to
discuss whether changes in the requirements for admission were advisable.

The discussion took place at the Sheraton-Palace Hotel in San Fran-
cisco, and in addition to nine regents in attendance there were two chancellors, including Clark Kerr, Berkeley's chancellor; the university's president,
Robert Gordon Sproul; its legal counsel, Thomas Cunningham, two leading professors, Edward Strong and Nixon; and the director of admissions,
Herman Spindt. They began with Sproul noting that the present size of the
university was about 38,000 but that by 1970 it could be 112,000. In 1956,
of California's 41,000 high-school graduates, 11 percent met the subject and
grade distribution to be eligible for admission to the university, but only 4
percent were actually taking advantage of the opportunity to enroll.[49] For
the university to fulfill its constitutional mandate from the State of California to educate all eligible graduates now and fifteen years hence, it would
need to adopt a new course of action. The university had three choices. It
could redefine admission's eligibility to "restrict growth in numbers of students"; it could "increase the facilities of the present University campuses
and/or . . . create new campuses."[50] The regents, chancellors, and faculty did
not entirely agree on which option would be optimal.

Regent Donald McLaughlin thought that more students would be worse
students, and he wanted the university to maintain "its elite position" not by
adding campuses, but by turning the present campuses into citadels for "real
scholars." McLaughlin "considered it the responsibility of the University
to educate the intellectually elite. . . . [E]ducation for the masses was the
responsibility of the state colleges and junior colleges."[51] McLaughlin proposed, and the awkwardly worded motion was approved, "The University
maintain its present high *or higher* standards of admission." And Professor
Strong assured everyone present, "The [academic] Senate Committee would
accept such an amendment, adding that the Committee is of the opinion that
admissions standards should be comparable to those of the leading institutions in the country."[52] The university's faculty, regents, and administration
were all in agreement on California's need to keep pace with the nation's
top, mostly private, universities.

McLaughlin's desire to cultivate an intellectual elite, however, was not shared by all of the regents. A university inhabited exclusively by scholars and scientists would not allow it to play Yale's game of selecting and educating leaders. Regent Cyril C. Nigg wanted to relax intellectual standards to accommodate society's future leaders. He said, "One of the fundamental responsibilities of the University was to train leaders, and the leaders were not always to be found among the brilliant students. . . . [H]e felt that consideration [in admissions] should be given to leadership qualities." The next speaker, Kerr, reassured Nigg "that a method of selection could be formulated which would result in terms of leadership."[53] The meeting resolved to investigate the feasibility of expansion, of building new facilities and new campuses, of recruiting new faculty, and of revising admissions policies.

Moving swiftly, the Office of the Director of Admissions and Relations with Schools issued a report in December 1956 for the regents and other university leaders involved in the policy discussion. The report, "A Comparison of Entrance Requirements at the University of California and at Selected Other Colleges," set out context, provided detailed comparisons, and suggested options. Leading universities worthy of California's consideration were identified, in this order, as Harvard, Columbia, Yale, Princeton, Stanford, and Michigan. Later in the document Reed College, MIT, California Institute of Technology, Barnard, and Chicago were also mentioned as institutions from which California received sufficient transfer students as to make some comparison of their grading scales with California's possible.[54] Of the list, only Michigan was a public university, truly comparable to California in mission and size. The dominance of private institutions on this list testified to their success in occupying the academic high ground.[55]

The report understood that California and Michigan were similar in a number of essential respects. The two land-grant public universities had an "insistence on a fixed pattern" of classes to establish one's eligibility. And at both "all eligible applicants are admitted while in the private colleges the number to be admitted is fixed, and selection is made on a competitive basis." California stood alone, however, as the one who treated high-school graduation as sufficient "evidence of good character."[56]

On how the various colleges evaluated scholastic ability, the report approvingly quoted from a Harvard admissions handbook, "Rank-in-class is the best single index." The California author of the report noted that Harvard drew 90 percent of its students from the top 21 percent of secondary-school graduates, that Michigan found 75 percent of its undergraduates from the top 25 percent of high-school graduates, and that California's "admissions requirements probably qualify not more than 15–17 per cent of the high school graduating classes in the state."[57] One might assume that California's greater selectivity from the high-school talent pool would make it academically stronger than the rest, but that was not the conclusion drawn by the report.

In the minds of California's admissions officers, there were two qualifications that put questions marks over their students' quality as measured by rank-in-high-school: private colleges in 1956 drew largely from private secondary schools and private colleges used the SAT. It was inappropriate, the report asserted, to equate the quality of Harvard's private-secondary-school youths with California's public high-school graduates.[58] They implied that class rank at Andover would be different from class rank at San Diego High not only because of differences in size, but also because private schools would be more academically rigorous than "the comprehensive high school of the mid-west and west."[59] No evidence in support of this claim was offered. For a meaningful comparison of California's student quality with the rest, the report left behind the land-grant institution's home ground, high-school performance, and ventured onto the private colleges' turf, SAT test scores.

Although the university did not require the SAT for admissions, a percentage of applicants each year had the College Board send their scores to California. One may safely assume that some of the youths in question were applying elsewhere in addition to California, perhaps to a private college on the East coast. The other reason a student's SAT score would be available to California was because she or he was applying with a poor high-school record but with a few years of junior college under her or his belt.[60] In the 1950s, the university required junior college transfer applicants with high-school grades below a "B" average to take the SAT. Consequently, at least some of the available SAT scores for California to work with were from relatively weak students.

To compare students' SAT scores among, in this order, California, Michigan,[61] Harvard, Yale, Reed College, MIT, Princeton, California Institute of Technology, and Stanford, the California's admissions office was willing to make a questionable leap in logic. "Assuming for present purposes," they

wrote, "that the group who sent us Scholastic Aptitude Test scores is a reasonably satisfactory sample, we can make some direct comparisons."[62] It was a stretch, statistically unwarranted, to treat those youths with SAT scores as representing a valid representative sample of California's undergraduates. If most students in the sample were there because they were junior college transfers or multiple applicants who did not get into a college back East, then the available California SAT scores would be biased downward.

The author of the report, nonetheless, concluded, "It can be accepted that our freshman class as measured by the College Entrance Examination Board Scholastic Aptitude Test is above that of Michigan, but below the other colleges listed."[63] Berkeley was judging itself to be weaker than the private sector. We know now that in 1968, the dean of admissions at Harvard would come to the opposite conclusion, putting the caliber of Berkeley's students above Harvard's[64]; in retrospect, it would be reasonable to assume that the same was true in 1956. At the time, however, the prestige of private colleges, and their preference for the SAT, sufficiently clouded the judgment of Berkeley's admissions officers that they downgraded their estimate of their students' intellectual caliber in comparison to Harvard, Yale, and the other private colleges on their list.

The preeminence of the elite private sector was further attested to by the Berkeley office appending to its report extensive excerpts from Harvard's advice on admissions given to its alumni interview committees. No other written materials from any other university were shared in the discussion. Just like Yale, Harvard wrote handbooks and issued reports to guide its alumni in the field doing the crucial interview work with applicants. And Berkeley reproduced enough of the handbook as to leave little confusion in the minds of California's leaders on how Harvard, and by inference the other elite colleges on its list, did admissions.

Harvard's handbook could have been written by the admissions dean at Yale, the two colleges were so similar. Naturally, Harvard wanted only "the best," and was well aware that the "problem is how to define the 'best.'" Harvard would not err on the side of scholastic brilliance by defining the best "solely in terms of academic ability." The handbook noted that there are those who believe that Harvard selects only youths "with the highest I.Q.'s and that our ideal is a college consisting entirely of 'A' students. These assumptions are incorrect." Harvard does, however, exclude from consideration those who could not "do work of minimum Harvard standards."[65] It also turns away "applicants about whom there is evidence of serious weakness of character," and "applicants with serious personality problems are rejected." Harvard was, however, willing to make allowance for some neurotic youths but not for those with character flaws. Harvard wanted to go beyond "a student body composed solely of excessively normal extroverts. Some of our most interesting and promising students, . . . have neurotic traits. . . . [T]he greater the talent the more willing we are to take chances on apparent personal idiosyncrasies."[66] Normal extroverts with dry and firm handshakes may be the typical Harvard or Yale man, but a few neurotic creative types would not hurt.

Once the academically ill-prepared, and defective or dysfunctional personalities were eliminated from consideration, Harvard's admissions office was left, like Yale, with many more times the number of candidates than available seats in its first-year class. How should it select from the rest? Harvard's answer, again like Yale's, was to set out a list of categories, some with explicit percentage targets, to capture "the best student body." Harvard's categories were ten in number.

First, there was room for between 10 and 20 percent of each class to be filled by youths with "outstanding intellectual ability. . . . Students of this sort constitute perhaps five to ten percent of the College at present."[67] Previous classes had been limited to no more than 10 percent intellectuals, but now the admissions office would entertain the notion that as many as 20 percent could fit that description. The second, third, and fourth categories were given without elaboration to be "outstanding qualities of character. . . . Outstanding capacity for leadership. . . . Unusual attractiveness of personality."[68] Having a magnetic personality, with a proven record of leadership and evidence of good moral fiber would surely get one a high score at an interview. The fifth category was "creative ability . . . in literature, music and the arts." Be a seventeen-year-old author, composer, or painter and one might find a place at Harvard. The sixth group, athletes, included the cautionary note, "Experience has made us leery of the highly touted schoolboy athlete who has been spoiled by too early fame, has developed false standards, and thinks that the world owes him a living." No doubt some alumni took offense and wrote letters condemning Harvard's slur on the virtue of young athletes. The seventh category covered legacies; just as at Yale, "about 20 percent of our students are sons of Harvard alumni. The son of a graduate has a definite advantage in the competition." Eighth was geography, "Harvard wants to be a national college." Admissions staff should strive to balance metro and regional areas to ensure representation from across the country. The ninth category, "maturity and strength of motivation for a liberal education" was given without elaboration. One may assume they had in mind the upper-class attributes spelled out by Yale's admissions dean, Arthur Howe, in his comments on Harvard's policies.[69] The final category, "intensity of desire for Harvard"[70] was equally open to social-class biases. How was one to measure and weigh an applicant's desire? Surely an Andover legacy would not express "intensity of desire" the same way as a first-generation college applicant from Brooklyn.

The handbook made explicit that "in choosing among the average candidates, . . . we believe that other factors are of considerably greater importance than academic factors." And, as was true at Yale, "each increase in the number of candidates underlines the importance of really searching interview reports."[71] The alumni interview was the most important item determining the fate of the applicant's file. The University of California's leaders should have read this appendix as a caution against seeing Harvard as a model of academic meritocracy.

Berkeley's admissions office did wrap up its own report with an explicit appeal to distance California's policies from Harvard's. The author wrote,

> I doubt that we should base our policy on "keeping up with the Joneses." Certainly we should be "respectable" in the eyes of the most severe of our neighbors, but our primary problem is not measured by comparison with others, but whether we are properly meeting the function that has been assigned to us by the State.[72]

It would be a mistake for California to pursue greater selectivity when its constitutional mandate was to make room for every eligible high school graduate. The report's author may have been unduly impressed by elite private colleges, and he may have been too willing to relegate Berkeley to the academic second tier because of its patchy SAT scores, but he did not waver from the public service mission of the institution. The university was there for all of California's citizens who were prepared to benefit from a quality higher education.

In the discussion that followed, tensions between access and excellence, between California's public mission and its desire to compete with Harvard and Yale, were felt. Faculty, regents, and administrators were themselves divided on whether it was more important to establish the university's credentials in the top tier or whether its commitment to provide places for all eligible citizens came first. Not all regents favored the elitist approach, not all professors cared only about peer-group standing, and not every admissions officer was committed to democratic access. Some individuals seemed to be of two minds on the problem. Getting the balance right between excellence and equity was a structural dilemma facing a public university that private colleges could choose to ignore.

Within five months, the regents' Committee on Educational Policy and the faculty's Senate Committee submitted a combined report, a "Second Progress Report on Admissions Standards"[73] to the office of the president. The report provided an update on the most important elements of California's admissions system and sixteen pages of proposals and policies. The first three proposals looked as though single-minded backers of elite excellence had trumped the supporters of democratic access. The committee recommended that California should require all candidates to take the SAT. California should start using the SAT for "improving selectivity within" California's top 15 percent of high-school graduates,[74] the SAT should be required, if possible, of all applicants to the fall 1959 class, and the university should announce a policy that it may, and "without advance notice," limit enrollments.[75] Restricting the size of its first-year class and selecting from among California's top high-school graduates based on their SAT scores looked like a very clear victory for the elitists on the Board of Regents and for faculty who cared more about being included in the top tier than about student access. In practice, the full effects of those three policies were not as elitist as they sounded because they were designed to address one particular problem, overcrowding.

The report clarified that the SAT should not be used to eliminate anyone qualified for admission under the university's old policies. "The Committee does not intend, by these 'Proposals,' to . . . reduce the proportion of students eligible for admission to the University at the time of high school graduation."[76] Rather, the SAT should be employed as a temporary way to allocate the available seats on any particular campus in the University of California system, when demand for places at that campus exceeds carrying capacity. SAT scores would factor in when adjustments had to be made "to keep numbers admitted from exceeding the maximum which can be cared for by staff and facilities."[77] A high SAT score would give an eligible student his first rather than second campus choice, for example, Berkeley over Davis, and a low score would have the opposite effect. It was possible that student demand at all campuses would exceed the system's total capacity, in which case until more facilities or campuses were built, the SAT could be used to draw a temporary cut-off point in the applicant pool.

The SAT was not, however, intended to make California's standards more exclusive to emulate Harvard. The report stressed,

> During prosperous times, many more applicants present themselves than Harvard is willing to admit. Standards of selection are raised as need be to eliminate students in excess of a predetermined quota. This is a feasible procedure for a private University. The University of California cannot defensibly decide to admit only so many undergraduates and no more. . . . [T]he University has . . . to provide for students eligible for admission under . . . [its] standards.[78]

And California's standards were those of a land-grant university in partnership with certified high schools. If a youth got good grades in particular subjects from an accredited public high school, then California held open its doors.

The democratic thrust of California's admissions policies were amplified in the report's comments on the university's partnership with high schools, and by its commitment to transfer students from California's junior colleges. Approximately 90 percent of the University of California's first-year students were admitted directly from high schools; they were made eligible for admission by achieving at least a "B" average in five subjects: history, English, mathematics, a laboratory science, and a foreign language, plus they had to receive at least a "B" in one advanced-level course in math, science, or foreign language.

The university did the work to statistically match the grades received in high school with those given at the university to help schools keep up their standards, not to predict academic performance in advance of admissions as was the practice at Yale. The report noted that California

> correlates the performance of freshmen with their high school grade records. An index is thus provided of the reliability of grading in the high

schools sending students to the University, and the schools are kept informed of the findings with respect to their own students. . . . In informing the high schools of records made by their students in their freshman year, the University performs an important service. The high schools are put on their mettle to improve a poor showing or to maintain a demonstrated excellence in the preparation of students for college work.[79]

The working relation between the university and schools was a contribution to the public good not performed by Yale.

California also kept its promise of providing access to the citizens of the state through its relations with junior colleges. There is nothing in the University of California's archive that suggests anything other than a positive, even collegial, attitude by the university to the state's junior colleges. No stigma was attached to youths coming out of the junior college system. The report noted that many high-school graduates, even from the top 15 percent in class rank, selected to attend a junior college straight out of school. To those, as well as all the rest without the subject grades in high school to qualify for direct entry, the university wanted to provide a second chance. Any determined individual capable of achieving "B" level grades in junior college could work his or her way into the university. Because junior colleges have essentially open-door admissions, there is always a way for upward educational mobility in California. The method has been used extensively. At present, the University of California receives approximately 25 percent of its students through the junior college route.[80] No private tier-one college in the nation has anything like California's contingent of students with junior college backgrounds.

The 1957 report made it clear that California would stick to its mission and its certification method of determining admissions. It wanted to call on the SAT when numbers ran higher than normal, but not to reduce the ranks of eligible Californians.

The second report said nothing about the idea raised by Regent Nigg on selecting for leaders. When he brought it up in 1956, Chancellor Kerr gave the proposal credibility. The idea must have continued to float around within the university's administration because the point was addressed at a meeting in May 1958, by the Committee on Educational Policy.

The official agenda was to report on programs at Berkeley and Los Angeles, but the meeting also took up the unresolved issues on admissions from the two previous reports. The use of the SAT had still to be implemented, CB subject achievement tests had not been properly considered, and the matter of leadership selection was left open. The report from the meeting stated,

> The Committee on Educational Policy has (with the concurrence of the Board of Admissions and Relations with Schools) previously recommended incorporating a scholastic aptitude test "into the regular procedures for admission to the University . . . " The Committee has not, however, recommended the use of achievement tests. The Committee strongly recommends, nevertheless, that the Board of Admissions continue to study the form and content of achievement tests that might be used in admission procedures. The Committee questions the desirability of using "information about leadership ability" as a factor in admitting students. The use of each nonobjective data as a factor in undergraduate admission would, in all likelihood, create serious or even unmanageable problems for the Office of Admissions.[81]

The committee wanted forward motion on the SAT, an exploration of scholastic achievement tests, but it did not see the point in following Yale in the chase for leaders.

In 1958, Kerr became president of the statewide university system. Within two years of taking office, Kerr got the State of California legislature to adopt his famous Master Plan. The plan integrated all three tiers of California's higher education, the junior colleges, the state university system, and the University of California into one big system. The legislature agreed to make higher education accessible to every citizen in the state by dividing the ability pool of high-school graduates. The top 12.5 percent of each high-school graduation cohort were to be eligible for the University of California's campuses, the California State system (such as Cal State Long Beach) should draw from the top 25 percent, and junior colleges would take care of all the rest. The Master plan bears much of the responsibility for California having more students than any other state in the nation, and for putting it into a first-place tie with Massachusetts for having the most adults, over 20 percent, with four or more years of college.[82]

The Master plan announced the democratic principle of making all levels of education available to every citizen. Every high-school graduate would be entitled to a taxpayer-supported higher education. Free or very low cost public education would not end in secondary school. The democratic thrust of the plan was, however, tempered by an element of elitist selectivity. The plan made into law the idea of using standardized tests for university admissions.[83]

California's interest in standardized tests was seen by the College Board and its independent corporation for running the SAT, the Educational Testing Service (ETS), as a great opportunity. California had the largest university system in the country, it was a public system, and it was on the West Coast. If California adopted the SAT, the educational legitimacy of the test, as something other than a tool of private northeastern colleges, would receive a significant boost. The ETS took advantage of the opening by offering a free trial of the SAT for California's students, and the university accepted the gift. Subsequently, the SAT was "administered to all freshmen entering UC in the fall of 1960."[84] It was to be an experiment to see what additional information above high-school records the SAT could provide on the intellectual caliber of California's students.

The experiment, from the university's perspective, worked, but the SAT did not. The project successfully demonstrated that the SAT was unhelpful. The university's Board of Admissions and Relations with Schools (BOARS) "concluded that the study did not indicate any additional predictive power associated with the SAT."[85] The university did not institute the policy requiring all California high-school applicants to UC to take the test.

In January 1962, Frank Kidner, who held the newly established position of university dean of Educational Relations,[86] sent a confidential memo to members of the president's cabinet and chief campus officers, pointing out the uselessness of the SAT. The board had conducted rigorous multiple correlation analyses evaluating the virtues of the SAT for admissions and determined,

> (1) that very little increase in precision may be achieved through the use of Scholastic Achievement Test scores at the level of freshmen admissions, and . . . all indications point to the probable elimination of the Scholastic Aptitude Test score as a condition of admission in advance standing where . . . it has even less validity than it does at the level of first semester admissions.[87]

The SAT did not improve California's ability to select first-year, and it helped even less with transfer students from junior colleges. In 1962, all use of the SAT for admissions, whether of transfer students or even of out-of-state applicants, was discontinued.

As Nicholas Lemann correctly reports, the ETS took this as a disaster requiring a counter offensive to recapture California. California was the largest potential student market in the nation for the SAT, but cash was not an immediate concern. The ETS needed California to protect its prestige.[88] The academic legitimacy of the SAT was undermined by California's withdrawal from the test.

The ETS and CB strategy was to woo the administration, especially President Clark Kerr. Their efforts apparently worked. Kerr would not let go of the idea; he kept the issue on the desk of the dean of Educational Relations, Kidner. And the Board of Admissions and Relations with Schools "would return year after year with a proposal to require the SAT."[89] There were a number of institutional dynamics that were helping the College Board's cause.

Within the university there were new opportunities that were pressing to distance it from the high-school certification system. Federal funds provided an extraordinary opportunity for the university's scientists to build little research empires. Federal funds had been dramatically increased by Congress' National Defense and Education Act, passed because of fears raised by the Soviet's launch of the first spaceship Sputnik in 1957 that we were losing the Cold War. It was thought that we were in a struggle for the survival of our civilization in which victory depended on scientific breakthroughs. Federal money fast became the second largest item in the university's budget, after State of California funds.[90] Those funds allowed the university to move into the top ranks of research universities nationally.

Large research grants helped unleash a logic of professionalization for California's academics. Junior faculty were being hired and promoted based on publications and grants. Senior faculty cared more about peer group ratings than college teaching or certification activities with public schools. Publications and grants were easy to count as solid professional accomplishments, whereas student evaluations of teachers were fuzzy and discounted as personality contests. Time spent off campus on public schools was even more difficult to evaluate.

The university's partnership with high schools was a public service that increasingly came to be seen within the university as an unrewarding burden. And by the early 1960s, California's high schools had an administration and bureaucracy interested in running its own show. With little opposition, Kerr cut at the roots of California's admissions methods by discontinuing the university's role in high-school accreditation. The proposal to end accreditation came from BOARS. In the policy discussion, BOARS played the prestigious peer-group card. Its report noted, "Many outstanding universities and colleges, including Harvard, Yale, Columbia, and Princeton, do not require graduation from an accredited high school."[91] In 1963, the university stopped accrediting the state's high schools. The partnership between the university and public schools was over.

Kerr, the College Board, and the ETS saw research as the candy to entice California's admissions experts. If the SAT I aptitude test was of little use to California, perhaps the SAT II's achievement tests could provide data on students' preparation in particular subjects that California would find interesting? And if California started using achievement tests, then it might only be a short while before it relented on the SAT aptitude test.

Dean Kidner wrote to Kerr in January 1963 about his "conversations with officials of the College Entrance Examination Board." He began by reminding Kerr of the inadequacies of the SAT I. He wrote,

> You are aware that the scholastic aptitude test was found to be of only limited usefulness in the possible refinement of admission criteria. On the other hand, it may well be possible to learn a great deal about the characteristics of our student body, . . . were we able to obtain College Entrance Examination Board achievement tests scores for entering students.

The cost of using achievement tests would be a burden on students, but the College Board was putting it on the table for free. His letter explained,

> I have been reluctant to propose that College Entrance Examination Board achievement tests be required of all entering students as a condition of admission because of the financial hardship and the time commitment which is imposed upon the entering student. . . .
>
> Discussions with the College Entrance Examination Board suggest, however, that the board would provide the University with several batteries of achievement tests and if the University were itself to administer the tests to an incoming freshmen [*sic*] class would be willing to score the tests and provide the University with the results in a form best adapted to modern data processing methods and without cost.

The tests could be conducted without stirring up a controversy among the faculty, because they would be purely for the purpose of research and not for admissions. Kidner concluded, "I do not believe that it would be necessary to seek approval of the Academic Senate for such an experiment since no change in admission requirements would be involved."[92]

Kerr gave his approval to the plan, and it was put in action for first-year students entering the university system in the fall of 1963.[93] If the use of the SAT I was blocked, then the administration might be able to ease CB exams back into the university with achievement tests.

Kerr also kept the regents aware of elite private college admissions' practices. In June 1964, for example, Kerr sent each regent a letter summarizing a Harvard report on its current policies. He said that the report shows,

> An effort to have a nationally rather than a regionally selected student body. . . . A trend toward greater emphasis on 'personal rating' and lesser emphasis on test scores. . . . Attention to athletic ability and to sons of alumni and faculty. . . . The active recruitment, with the help of alumni committees, of outstanding prospects. . . . The desire for a diverse student body with prospective leadership capacity in many areas of human endeavor.[94]

Again, the contrast between California's high-school-class-rank meritocracy and Harvard's mix of personal factors, in particular athletic or legacy status, and leadership potential, was clear. And Kerr implied that the difference was not to California's credit.

The regent most in favor of intellectual elitism, Donald McLaughlin, responded quickly. He was not in favor of shifting California's admissions in the direction of personal appraisals. He preferred UC's use of high-school rank. McLaughlin wrote to Kerr,

> It seems to me that their [Harvard's] problems are really very different from ours. I doubt if we would be justified in attempting to make such careful and expensive appraisals of entering students—and I am not too sure that even with greatest care subjective judgments can be avoided when qualities such as they are emphasizing are given rather special weight.
>
> With our acceptance of any applicant who ranks in the highest eighth in academic standing, we probably get a broader coverage and catch a few good men Harvard misses.[95]

There is no record of Kerr's response to McLaughlin's defense of California's current practice.

In the administration, Kerr was not alone in feeling the magnetic status pull of Harvard. Berkeley Chancellor Edward Strong wrapped up a speech to the Board of Trustees for the University's Alumni Foundation, with these words, "To maintain the margin of greatness—the margin achieved at Berkeley in coming abreast of Harvard University—is our continued resolve and task."[96] Even if Harvard was not the measure of all things academic, it certainly seemed to be Berkeley's mark.

Whatever opposition there was in the university to CB exams was overcome in the next few years. Again, arguments about growing enrollments and overcrowded campuses carried significant weight. The attraction of the tests came less from educational research than from "pragmatic needs to reduce the size of the eligibility pool and to rank-order applicants to selective campuses in a simple, efficient way."[97] By 1968, the faculty signed off on the proposal and the university required, as of the entering class for that fall, the SAT I and three SAT II achievement tests.[98] California now made it mandatory for its candidates to take more CB tests than applicants had to face getting into Harvard.

California Admissions with the SAT

California used the SAT I and SAT II for thirty-five years before the exams became items of hot controversy again in 1999. When the SAT came under fire, the spark was provided by a vote by the regents on affirmative action. It is important to understand something of California's experience with diversity to see how the university ended up looking for answers to affirmative action controversies in its tools for measuring academic merit.

After 1968, California admitted youths mainly based on their high-school records and test scores, tempered by concerns about diversity and equity by race, gender, residence, and socioeconomic status. In the beginning, the university set aside up to 6 percent of its seats for "special action" cases, which were originally mostly athletes; by the late 1970s, they were often Blacks. Minority recruitment ran at approximately 6 percent for Blacks and for Hispanics until the late 1980s, when minority representation just about doubled. For example, at Berkeley among entering first-year students in 1987, Blacks were 12 percent, and Hispanics were 17 percent.[99] The growth of Asian enrollments, however, really tested California's commitment to diversity.

Although Asians were a minority in the state, at fewer than 10 percent of California's residents, they were not an affirmative action target group for admissions. Asians were excelling in high school. They had the highest high-school graduation rate, 89 percent, of any racial group; Whites were at 71 percent, Blacks at 53 percent, and Hispanics at 52 percent.[100] And their academic records made more Asian high-school graduates eligible for admission to the University of California than any other group. UC-eligible seniors were 16 percent of White high-school seniors, 5 percent or less of Hispanic and Black seniors, but fully 33 percent of Asian seniors.[101] High-school preparation paid off. By 1981, the University of California was 26 percent Asian, and only 58 percent White.[102]

Despite the Asian relative success at California, the Berkeley and Los Angeles campuses were, along with Brown, Harvard, Princeton, Stanford, and Yale, accused in the late-1980s of discrimination.[103] The situation replicated many of the features of East Coast anti-Semitism of the 1920s. As a scholar of the controversy reports,

> In early 1987, Professor L. Ling-Chi Wang told Robert Lindsey of the *New York Times* that bias against Asians bore an uncanny resemblance to the Jewish quotas at Harvard, Yale, and Princeton earlier in this century. Apparently, the comparison . . . struck gold with the media.[104]

Brown and Stanford were the first to acknowledge bias. Then, Berkeley's Chancellor Ira Michael Heyman expressed his regret and conceded in two public apologies that "decisions . . . made in the admissions process . . . indisputably had a disproportionate impact on Asian applicants."[105] Steps were taken to rectify the bias and Asian enrollments jumped up. By 1996, Asians were 33 percent of all UC undergraduates, whereas Whites had fallen to 37 percent.[106] At the most academically prestigious campuses, Berkeley and Los Angeles, Asians were approximately 40 percent and 38 percent respectively at each.[107]

Although California may have responded more slowly than its critics would have liked, the university did concede the point and took steps to open its doors to Asian academic high performers. Harvard and Yale, in contrast, have maintained that they did not in any way discriminate against Asians. Their records, however, continue to raise questions. Before the controversy, Asians were approximately 6 percent of Harvard's and Yale's undergraduates; afterwards their percentage jumped to 11 percent, which critics still find too low.[108]

During the Asian controversy, the California regents reaffirmed the university's commitment to "provide places within the University for all eligible applicants who are residents of California." And it stated again that eligibility meant the "top one-eighth of the state's high school graduates."[109] In 1989, the faculty's voice was heard across a whole range of admission's issues through a report adopted by the Academic Senate for Berkeley, "Freshman Admissions at Berkeley: A Policy for the 1990s and Beyond."[110] It is known as the Karabel report because the chair of the committee and chief author of the report was the Berkeley sociologist Jerome Karabel. The report called for increasing the weight of academic criteria in the admissions process, for softening race-based affirmative action, and for formalizing socioeconomic affirmative action. Youths from the low end of the socioeconomic scale should receive some special consideration in admissions.

The Karabel report did not, however, raise any questions about the use of CB tests. No connections were drawn between the SAT and socioeconomic disadvantages in admissions. That step came, ironically, only after the regents voted in 1995 "to end the use of race, ethnicity and gender in admissions."[111] The ruling is known as Special Policy 1 or SP1. The politics of the decision were clearly conservative, part of a national as well as California reaction against affirmative action. The faculty and admissions staff were caught off guard.[112]

The response by BOARS was to reexamine the academic tools that were left to them. If considerations of diversity were ruled out, and admissions were to be based almost entirely on academic measures alone, what exactly could BOARS tell by a student's grades and test scores? What combination of academic measures produces the most valid and reliable results? Special Policy 1 led BOARS to reopen the case for and against the SAT.

California Votes to Eliminate the SAT

As dean of admissions at Yale, R. Inslee "Inky" Clark, Jr., in the 1960s investigated and rejected Berkeley's admissions model as too exclusively based on numbers. Yale preferred its type of subjective meritocracy to Berkeley's objective one. Berkeley was not afraid of playing a numbers game because it was looking more at academic performance than at personality. In 1977, the University of California refined its quantitative approach further, instituting an eligibility index based on GPA and SAT score. Admissions were now primarily based on students' scores. Although the university required five standardized tests, the SAT I's verbal and math tests plus three SAT II achievement tests, it calculated a youth's index score using only high-school GPA and the SAT I.[113]

After SP1 was put into effect in 1995, BOARS decided to reevaluate all of its available inputs to see which ones contributed to California's ability to predict university performance. It started in 1997 by doing a study of the relative merits of using SAT I over SAT II tests in calculating the eligibility index.

BOARS began by statistically analyzing which combination of GPA, SAT I, and SAT II tests best predicted first-year grades—precisely the same task Yale had abandoned in 1972. California found that SAT II tests were significantly better than SAT I at the job. As BOARS explains, their 1997 "study suggested that the superior performance of SAT II's in predicting first-year grades might be 'due to the somewhat different nature of the SAT II exams, which are curriculum driven . . . in contrast to the SAT I which [is a] general reasoning test.'"[114] As a consequence of their research, "the Eligibility Index was revised in 1999 to reincorporate SAT II scores, weighting them twice as heavily as SAT I."[115]

The BOARS finding, yet again, against the usefulness of the SAT I reinforced California's President Richard Atkinson's objections to the test. In February 2001, he asked the "faculty to reconsider UC's current testing policy."[116] BOARS took as its mandate three questions:

1. To what degree do admissions test scores contribute to the UC's ability to identify which students will succeed at the University? . . .

2. Can admissions tests be used to identify reliably students with as-yet undeveloped talent who are likely to be high achievers at UC despite relatively lackluster high school records?

3. Does analysis of admissions test scores for UC students reveal any evidence that the scores are inappropriately correlated with other factors, such as socioeconomic status?[117]

For its analyses, BOARS had the full files of 77,893 first-time first-year students, all of whom entered the University of California between 1996 and 1999.[118] BOARS had data on gender, race, family income, parental education, high-school GPA, SAT I, SAT II, and everything else relevant from the applicants' records. California's analyses may be taken as the definitive test on what each part of the admissions formula adds to our ability to predict college grades or to identify late-bloomers in the talent pool.

UC discovered that the SAT I was inadequate as a predictor of college grades. The "SAT I was not statistically significant for two of the four years studied"[119]; in other words, with their data the SAT I did not contribute any information to the prediction of college grades half of the time. For the other two years, the weak statistical power of the SAT I depended on not including socioeconomic variables in the regression model. When one added family income and parents' education to a regression model predicting first-year grades, the SAT ceased to have any statistical value. The authors of the report wrote, "Once socio-economic variables are included, SAT I scores do not add to the prediction of freshman grades."[120]

The SAT I's statistical power was borrowed from family background characteristics. The SAT's predictive value, weak to start with, was, apparently, spurious. The university's researchers reported, "Much of the apparent relationship between the SAT I and UC freshman grades is conditioned by socioeconomic factors."[121] The same was not true of the subject specific tests, the SAT-II. They came through as statistically significant, and their effects were strengthened by adding information on parental education and income.

The answers BOARS found to its three questions were that the SAT I verbal and math tests do not help predict college grades, but SAT II subject tests do. Neither type of test helps to identify the disadvantaged or late-bloomers. And the SAT I is too contaminated by socioeconomic background factors and its historical association with IQ tests to be suitable for the University of California. SAT II achievement tests would be preferable to SAT I tests.

The members of the committee wrote

BOARS is strongly persuaded that achievement-type tests offer the University a number of advantages over aptitude-type tests. . . . [A]chievement exams are more suited to measuring mastery of the high school curriculum. . . . Focusing on achievement tests rather than aptitude tests also avoids the historical association of aptitude tests with intelligence tests.[122]

In addition to dropping the link to the eugenic movement's IQ instruments, subject specific tests reestablish a connection between high-school work and entry to college. The authors continued,

> In the view of BOARS, achievement tests reinforce this message: students who take challenging courses and work hard [in high school] will see their effort pay off. . . . This message is consistent with, and underscores, current efforts to improve the quality and rigor of K-12 education in the state.[123]

BOARS and the UC president's office presented the evidence to the faculty senate, which voted to eliminate the SAT I from the admissions process.[124] Cutting through the statistical niceties of California's analyses, the message was clear. The SAT I was too contaminated by family social class to be a good measure of academic aptitude. Because California had no vested interest in hiding the connection between SAT score and family socioeconomic status, it could expose the test for what it was and discontinue its use.

When California voted to drop the SAT I test, it in effect forced the ETS and College Board to abandon it.[125] They had to or the ETS would lose its single largest student market, and it would lose intellectual credibility if it limped along without California. If Berkeley, Los Angeles, and the rest of the UC system all said that the SAT was an unacceptable test for college admissions, then the SAT's credibility would be in tatters.

The College Board and the ETS reached a settlement of sorts with the University of California. The settlement was that the UC would continue to use ETS tests if they would eliminate, as of the test-taking cohort of 2005, the test's most contaminated component: the verbal analogies. They would be replaced with essay questions written to connect directly to what is taught in high schools. California may take credit for exposing the SAT's class bias and of moving the test in the direction of the high-school curriculum. The old SAT was gone.

The Social and Racial Biases of the Verbal Analogies

There is strong evidence, in addition to that offered by the UC, that the verbal section of the SAT, which Yale valued above the math section and subject tests, was the most biased part of the SAT. Family background, race, and gender do translate into vocabulary differences, as Betty Hart and Todd R. Risley's transcripts of everyday language in American households shows.[126] And those family differences in vocabulary have lasting effects on educational attainments.[127] Furthermore, although some over the years have maintained that the SAT was above content bias,[128] the suspicion has grown recently that it was not.[129]

Several months after the ETS announced that it would drop the SAT's verbal analogies and replace them with something acceptable to California, a talk was given at Yale on the problem of bias in question selection for the SAT. The speaker was Jay Rosner, vice president of the Princeton Review. The presentation in the afternoon of October 10, 2002, was publicized as being on racial bias in question selection for the SAT. Bias problems with the SAT were topics of serious discussion and research at the time, yet no one from Yale's admissions office or its Office of Institutional Research bothered to attend.

Rosner's lecture recounted how seemingly neutral verbal analogies could inadvertently become, purely for statistical reasons, a means of discrimination. Rosner explained the social consequences of taking new questions for future tests from the experimental sections of old ones. If there are racial differences in performance on verbal analogies, and if those questions on which Blacks did well from previous experimental sections were eliminated for statistical reasons from future SAT exams, then a racial test score gap would be created or widened.

Rosner was able to see the mechanics of bias in results from the experimental section of the SAT test, the section from which questions are selected for next year's test. Looking at the experimental questions, he found something both surprising and disturbing. There were verbal analogy questions on the experimental section of the test that Blacks did better on than Whites. On average, Blacks who are concentrated in poor neighborhoods with resource-starved schools are supposed to be less well prepared academically than Whites, so the finding that Blacks performed better on some verbal questions was in itself news. Rosner called those analogies "Black preference" questions because a larger percentage of Black SAT takers got those questions right than White test takers. Not one of those "Black preference" questions survived the ETS analysis and made it onto next year's test. Yet, on questions where a substantial percentage of Whites got the correct answer and a lower percentage of Blacks got the right answer, those "White preference" questions were placed onto next year's SAT. Indeed,

Rosner argues that not one Black preference question has been used by the SAT in at least the last ten years. And, "while all the questions on the October 1998 SAT favored whites over blacks, approximately one-fifth showed huge 20 percent gaps favoring whites. Skewed question selection certainly contributes to the large test score disparities between blacks and whites."[130]

Whites have benefited from a content bias, according to Rosner, because verbal analogy questions that Whites do better on than Blacks will always be preferred by the ETS when it decides which experimental questions to use on next year's test. This is not because of conscious racism, but because of the logic of question selection. Rosner wrote, "if high-scoring test-takers— who are more likely to be white—tend to answer the question correctly in pre-testing, it's a worthy SAT question; if not, it's thrown out. Race/ethnicity are not considered explicitly, but racially disparate scores drive question selection, which in turn reproduces [racially] disparate scores in an internally reinforcing cycle."[131] Rosner raises the question of whether the SAT test score gap between Blacks and Whites is an artifact of biased question selection. One could close the racial SAT score gap by changing which questions are used from the experimental section of the SAT. Rosner's findings were published in *The Nation*.[132]

Rosner tried to document a racial bias in question selection, but he did not offer any explanation for why Blacks do better on some questions and worse on others. For a possible answer to the question of racial performance on the SAT, one should look to the work of Roy O. Freedle. Freedle retired in 1998 from thirty years of research at the ETS on language and tests. Freedle was uniquely positioned to tell us about the mechanics of racial and SES correlations with particular types of verbal questions. He published a summary of his findings in the *Harvard Educational Review*.[133]

Freedle and others have found that racial identity matters most for verbal analogies and antonyms and least for reading comprehension questions and that there are statistically significant differences in the performance of Whites and Blacks depending on whether the analogies and antonyms are "*hard*" or "*easy*."[134] Researchers at the ETS rate verbal analogies as being *hard* or *easy* in degree of difficulty. The same points, however, are awarded for getting a *hard* one right as for getting an *easy* one.

Freedle provides us with the unexpected finding that Blacks do best on the *hard* analogies and least well on the *easy* analogies; conversely, Whites do better than Blacks on *easy* verbal analogies, and less well on *hard* ones.

Why do Blacks do their best on the *hard* questions? Freedle is confident that a "culturally based interpretation helps explain why African American examinees (and other minorities) often do better on *hard* verbal items but do worse than matched-ability Whites on many *easy* items."[135] Freedle writes, "*Easy* analogy items tend to contain high-frequency vocabulary words [such as 'canoe'] while *hard* analogy items tend to contain low-frequency vocabulary words," such as "intractable."[136] *Easy* analogies are everyday conversation terms, whereas *hard* analogy terms "are likely to occur in school-related contexts."[137] The more everyday a verbal analogy is, the more likely it is to transmit racial differences. *Hard* analogies, employing rare and precisely defined terms, more often learned in school than acquired in the home or neighborhood, do not communicate as much bias as *easy* ones. Blacks who take the SAT are drawing more effectively than Whites on average from their formal schooling, but they lack the cultural knowledge that White youths have as contextual background, enabling Whites to do better than Blacks on the *easy* questions. Freedle shows us that if one relied only on *hard* verbal analogies, the scores of Black youths would improve by as much as 300 points.[138]

The ETS disputes Freedle's findings, claiming his evidence is thin. And they have threatened legal action if he has in retirement any SAT data from the ETS to thicken his analyses.[139] In effect, the ETS told Freedle, you cannot prove this, and if you have the data to attempt a proof, we will sue you. They would like him to be silenced and ignored. The ETS had enough problems satisfying the University of California with a new SAT, it did not want to put out additional fires on charges of racial bias.

Yale and Harvard have been quiet on the death of the old SAT and the creation of a new one. Why was the University of California the first to offer the public sophisticated research on standardized tests, college admissions, and the inadequacy of the SAT? Why did Yale fail to lead the world of higher education on this issue? As the sponsors and creators of the old SAT, and as America's premier universities, why have Harvard and Yale been absent from the public discussion of the new post-2005 SAT?

The suspicion remains that Yale's silence on the new SAT has something to do with the old SAT's value in capturing 60 percent of its undergraduates from families at the top of the income scale. The College Board provides tables on the breakdown of scores by family income and parents' education. For income groups ranging from less than $10,000 per year to $80,000 per year, each $10,000 increase in a family's income is worth to its offspring approximately 24 points on the combined SAT. For example, combined mean scores for youths from families earning less than $10,000 in 1996 were 873; the mean for youths from families making between $40,000 and $50,000 was 1016; the mean for test takers from families with incomes between $70,000 and $80,000 was 1064. Youths from families near the top of the income scale, earning $80,000 to $100,000, had a mean score of 1085. The income–SAT score boost, however, was greatest at the very top. The top group's mean score was 1129. Being in the over-$100,000 league gave one a boost worth 44 points over the $80,000 to $100,000 category. The over-$100,000 category included 11 percent of all SAT test takers in 1996, in raw numbers they were 100,429 individual students.[140] Those 100,000 are Yale's main applicant pool.

Family incomes correlate with SAT scores. And in any given year, Yale typically gets 50 percent of its students from the top 11 percent of SAT scores; another 50 percent from the next 42 percent of SAT scores; avoiding as much as possible the bottom 47 percent. Even in the 1990s, one could get into Yale with a 540 verbal SAT, but half of one's classmates would have scores at or above 660. In income and financial aid, as mentioned before, about 60 percent of one's classmates would be from the top 10 percent of family incomes and the other 40 percent would be receiving some financial assistance. Those numbers have been pretty steady since the late 1950s. Need-blind financial admissions, race sensitive admissions, and opening the door to females did not change the basic distribution of students in Yale by family income or by SAT scores. The post-1950s era of "meritocracy" witnessed a diversification of the racial and gender composition of Ivy colleges, but not of their economic composition.

Academic selection is disguised social selection if the criteria systematically favor one social group over another. In the competition for seats at selective colleges, wealthy Whites have benefited from a preparatory system of expensive private or affluent suburban public schools, from a home environment rich in cultural and educational resources, and from racially and socioeconomically biased standardized tests. CB tests have always been measures of academic ability, but with class and racial disparities built in. Sometimes those biases were there by intentional design, as in the 1930s; other times those biases were there because of unexamined assumptions about vocabulary and logic, as in the period that ended in 2005. The elite private sector has been able to benefit from the disguise of social-class selection by the seemingly neutral device of standardized aptitude tests. At best, elite private colleges have been merely complicit in the misrecognition of social class as academic merit, but it is hard to imagine that Arthur Howe's intent to capture 60 percent of Yale's students from the top of the income pyramid has not been a factor in the construction of a rigged game. Selective college admissions throughout the twentieth century appear to have been a case of, to borrow a phrase from a Berkeley book, inequality by design.[141]

If elite private colleges set their sights on the economic upper class, that leaves open the question of whether their fixation was mutual. Did the upper class or fractions of it look to elite private colleges as a means to pass on its privileges to the next generation? The question is still open about whether private colleges perform a necessary function in the intergenerational reproduction of class privilege.

CHAPTER SIX

Top-Tier Colleges and Privileged Social Groups

The relations between top-tier colleges and privileged social groups are long-standing, complex, and fraught with institutional and public consequences. We have encountered in our narrative two very opposing views on the topic, a favorable one expressed by Yale's Arthur Howe and Kingman Brewster, and a highly critical one articulated by Pierre Bourdieu. Howe and Brewster saw the excellences of America's best private universities as rooted in their historical relation to society's economic upper class. According to this view, the academic pursuit and transmission of knowledge flourishes in privately endowed and resource-rich universities because they are in the best position to set their own direction and to resist external control.[1] The opposing case alleges that the university's mission is corrupted, its curriculum warped and ethos diluted, when it acts as a finishing school for apprentice members of the upper class. Bourdieu might say that the liberal-arts tradition of nurturing a whole, rounded individual is just an antiquarian disguise for pandering to the whims of privileged youths. And he would point out that scientific research is doing just as well or better at public universities, such as California, Wisconsin, and Michigan, as at Harvard, Yale, and Stanford.

Both sides would acknowledge that there has never been a university in America or Europe that could pay its own bills without donations from individuals, organizations, or the state. All universities and colleges must strive to acquire from students and patrons the resources needed to sustain academic excellence and freedom in teaching and research. And during the nearly four centuries of higher education in America, our colleges have gladly or grudgingly exchanged some of their freedoms for economic security.

Private colleges, religious colleges, and public universities are all in a similar position. Private secular colleges are economically dependent on privileged social groups; religious colleges are dependent on church coffers; and public universities are dependent on the state's budget. When a religious group or a political authority covers a substantial chunk of a college's operating expenses, academics learn to live with restrictions on the practice of their profession. Methodist, Baptist, or Catholic churches, for example, may exchange funding for seats on the university's highest governing body. An institution's spiritual affiliation may make religion a course requirement and place some materials or campus events beyond the pale. When the state is the paymaster, universities struggle to maintain their integrity and self-governance against political hot air and bureaucratic humidity. Faculty pay scales, admissions criteria, such as the consideration of race, and even areas of work, such as stem-cell research, may be regulated by political temperatures. If the upper class is the overlord, however, the interference is less direct than a politician's and more subtle than a church warden's. Having a diverse affluent class to draw on puts an institution in a relatively good position from which to maneuver. Although the college may absorb some of the culture of the upper class, it can resist direct interference from that class. Any particular individual may be turned down at the admission's gate, and any particular benefaction with unacceptable conditions attached can be refused. The threat of external interventions looms larger from the state or from a church than from wealthy individuals—and that is an advantage for the private sector from the standpoint of the academic profession.

Private colleges have historically depended on tuition fees and alumni donations to fund themselves. The balance between those two sources of funding has been shifting away from tuition and in favor of the endowment since the 1980s. Today, contributions from the past sustain the present to an unprecedented extent. Harvard, oldest and far in the lead for gathering donations, had an endowment in 2006 of over 26 billion dollars. There are 39 other colleges with endowments worth more than 1 billion, and 51 more colleges have more than a half billion in the bank. In total, there are nearly 300 institutions with more than 100 million dollars to invest.[2] In the top tier, alumni participation rates in capital campaigns average around 40 percent.[3] The big bucks, however, flow from a small percentage of donors. Approximately 90 percent of the value of gifts to tier 1 colleges comes from about 10 percent of alumni. Just one in ten of one's graduates will keep the college's liquidity afloat. Colleges cannot know, however, who will be the big benefactor of tomorrow. It is likely that the best single variable predicting a major contributor is not legacy status but whether the graduate goes on to earn an MBA.[4] In Arthur Howe's days at Yale, however, annual tuition fees were a much greater concern than they are now. And it was from Yale's need for tuition income that Howe derived his formula for its dependence on the rich.

Howe calculated that for America's prestigious private colleges to pay their bills, 60 percent of their undergraduates would have to come from families in the top 5 percent of the income index. In Chapter 3, Table 3.1, we saw clear indications of Yale's success at capturing 60 percent of full-fee-paying undergraduates from affluent families for the last half-century. Even with needs-blind admissions after 1964, because of the correlation of family income with SAT scores, Yale never had to look at a candidate's ability to pay. What about the rest of the top tier? Were they, like Yale, attracting 60 percent of their students from those with the highest ability to pay? How many of their students were drawn from the upper class? How does their economic composition compare with our exemplar of a public university system, the University of California?

American universities rarely release information on the economic backgrounds of their students. When they do, it is most often to satisfy requirements for taxpayer subsidies and then the statistics are usually on students from low-income rather than high-income families. With the exception of the University of California system, we have to work with data from the best available source on family income and educational outcomes and that comes from the U.S. Department of Education's *National Educational Longitudinal Survey* (NELS). NELS followed a nationally representative sample of American youths and their families from eighth grade to beyond the age of college graduation, from 1988 to 2000, affording researchers the opportunity to evaluate the impact of a great many things, ranging from home environment to extracurricular activities, on educational attainments, jobs, and earnings. There are, however, limitations to NELS. With NELS, we cannot see how well Howe's top 5 percent are doing; NELS does not provide precise dollar amounts above a cutoff point. We can, however, see how the top 10 percent are faring. We can see how many undergraduates from families with incomes in America's top 10 percent in 1988 went by the year 2000 to each of our seven college tiers.[5] And we can compare the economic composition of our tier 1 private colleges with the pubic universities in California. The president's office at the University of California, because of the faculty senate's adoption of Jerome Karabel's plan for socioeconomic affirmative action, has the will and the statistics to provide us with answers to our questions about its composition.

From Table 6.1 we can see that Howe was not far from the mark. One can quibble about the substantial differences between families in Howe's top 5 percent and those in our top 10 percent, but in either case, we are dealing with the summit of America's income structure.

Tier 1 derives 64 percent of its undergraduates from families in the top 10 percent of our income pyramid. Whether from fiscal necessity or institutional choice, private prestigious colleges pick the majority of their undergraduates from America's top tenth. The overrepresentation of families with the highest incomes in our seven-tier college hierarchy is not eliminated until one drops down to tiers 6 and 7.

The contrast with California is impressive. The percentages reported here for the University of California (UC) are six-year averages, from 1991 to 1996. The representation of wealth in the UC system is neither as small nor as concentrated at the most academically prestigious campuses as one might expect. Berkeley and Los Angeles are not the most economically exclusive. Santa Barbara holds that distinction. Berkeley (with 27.6) falls just slightly below San Diego (at 28.3), whereas Santa Cruz, Davis, and Los Angeles draw about a quarter from the top income decile. In comparison, Irvine and Riverside are positively egalitarian institutions.

With nearly one out of every four undergraduates in the California system coming from very affluent families, even the UC's campuses draw disproportionately from the top of the income scale. They do not do so, however, with anything like the large disparities displayed by the private colleges in tier 1. The gap between tier 1's 64 percent representation of the top tenth and Berkeley's 28 percent record is consistent with this book's evidence that processes other than academic performance have been at work in matching youths with particular colleges.

TABLE 6.1

Top 10% Family Income by Tier and by University of California Campus.

%students from top 10% family income:	%
Tier 1	64
Tier 2	44
Tier 3	32
Tier 4	21
Tier 5	20
Tier 6	11
Tier 7	11
University of California Campuses:	
UC Santa Barbara	31
UC San Diego	28
UC Berkeley	28
UC Santa Cruz	24
UC Davis	23
UCLA	23
UC Irvine	18
UC Riverside	15

Estimates based on weighted observations. *National Educational Longitudinal Study Restricted-Use Data, 1988–2000,* Data License Control Number: 06011044. University of California data supplied by Mark Langberg, Office of the President. UC percentage represents a six-year average, 1991–1996.

Does the Top Tier Play a Reproductive Role for a Class or Status Group?

All tier 1 colleges share with Yale a similar socioeconomic market. All of them understand, reluctantly or complacently, that their "natural clientele" are families with high incomes. They all find, unhappily or not, that their criteria defining academic merit are qualities concentrated in privileged families.

To say that tier 1 colleges are oriented toward families with incomes in the upper decile is not, however, the same thing as claiming that those colleges play an essential role in the life of rich families. In order for elite colleges to be fully in partnership with an economic class as a whole, a substantial proportion of youths from that class must pass through them. If top-tier colleges service a small fraction of privileged youths, then what may be an obsession from the college's standpoint is only a sideline from the perspective of the economic class.

An economic class may have a disproportionate share of a positional good, in this case an elite college education, but possession of that positional good becomes defining for the class only if most bother to participate in the market for it. Positional goods are by definition scarce; there is, for example, only so much room on a mountaintop. If, however, a particular economic class is indifferent to alpine views, then regardless of the attractions of elevated vistas for some, mountain residences will not count among the qualities that draw boundaries between members and nonmembers of that class. What is true of residence is also true for education. If only a fraction of an economic group participates in the acquisition of an elite education credential, then that credential may help define the identity of a status subgroup within the larger economic class, but not the identity of the class as a whole. Are top-tier colleges in partnership with a social group? Are elite colleges really upper-class institutions playing a role in the intergenerational reproduction of an entire economic class, or are they a prestige badge worn by a small status group?

There is a literature on how to evaluate whether or not a group participation rate in an educational sector reaches a level at which one could be confident that a significant mutual relation exists. And much of that literature derives from our critical sociologist, Pierre Bourdieu.

Bourdieu's Theories of Elite Reproduction

Bourdieu's signature intellectual contribution was to investigate the role of what he called "cultural capital" in the relation of dominant-class families to the elite sector of the educational system.[6] Turning the concept of "human capital" on its head, Bourdieu coined the phrase "cultural capital" to describe the abilities that dominant-class "students owe first to their home background."[7] Although human capital was supposed to be the fruit of individual investments in economically relevant skills, an equal-opportunity resource that anyone could accumulate through years of education, cultural capital was a highbrow sensibility and personal style that was bred at home.[8] Cultural capital was a resource, passed down within privileged families, of "shared, high status cultural signals (attitudes, preferences, formal knowledge, behaviors, goals, and credentials) used for social and cultural exclusion."[9] Dominant-class offspring have, allegedly, a homegrown "natural ease" with those signals that are rewarded over time by "key gatekeepers."[10] Bourdieu saw an intergenerational transmission of a cultural style facilitating upper-class mutual recognition at key transitions in life; it worked best on its home ground, in the networks of privileged families and their institutions, especially their elite schools and occupations. Outside an elite context, and in the hands of lower-class parvenus, cultural capital allegedly lost its potency, no matter how ardently its non-dominant class emulators embraced it.

Bourdieu's model of society included three basic social classes[11] (the working class, the middle class, and the dominant class), each with multiple internal fractions (such as, for the dominant class: private-sector executives as one fraction and professionals as another); whose relations were structured by three types of capital (economic, cultural, and social) as well as geography.[12] By *economic capital*, Bourdieu meant income and fiscal assets; *cultural capital* meant personal taste, highbrow cultural objects, and elite educational credentials; and *social capital*, for Bourdieu, meant the social networks that supply one with support and information. Economic, cultural, and social capital were all unequally distributed to the various class fractions, and the clout or value of different types of capital varied depending on one's location in the field of power. Each class or class fraction was, for Bourdieu, constantly struggling to transmit to the next generation its share of desirable social and material goods.

Bourdieu's focus was on the upper class, which he most often referred to as the dominant class. It was dominant because the members of that class were in the highest paying occupations and they exercised corporate, governmental, or cultural power. In a managerial-capitalist society, where dominant-class parents could not just hand over their own occupational positions to their children, Bourdieu saw elite schools and colleges as providing the credentials and networks that made intergenerational dominant-class reproduction possible. Bourdieu identified the dominant class as six occupational fractions that in combination added up to only 8 percent of the working population in France.[13] The main "fractional" division within the dominant class was between those in professional occupations, such as lawyers and doctors, and those in the corporate sector, such as bankers and executive officers. He distinguished between fractional and class reproduction. For example, fractional reproduction was when a lawyer's son went into the same profession; class reproduction was when a banker's son became a lawyer. Class and fractional reproduction for Bourdieu was far from perfect; no category achieved anything close to 100 percent. Bourdieu's highest rate of father/son fractional reproduction was 33.5 percent for industrial employers. Class reproduction was strongest for the professions, which drew 41.5 percent of their members from across the dominant class as a whole.[14]

When dominant-class offspring were a majority or a significant percentage of the students in an educational institution, then he found that institution guilty of facilitating dominant-class reproduction. To illustrate what a disproportionately privileged composition looked like for France's elite institutions, Bourdieu gave us the percentage "of the top establishments [composed] by the most privileged students;" in 1962, 57 percent of students at the *École Normale Supérieure* and 51 percent of students at the *École Polytechnique* were from dominant-class families, and just 2 percent were from families of industrial workers.[15] He did not, however, tell us from the perspective of the whole social group the percentage of dominant-class youths who each year attended elite colleges. We know that dominant-class youths predominate inside the *École*, but not that the *École* defines what it means to be highly educated for most dominant-class youths.

We are left, then, with some guidelines on what should rate as an elite college and what should count as dominant class reproduction. If 50 percent or more of a college is drawn from the dominant class, then Bourdieu would classify that college as elite. And we may extrapolate from Bourdieu's work on group reproduction a one-third rule. If a group in the dominant class has a participation rate of sending 33 percent or more of its youths through elite colleges, then that group is using those colleges as a means of passing its privileges to the next generation. One-third may seem like a rather modest standard, but even privileged children are not all interested in college and elite careers. If one out of every three youths from any social strata passes through the same set of universities, that is an achievement.

Using this as our metric, a generous test of Bourdieu would be to say that for a reproductive relation to exist at least 33 percent of the youths from a social group must apply to and attend a type of college. Of course, the higher the percentage, the more conclusive is the test. We know that 64 percent of undergraduates in tier 1 colleges are from families with incomes in the top 10 percent, making those colleges, for Bourdieu, unambiguously elite—but what percentage of youths from that dominant class attends elite colleges? Does America's top tenth have a one-third or higher reproductive relation to those colleges? If not, is there any group in the dominant class whose participation rate in America's elite colleges reaches or exceeds 33 percent?

To test the reproduction hypothesis with the best data available, we[16] have divided the participants in the *National Educational Longitudinal Survey* from 1988 to 2000, into five class groupings; those categories represent attempts to translate Bourdieu's French social-class fractions into American terms. NELS began in 1988, so we have taken those families whose 1988 incomes were in the top category of our sample (annual incomes of $75,000 or more) and divided them into those working in professional occupations and those who were not. Those two groups, the top-income professionals and the top-income non-professionals, correspond to Bourdieu's two main fractions within the dominant class. Bourdieu expects professionals in the dominant class (such as architects, doctors, lawyers, and professors) to be richer in cultural capital and more reliant for their reproduction on elite educational credentials than any other social strata, including corporate managers or executives. By dividing our top income category into a professional and non-professional group, we can test his hypothesis. Our third group corresponds very roughly to Bourdieu's conception of the "middle class." These are families with annual incomes in 1988 of $50,000 to $74,999. The fourth group had family incomes ranging from $20,000 to $49,999; it matches Bourdieu's working class. Lastly, we have separated out those families with very low incomes, from 0 to $19,999, into a lower-working-and-poor class. Our working-class and lower-class categories correspond almost exactly to the bottom two income quartiles in the United States when NELS began collecting data in 1988.[17]

Class Composition and Characteristics of America's Seven Tiers

From Table 6.2, it is possible to discern the logic of class reproduction as theorized by Bourdieu. The hierarchy of college tiers and social classes looks harmonious.

The professional fraction of the dominant class provides fully 41 percent of the students in the top tier, and that is quite an accomplishment. In a database weighted to represent the entire U.S. population, this group provided approximately 8 percent of the national youth cohort in the longitudinal study. Those youths were nurtured, groomed, educated, drilled, and driven to extracurricular events until they were capable of wining two out of every five seats in colleges like Yale. They outperformed their rich, non-professional cousins at a rate of nearly two to one. And when one adds those two dominant class fractions together, one gets 64 percent, an absolute majority of tier 1. Tier 2 also receives the largest percentage, 44 percent, of its students from those two groups. The nexus of class and tier is obvious; as one moves down the ranks, the presence of dominant-class groups declines, whereas the middle and working class increase.

The distribution of attributes, such as test scores, across the tiers replicates the class hierarchy. Tier 1, for example, has the highest SAT average; the highest percentage (63 percent) of parents with postgraduate degrees; the lowest percent (10 percent) of parents without college degrees; the most (45 percent) graduates from private secondary schools; the greatest concentration of cultural capital, as gauged by our most reliable indicator of a family's commitment to the highbrow, parent and youth (72 percent) art museum attendance[18]; the greatest percentages of leaders in sports, student government, publications, and academic clubs; and the highest percentage of parents (75 percent) expecting their eighth-grade child to go on to achieve a postgraduate degree. All of those qualities matter to educational attainments, and they are distributed in dwindling percentages down across the remaining college tiers.

Unquestionably, the characteristics of youths in the tiers of higher education replicates the architecture of our social classes and Bourdieu's theories look confirmed for America. And yet, perhaps things are not as neatly wrapped up as they seem. We still must consider whether the dominant class is as dependent on top-tier colleges as the colleges are on them. Is there a dominant class group in which 33 percent or more of their offspring get into one of America's elite colleges?

Class Reproduction?

From Table 6.3, we can see that nationally youths from top-income families are not in a reproductive relation to America's top college tier. There is not a single case of any class grouping approaching our baseline of 33 percent of its youths entering or graduating from any particular tier in the system.

In our two groups within Bourdieu's dominant class category, 64 percent of youths from non-professional families do achieve a college degree, but half of those do so in tiers 3 and 4. Thirty-six percent of youths from those non-professional families skip getting a college degree at all. The relation of affluent professionals to the tier structure is, however, in the direction but not near the scale anticipated by Bourdieu. Professional families in our dominant class invest in elite colleges at twice the rate of their non-professional cousins. Between our two dominant-class groups, there are larger percentages of professional-family youths than non-professionals in tiers 1, 2, and 3. Both fractions of the dominant class avoid tiers 5 and 6, but apparently feel comfortable at the bottom, where 12 percent of each settle.

The structural symmetry of social class and college tier displayed in Table 6.2 is not perfectly replicated in the distribution of social classes into the tier system, as demonstrated in Table 6.3. There are areas of overlap. The representation of the dominant class was discussed earlier. On the other classes, there is a tendency for the middle class to cluster in tiers 3, 4, and 7, and for the lower classes to divide between tiers 4 and 7. Although there are correlations between particular social groups and particular college tiers,

TABLE 6.2

Descriptive Statistics by College Tier.

Student Characteristics by College Tier	Tier 1	Tier 2	Tier 3	Tier 4	Tier 5	Tier 6	Tier 7	Total Data
Family Social Class in 1991:								
% of Students from Top Income Professional Career Families	41	25	19	10	13	5	5	8
% of Students from Top Income Families (non-professional occupations)	23	19	13	11	7	5	5	5
% of Students from Middle Class	23	40	44	47	41	52	40	37
% of Students from Working Class	6	8	11	17	17	15	22	20
% of Students from Lower Working Class & Poor	7	8	12	15	22	22	29	30
Neither Parent Graduated from College:								
% of Students	10	22	42	53	57	62	70	56
At Least One Parent Has an Advanced Degree:								
% of Students	63	53	33	20	28	14	13	16
% Female	43	45	50	55	57	50	54	53
Racial/Ethnic Groups:								
% Asian	14	8	5	4	2	3	4	5
% Hispanic	3	10	6	4	12	7	7	6
% Black	5	4	5	10	4	17	10	9

High School Type:

% Went to Catholic High School	23	16	15	8	8	9	7	10
% Went to NAIS* Private High School	21	8	2	2	0	0	0	2
% Went to Other Private High School	1	2	4	4	1	2	5	4
% Went to Public School	55	74	79	85	91	88	87	84
% Live in Northeast	53	40	29	24	8	14	20	23
SAT/ACT Mean	1260	1147	1050	983	1002	915	886	969
Attended Art Museums % Both Parent and Student:	72	55	47	38	33	35	27	36
% Captain/Officer:								
Team Sport	23	11	17	13	15	16	11	13
Individual Sport	20	17	9	7	10	6	3	7
School Government	23	14	11	8	10	6	6	8
Yearbook or Newspaper	29	11	8	7	8	5	4	7
School Academic Club	19	9	8	5	8	5	5	6
% Parents Expect 8th Grader to Receive Advanced Degree	75	59	38	30	21	21	20	29
% Students by Tier	4	8	14	24	6	9	35	100

Estimates based on weighted observations. Restricted Access Data License Control Number: 0601044.

*NAIS refers to the National Association of Independent Schools. Numbers may not add to 100 due to rounding.

TABLE 6.3

Breakdown of Class Groups by Offspring's College Tier and Those Not Attending

% of Total Data	Distribution of Class Groups into Tiers:	Tier 1	Tier 2	Tier 3	Tier 4	Tier 5	Tier 6	Tier 7	Did Not Attend College	% of Class Group
8	Top Income Professionals	10	12	20	19	4	3	12	19	100
5	Top Income Non-Professional	5	9	12	20	2	2	12	36	100
37	Middle Class	1	3	7	15	2	4	19	49	100
20	Working Class	(.5)	1	3	9	2	2	18	63	100
30	Lower Working Class & Poor	(.3)	1	2	6	1	2	16	71	100

Estimates based on weighted observations. National Educational Longitudinal Study Restricted-Use Data, 1988–2000, Restricted Access Data License Control Number: 06011044. Percentages may not add up to 100% due to rounding.

there is not a clear reproductive relation in which 33 percent or more of a group passes through any particular one. We cannot say that any tier defines membership for either of the two dominant groups, and the absence of any college experience seems to play a role in drawing the boundaries of the two most subordinate classes.

It is possible that NELS data are inadequate or our categories are not subtle enough to test Bourdieu's theories. Perhaps the top tier, with just forty-four institutions and 4 percent of America's students, is too small to have an impact that shows up in a national sample such as NELS. And our national sample of top-income professionals may require refinement before we uncover a reproductive relation to elite colleges.

We think it is worthwhile to try two additional ways of tackling Bourdieu before we abandon the question of dominant-class reproduction. First, we will enlarge the reference group for elite colleges to include all institutions in the second tier. Other scholars have classified elite institutions as a combination of the first and second tiers. Three of the economists who participated in the debate reviewed in Chapter 5 on college tiers effects on lifetime earnings worked with models that combined tiers 1 and 2 because the top tier with only forty-four institutions was, except for three military academies, entirely private.[19] And there is a scholarly book on low-income students that views the top as a combination of tiers 1 and 2.[20] Most importantly, however, Bourdieu would have no difficulty classifying all of those colleges as elite because youths from the dominant class provide 50 percent of their combined total of undergraduates. Looking back at our Table 6.2, the reader can see that the dominant class is the largest single group represented in tiers 1 and 2.

Tier 2 has eighty-five institutions in it, including sixty-five private university and colleges, such as Barnard, Carnegie Mellon, Emory, Hamilton, Kenyon, Lehigh, Mount Holyoke, NYU, Oberlin, Reed, Smith, Vanderbilt and Vassar.[21] Those private colleges are sufficiently elite to make it onto most professional class families' mattering maps. And the tier has twenty of the best public universities in the nation, including: UC Berkeley, UCLA, University of Illinois at Urbana-Champaign, University of Michigan at Ann Arbor, and the University of North Carolina at Chapel Hill. We will see what difference a larger, but still elite group of colleges and universities make to the reproduction question. And we will see if there are any statistically discernable differences for fractions of the dominant class between the twenty public universities and the sixty-five private institutions in the second tier.

Second, we will redraw the boundaries for our top-income professionals by separating those with home residences in the Northeast from the rest. Bourdieu saw social class as being structured in part by geography. He found a relation between a fraction's "position in social space . . . and its distribution in geographic space."[22] Physical location, proximity to strategic center points for cultural capital, such as Paris or New York, matters. If there is a group with a reproductive strategy that relies on elite colleges, that group should be physically clustered in an area that is rich in cultural capital.

For the United States, the northeast region in NELS is a reasonable proxy for the geographic heartland of cultural capital. Although highbrow culture is available in all metropolitan areas in the United States today, it originated in and continues to be most prominent in a northeastern geographic zone that extends from Boston, down to Washington, D.C., and over past Philadelphia.[23] Consequently, we will see if northeastern professional families in the dominant class have a reproductive relation to elite colleges calculated as our combined tiers 1 and 2.

Northeastern Professionals in Elite Colleges

We found that northeastern top-income professional families have youths who apply to and graduate from elite colleges at higher rates than any other group. And, most importantly, as one can see in Table 6.4, they achieve a reproductive relation as judged by our minimum standard of 33 percent or more of every youth from that group receiving a degree from an elite institution.

When we look at the enlarged elite college list, 53 percent of the northeastern professional group applies and of those 68 percent are admitted, for a group total of 36 percent reproduction. If we exclude those who did not attend college (and they are 19 percent of all professional-family offspring), then of all youths with college experience in our northeastern-professional fraction 40 percent pass through elite colleges. Regionally, high-income

TABLE 6.4

Distribution of Dominant Class Fractions into Combined Elite Tiers.

Percent of Youths in Each Category:	NE Top Income Professional Class Fraction	Non-NE Top Income Professional Class Fraction	Top Income Non-Professional Fraction	Our Three Dominant Class Fractions Combined
Total % of All Youths in NELS in Class Fraction	2	5.7	4.6	12
% Appling to Tiers 1 & 2	53	26	17	27
% of Those Applying Admitted by Tiers 1 & 2	68	75	56	68
% of All Youths In Class Fraction Admitted to Tiers 1 & 2	36	19	10	18
% of All Applicants to Tiers 1 & 2 From Class Fraction	13	19	10	42
% of All Admits to Tiers 1 & 2 From Class Fraction	15	24	10	49
% of All Graduates of Colleges in Tiers 1 & 2 from Class Fraction	15	21	12	50
Of Youths with College Experience in Class Fraction % Who Are Graduates of Tiers 1 & 2	40	23	22	25

Estimates based on weighted observations. *National Educational Longitudinal Study Restricted-Use Data, 1988–2000,* Data License Control Number: 06011044.

professional families appear to have a class reproductive relation to those institutions. If we shift our focus and look at dominant-class professional families nationwide, they have a better record with the combined tier than in tier 1, but not one good enough for a strong reproductive relation to exist. Outside the Northeast, 26 percent of professional class youths apply, and of those 75 percent are admitted, giving that group a youth participation rate of 19 percent at elite colleges.

Dominant-class northeastern professional families outperform every other group in the race for filling seats in elite colleges. Even though they represent only 2 percent of all U.S. families, they supply 15 percent of all graduates from elite colleges. They are approximately one-third the size of their national professional-class cousins and yet the Northeast provides 42 percent of their combined total representation in elite colleges. As Bourdieu's theories predict, nationally high-income-professional families do better than high-income non-professionals at elite college applications, acceptances, and graduation.

Out of America's thousand of colleges and universities, 129 enrolling about 12 percent of our total undergraduates provide the elite educational credentials that assist in the reproduction of northeastern professionals. Bourdieu's theories and empirical generalizations do apply to the professional fraction of the dominant class in America's Northeast.

Why did we have to combine tiers 1 and 2 to uncover any signs of a dominant class reproductive relation to elite colleges? Did professional class offspring find the admissions standards of the top tier too rigorous for it to gain entry in large numbers? Have families in the dominant class defected from the private sector to the public sector because it is cheaper? If northeastern professionals are sending their children to public universities, we cannot evaluate whether the switch was made acceptable because of enhanced prestige or low cost. But we can see which mix of qualities goes with applications and admissions for our northeastern dominant-class fraction at public versus private institutions in the second tier.

We looked carefully at the data and found the private sector was still commanding dominant-class loyalties, but there was an interesting reversal in admissions criteria at work between the pubic and private institutions. In the second tier, a larger percentage (63 percent) of northeastern professionals was in private colleges than in public universities. And those who went into the second tier at public universities (37 percent) were weaker academically but stronger in extracurricular activities than those entering private colleges. It appears that the competition was fiercest in the Northeast for entry to the top tier and professional-class youths with more academic than extracurricular accomplishments found themselves moving on to their second-choice private college. It was likely that private tier 2 colleges selected less for personal promise and more for academic performance than tier 1 colleges. The research discussed in Chapter 5 on personal qualities by the College Board senior scientists, Warren Willingham and Hunter Breland, found that as one moves down the prestige scale at private colleges, academic factors matter more in college admissions.[24] And, in a role reversal, the public institutions in the second tier were capturing more high-school presidents and athletes with weaker academic files than were the private colleges.

It is possible that since the 1960s, as college has been seen by privileged families as more important than before, there has been an expansion of the elite market. One indication of this is that in 1966, *Barron's Profiles of American Colleges* put 43 colleges in tier 1, and 53 colleges in tier 2; in 1990 they classified 44 colleges in tier 1 and 85 institutions in tier 2.[25] Yale and the others at the very top have attracted so many emulators that there has been significant growth in the ranks of elite institutions in the second tier, and those institutions have won sufficient prestige for dominant-class professional families to find them respectable. Included in the group would be flagship public universities, such as UC Berkeley and the University of Michigan at Ann Arbor. The spread of northeastern professionals across the second tier is consistent with a historical narrative that sees an intensified competition within tier 1 and a trickle-down effect into the next.

Alumni Tier-1 Reproduction

Northeastern professionals have a reproductive relation to elite colleges, but what about alumni families? We know that legacies receive a big boost in elite admissions at the parental *alma mater*, but only a minority of elite alumni offspring even attempt to follow in the parental footsteps. How adept are top-tier alumni families at reproducing their tier's status with the next generation?

We can look at alumni surveys to gain some insight into the issue of alumni-tier family reproduction. Working with data on Yale alumni whose children attended college in the 1970s or early 1980s, we find that out of 1,054 families responding to a survey (a response rate of 67 percent), they had a combined total of 3,316 children, averaging slightly over three children per family. Of those children, 94 percent went to college, which is impressive in itself. And 53 percent of first-born, 48 percent of second-born, and 42 percent of third-born youths matriculated at one of our 129 elite colleges. Looked at in terms of family units, only 28 percent had total success with all of their children achieving elite college reproduction, but fully 82 percent of the families had at least one youth with an elite college education. And just 18 percent of Yale families in the survey experienced only downward educational mobility with all of their children.[26]

We can also draw on a survey of alumni families of Wake Forest University, an institution that moved into the top tier between 1980 and 1994. Its rise in status was assisted by severing ties to the Southern Baptist Convention and by broadening its national recruitment of students in the late 1980s and early 1990s. The survey requires some nuance in its interpretation because the parents graduated in the late 1970s when the institution would have been, at best, in the second tier and their offspring went to college roughly between 1990 and 2005, at which point the university was in the same tier as Yale.

The scientific advantage of the Wake Forest survey over the Yale data is that it was administered to a properly randomized sample, and of the families selected to participate, 73 percent responded. We can be confident that the Wake Forest study captured a representative sample. Those families raised a total of 321 college-age youths. Table 6.5 displays where those alumni offspring went.

This table shows how each family may be classified by taking the combined college tier ranking for each youth into account. For example, a family would be rated "all up" if every child went to a tier 1 college. "Up and Repro" is the classification for a family with its children divided between tier 1 and tier 2 colleges, and so on down the line. From this table, we can see that 87 percent of alumni families reproduced or increased their college tier status with their children, and only 13 percent experienced downward educational mobility. Even though 45 percent of families managed to get at

TABLE 6.5

Balance Sheet on Wake Forest Families with Upward, Reproductive, or
Downward Educational Mobility.

Mobility or Repro by All Children's Tiers	Families with All Children in Tier 1	Families with Children in Tiers 1 & 2	Families with Children in Tiers 1 & 3	Families with All Children in Tier 2	Families with Children in Tiers 2 & 3	Families with Children in Tiers 2 and 4	Families with Children in Tiers 3 & 4
All Up	22%						
Up & Repro		22%					
Up & Down			1%				
All Repro				42%			
Repro & Down					6%	2%	
All Down							5%

SOURCE: Author's survey.

least one child into a tier-1 college, only 22 percent had all of their children
there. The largest homogenous category was the second tier, which contained 42 percent of all families.

On balance, one can say that successful tier-status educational reproduction for families with top-tier alumni is the norm. Approximately half of the
youths from alumni families reproduce or improve on their family's educational attainments. Elite colleges and their alumni families are partners in an
association for the reproduction of educational privilege. The irony is that
education was supposed to be an equal opportunity leveler, but at the top, it
has become a mechanism of class stratification.

Regression Analysis of Who Applies to and Who is Accepted by Elite Colleges

Before we can be certain that class privileges are a factor in who applies
to and attends elite colleges, we need to sail through a series of statistical
tests. Social scientists use multivariate regression analyses to clarify which
characteristics or behaviors really matter to an outcome. Descriptive statistics such as we have been using so far in this book are fine, but they have

limitations. They cannot establish whether and to what extent something, like family income, is meaningfully correlated with something else, like attending a private college. A percentage can tell us how many people share a quality, but not whether that quality is in any sense producing a particular result. Black Americans, for example, on average watch more television than White Americans. A percentage chart on race and viewing hours would tell us that, but it would not give us any insight into what produces the pattern. A regression analysis allows us to do a statistical version of a controlled experiment to isolate what really counts. On the example of Blacks and television, a regression model with data on race, family income, occupation, and education would show us that what matters most to television viewing is education, not race. Whites and Blacks with the same level of education watch the same amount. Blacks on average have lower educational attainments than Whites, and the education gap explains what appears to be a racial difference in television patterns. In the remainder of this chapter, we will use logistic regression analysis to look at what statistically explains the type of youth who applies to and is admitted by elite colleges.

The following demographic and behavioral data on the families in the *National Educational Longitudinal Survey* have been coded as independent variables that may contribute to the outcomes in question: family's social-class classified as one of our six Bourdieuian groups; family's region of residence; parents' education; parents' expectations for their child to attain a postgraduate degree or not; the youth's sex and race; the type of secondary school attended by the youth; the youth's SAT scores; whether in school the youth took art classes; parents' and offspring's art museum attendance; the youth's secondary-school extracurricular participation in sports, music, theater, school government, academic societies, yearbooks or newspapers, service clubs, individual or team sports; and whether the youth was a team captain or officer in any of those activities.

We are asking about two outcomes: applying to and being admitted by an elite college, meaning any of the 129 institutions that we found to be important to the social reproduction of northeastern dominant-class professionals. We need two logistic models to find the characteristics that best predict our two distinct outcomes. Applying is a separate and prior process of self-selection in which the youth gets to decide; the admission decision is in the hands of the college.

TABLE 6.6

Logistic Regression Results for Applying to and Being Admitted by a Tier 1 or 2 College.

Characteristics That Are Statistically Significant at the .05 Level or Higher	Odds Ratios for Applying to Tiers 1 & 2	Odds Ratios for Being Admitted to Tiers 1 & 2	Missing Comparison Group: The Odds Are Calculated Relative to the Chances of This Group
Students from Top Income Professional Career Family in Northeast	3.39	Not significant	Working-class students
Students from Top Income Professional Career Family	2.03	Not significant	Working-class students
Student is Asian	1.75	Not significant	All other ethnic/racial groups
At Least One Parent Has an Advanced Degree	Not significant	3.09	Parents are only high-school graduates
Went to NAIS Private High School	4.23	2.36	Student went to a public high school
SAT Verbal	1.72	Not significant	Scale in 100-point increments
SAT Math	1.60	1.54	Scale in 100-point increments
Both Parent and Student Attend Art Museums	Not significant	1.85	Neither the youth nor the parent attend
Participate in Academic Honor Society in High School	1.94	Not significant	Does not participate
Captain Intramural Team Sport	.50*	Not significant	Is not a team sport captain
Participate in a Team Sport	Not significant	.43*	Does not do team sports
Officer in High School Government	Not significant	2.65	Is not an officer in student government
Parents Expect 8th Grader to Receive Advanced Degree	1.68	Not significant	Parent does not expect 8th grader to achieve advanced degree

Estimates based on weighted observations. Restricted Access Data License Control Number: 0601044.

* These are statistically significant but negative odds. Someone with this characteristic is less likely than those without it to have the outcome in question.

In a logistic regression model, when a variable is significant, it means that holding all else constant, we know that the variable matters, like education in relation to television in the example on race. When something matters, it correlates with or possibly even causes the outcome—in these cases, the self-selection of youths who apply, and the admissions committee's decision to reject or admit. In both cases, we cannot report a guaranteed result; there are no absolute certainties in the social sciences. Even in medical science, one can only offer estimates. Exposure to toxins does not result in cancer 100 percent of the time, but medical science can calculate one's level of risk, if your background and the nature of the exposure are known. The same is true in the social sciences. We can mathematically estimate the odds or the probability of a type of youth applying or getting in, but not whether any particular youth will do so. In reporting our results for the non-specialist reader, we will present only findings that are statistically significant and what their contributions are to one's odds of applying to and receiving a thick envelope in the mail from an elite college. (Anyone interested may download the entire regression results at www.wfu.edu/academics/sociology/soares.html.)

The beauty of the odds reported from a multivariate logistic regression equation is that they are adjusted to take account of everything else in the model. The regression analysis makes all else equal to isolate the precise effects of a particular variable. But the adjusted odds given in Table 6.6 are always relative to a reference group. And the reader needs to keep the reference group in mind when thinking about the magnitude of the effect.

Two separate models are reported in Table 6.6, a regression model on applying to elite colleges and one on being admitted. We can see from the table that not many things significantly contribute to the outcomes, and what matters to the application step does not necessarily matter to the admissions decision.

Professional-class membership is very important to the application process. Youths from dominant class professional families in the northeast are 3.39 times more likely than working-class youths to offer themselves as candidates for elite colleges. The regression analysis allows us to say that holding all else equal, youths with the same gender, race, SAT scores, and everything else included in the model have their odds of applying to an elite college increased by a multiple of 3.39, if the youth comes from one of those privileged families. Outside the Northeast, professional-class families give their children twice the odds of working-class youths of applying. Professional-class membership helps to place one in the applicant pool, but not in getting one selected. There were no statistical differences between any of our class fractions at the final stage of the admissions process. The entire applicant pool must be too privileged for differences in class backgrounds to differentiate between candidates.

There is an ethnicity effect in that being Asian increases one's odds of applying by a multiple of 1.75 over anyone else. The Asian effect works in harmony with the power of socioeconomic class. Social scientists have found insignificant class differences between Asian and White youths at elite colleges. We know that at elite colleges "the typical white or Asian freshman clearly comes from a professional or managerial class background."[27] There is, however, something about Asian family practices that gives their youths an edge in putting themselves into the applicant pool. Being Asian, however, does not help with the admit results.

Attending a private non-Catholic secondary school has a tremendous effect on the likelihood of applying to an elite college, and a very large effect on the odds of being admitted. Being a senior at a private non-Catholic school boosts one's odds of applying by a factor of 4.23, and it multiplies one's chances of admission 2.36 times, over public school seniors. Attending a private Catholic high school does not help or hurt one's odds relative to public school youths.

Having a parent with a law school degree, or some other postgraduate credential does not matter to the application stage, but it does have a large impact on admissions. A parent in the family with a postgraduate degree increases the youth's odds of admission by a multiple of 3. One would like to believe that the parental-postgraduate boost is due to the effects parents have on the cognitive and cultural development of their young, rather than anything as crude as an admissions officer giving top scores if the applicant mentions mom's medical degree. The regression analysis, however, gives us little room for optimism. The regression results tell us that between two equally strong candidates, the one who can report a parent with a postgraduate credential is three times more likely to be admitted. Gatekeepers are making judgments on families, and not just on the performance of individuals.

On SAT scores, each increase of 100 points on the verbal section of the test raises one's odds of applying by a multiple of 1.72, as it does on the math section by a factor of 1.6. At the admission's stage, there may be too little variation in the applicant pool's SAT verbal scores to matter, but math scores continue to differentiate between winners and losers. It is possible that this is because of elite colleges having more male than female students; women were 53 percent of all undergraduates in the data, but they were just 44 percent of the students in elite colleges (see Table 6.2). And males score higher than females on the math section of the SAT. On admissions, each 100-point increase in one's math score lifts one's odds 1.54 times. SAT scores are very important determinants of applicant self-selection and admissions committee action. And although SAT scores correlate with family socioeconomic status, academic work can stretch the class tether.

Cultural capital played no discernable role in the application process, but in the admissions contest, it comes through. When a youth and a parent share a taste for frequenting arts museums, it improves one's odds of being admitted 1.85 times. We doubt that the relationship of family art museum attendance and elite college admissions is direct. We find it hard to imagine that dropping a comment in one's personal essay about the most recent Picasso exhibition in town will get one admitted. Somehow in the personal essay, letters of recommendation, or alumni interview, the qualities of families with cultural capital must come through, but the precise mechanism remains undiscovered. We looked into the relation of groups in the dominant class to this variable, through the use of interaction terms, to see if we could tease out differences in the value of this practice to privileged and unprivileged groups, and we could not. We did not find evidence that cultural capital was exclusively available as a resource to the upper class; as other researchers have found, there appears to be a social mobility payoff for going to art museums.[28] Apparently one can draw on the fine arts to act upper class in real life, and not just in films, like *Six Degrees of Separation*.

The extracurricular activity most closely linked to intellectual effort is captured by the academic honor society participation variable. Hanging out with eggheads in high school increases one's likelihood of applying 1.94 times, but carries no weight with admissions committees.

Sports leadership and participation do not transmit any benefits, but they do carry some penalties. At the application stage, it hurts to be a captain on an intramural sports team. Former team captains are half as likely as non-captains to apply. And even being on a sports team in high school handicaps one at the admission's stage. Team members are only 43 percent as likely to be admitted as non-team members.

The sports results were a surprise, because we know that recruited athletes get the easiest ride through the admissions door.[29] To double check on the dynamics at work, we ran separate regressions for our questions using just the first and then just the second tier as our outcomes to see if tier differences were responsible for these unexpected results. The answer is yes. On sports, the two top tiers pull in opposite directions. In the first tier, being on a team or being a team captain helps, but not so much that it overcomes the negative effects facing the athlete in the second tier. If one is an athlete with a respectable academic record, one will do better at a tier 1, rather than a tier 2, institution.

Leadership as reflected in being an officer in the student government does not factor into who applies, but it pays off big on admission. It provides a 2.65 boost, making it one of the strongest effects in the data. The student government effect is one of the more equal-opportunity variables that matter. Anyone can run for a position in student government. Admissions committees who reward this, however, are implicitly endorsing Yale's view on the importance of selecting for leaders. And leadership selection has not hurt Yale's socioeconomic composition any more than SAT selectivity has.

Parental expectations play an important role in pushing or encouraging youths to apply. They lift a student's application odds 1.68 times, but they fail to make an impression on the admission's decision.

On balance, slightly more effects of class privilege are transmitted in the pre-admissions process of preparation and self-selection, but many carry through to the admission's office stage as well. Aspects of class privilege in these two models include being from a top-income professional class family; having parents holding postgraduate or professional-school degrees; attending a private secondary school; having regular family outings at art museums; and even the parental expectation that one will show signs by the age of thirteen of being destined for a PhD or MD, is a form of class privilege. Four of those advantages factor in to determining who applies, and three increase one's odds of getting picked.

Something left out of consideration is the effect of legacy status. There is not an explicit question about being a legacy in NELS.[30] It is likely that a parent with an elite college degree passes along unmeasured class privileges to her or his children. But we cannot see if there is such as thing as an elite-tier-legacy effect. NELS does not identify the colleges attended by parents; none of the existing data sets on educational attainments in the United States contain that information. Social scientists, politicians, and government agencies have not thought it worth asking the question. The full scale of legacy privileges at particular colleges today, and whether there are such things as parental-tier effects, remain hidden from view.

Overall, in answer to our questions on application and admission, all of our logistic regression results tell us that class background matters dramatically. An eighth-grade, working-class, public-school, Caucasian female cannot do academic or extracurricular activities that will turn her into an Asian, or put her family into a different social class, or earn her parents postgraduate credentials, or place her in a private school. The best she can do is work on academics, prep hard for the SAT, get into the student government, drag a parent along to an art museum, and hope her family moves to California.

In sum, with descriptive statistics and through regression analyses, we have found that Howe and Bourdieu are both largely correct. As Howe predicted, tier 1 colleges draw 64 percent of their undergraduates from families with top incomes. And, as Bourdieu predicted, students from families with top incomes and parents in professional occupations outperform all others in the race for elite places. This is a contest in which winning requires dedication and sustained effort from the youth and from the parent. The parental contribution weighs as heavily on the scales as anything done by the young. Professional-class parents are pros at making academic stars of their young.

The parental power to pass along privilege works most effectively in the Northeast. Within the historic home of highbrow culture in America, northeastern upper-income professionals transmit class power to the next generation through elite college credentials. Nationally, of the dominant professional class youths in NELS, one out of every five enters an elite college; in the Northeast, their record is one out of three. Limiting our comparison to just those going to college, the elite-college reproduction record nationally is one out of four, and regionally, it is two out of five.

Bourdieu's standards for dominant class reproduction have been met in the Northeast, but that still means that most children in the dominant class are happy to leave elite colleges to others. Most dominant class youths do not apply to elite colleges; those who do are successful 68 percent of the time. Odds are that a determined multiple-elite-college applicant from the dominant class will get into one. In elite colleges, they have a lock on 50 to 64 percent of the classroom seats, but that still leaves open 36 to 50 percent. There is room for more, if that is a family goal. We can only conclude that elite colleges have been more obsessed with the dominant class than it has been with them. Elite colleges have for the better part of a century used admissions criteria that were an academically disguised form of social selection. And a small fraction of the privileged classes in America have been willing to play the game. It is most unfortunate that many other Americans have been afflicted by the mad scramble at the top for superlative extracurricular resumes and high SAT scores. If youths and parents find the college application season exhausting, they should know now where to point the finger.

Conclusions

The American faith in the value of individual liberty is partially balanced in our culture by a fundamental desire to be fair. The inevitable conflicts between freedom and equity are not, however, easily reconciled. We want to be a land of opportunity where individuals can make of themselves what they will. We like competition, but believe it should be meritocratic; the contest should be honest with outcomes that are just.

Americans believe in education as the best way to sustain a meritocratic society. There is hardly anyone who does not want every youth to have the opportunity to attend good schools in the pursuit of academic excellence. Yet we have managed not to notice that our most prestigious colleges and universities are beyond the reach of most youths other than those from families earning in the top income decile. It was not supposed to work like that, according to both the optimistic and cautious versions of the meritocratic story summarized in our first chapter.

The optimistic authors discussed in this book offered us a morality tale on the triumph of merit over privilege, of the rise of talented newcomers over cronies and blood relations, of the emergence of a fair and efficient system of academic selection and rewards. Their stories flattered our premier private colleges and universities, seeing them as institutions that went from judging a White male by his character to becoming places that opened their doors to brains regardless of gender, race, and social class. Their tale articulated a vision of historical progress toward a democratic society, giving comfort and pride to our professional class. Enlightened professional people like us cleared a path through the thorns of privilege, making way for a better tomorrow, and now that merit really matters, we have an imperfect but basically equal-opportunity society. Those of us with degrees from top-tier institutions and professional jobs have earned where we are today. We were once the underdogs beneath the WASP establishment, and now we are the winners of the race, and what is more American than that? Unfortunately, it is a myth—a myth with some kernels of truth, but a myth nonetheless.

On balance, one can see that the optimistic version of meritocracy is at best inadequate. It is a myth that meritocracy came into a position of institutional hegemony by beating out an older elite, based on blood and property, replacing it with a new elite based on intellectual ability. Brainy parvenus did not displace family legacies. The ranks of legacies were thinned at Yale for all of six years; their comparative privileges over non-legacies, however, were never removed. In the post-meritocratic period, an explicit target was put into place, from 1974 to 1989, reserving for legacies the space to be approximately 20 percent of every entering undergraduate cohort. Admissions officers were not in open conflict with their institution's traditional constituency. The discontinuities between the two admission deans at Yale, the allegedly conservative Arthur Howe and the meritocratic R. Inslee Clark, were exaggerations. The most privileged groups held on to their share of seats at elite colleges. The proportion of undergraduates from families at the top of the income pyramid never changed. What changed was the applicant pool; it was larger but just as socially privileged as in the past. More affluent families than ever before were sending their young to college.

Although the optimistic version of the meritocratic tale falls short of its mark, what about the cautious version? Is it correct to say that starting in the 1950s, Yale selected youths primarily by academic rather than non-academic criteria? Did the machinery of admissions modernize even if the constituency remained unaltered?

Selective admissions from the 1920s to the early 1950s were never just about character. It is true that in the past Ivy gatekeepers did their best to exclude Jewish young men regardless of their proficiency in academic subjects, yet it is a mistake to infer the reverse and to think that White Anglo-Saxon Protestants (WASPs) were admitted on the basis of character regardless of their intellectual performance. Academic merit was always a large part of admissions. When Yale discriminated against Jews, the Ivies thought Protestant youths possessed a form of intelligence that was superior to that of Jews in very important ways. WASP male brains were supposedly more disinterested, more wise, more robust and subtle than the sort of grubby, rote, mechanical intelligence Jewish youths displayed. Of course, that was ugly anti-Semitic nonsense, but that did not deter those in a position of authority from embracing this misevaluation of intelligence. In the bad-old days, Yale's presidents and deans cared about intellectual merit, and they measured it as precisely as possible, given their eugenic upper-class assumptions. Poor academic performance would get one rejected, even if one's father was an alumnus and he owned a bank or worked in the White House.

The meritocratic narrative about the shift from character to intellect is mistaken. Character was not dominant in the old days, and intellect is not supreme now. The machinery to calculate and reward boys in the admissions contest based on individual academic performance was in place in the 1930s. The use of the Scholastic Aptitude (renamed Assessment) Test (SAT) and grade predictions from 1926 to the 1970s was not responsible, by itself, for ushering in religious diversity, or women, or racial minorities, and academic admissions criteria had no positive impact whatever on socioeconomic diversity.

What changed in the post-1950s "meritocratic" period was not the use of standardized test scores or some other mechanism of academic selectivity in admissions. It is simply not accurate to say, as Nicholas Lemann does, "Yale had changed [with Brewster]. . . . It would choose [hence forward] its students mainly on the basis of their predicted grades."[1] What was new inside Yale after the 1950s was its emphasis on leadership, on selection for personal character, which was exactly the opposite of what one would expect from the meritocratic narrative.

From roughly 1956 to 1974, determining who had the personal ability to play a leading role in society was what the admissions game was all about. Yale was there to nurture the leadership class in America and that social role provided the criteria enabling it to select from among its many academically qualified applicants. The admissions challenge was how to identify who had the most personal promise at the age of seventeen to become a leader. The correlation between leadership qualities and the performance records of youths from high-socioeconomic families was never seriously questioned.

The emphasis on leadership went uncommented on because of external changes in American society that drove up SAT scores. What changed on the outside of the Ivy League was the participation rate of middle- and upper-class families in higher education. There was literally a flood into elite colleges' applicant pool of academically prepared, affluent youths. The affluent decided in the late 1950s to invest in college preparation and in prestigious college educations. And the payoff for elite colleges was a five- to seven-fold increase over previous years in applicants who were academically acceptable and able to pay full fare. At Yale, SAT scores went up and up until 1970, consistent with the social composition and academic preparation of the applicant pool. And Yale's response to this embarrassment of qualified applicants was to sharpen its tools for leadership selectivity.

After 1974, the emphasis on leadership was broadened by a range of qualities that reflected Yale's internal models of personal success. Those personal success models were, in large part, responsible for current admissions practices being driven by the extracurricular resumes of applicants. If aspirants to elite colleges cram their after-school and summer hours with activities intended to communicate their extraordinary talents, we have elite college admissions based on predicting personal success to blame.

We know that the accounts of the rise of meritocracy are mistaken, but what of meritocracy's critic, Pierre Bourdieu? Does Bourdieu provide us with a better way of understanding the behavior of elite colleges and privileged social groups than the meritocratic authors? If things are not as good as our meritocratic authors would like us to believe, are they as bad as Bourdieu predicted?

Bourdieu's theories are on target about the policies and practices of elite colleges. In the meritocratic imagination, colleges and universities concern themselves primarily with the disinterested pursuit and dissemination of knowledge. Bourdieu's response is that regardless of academic ideals, all colleges occupy positions in a competitive market. From the perspective of each college, the educational market is structured by four interrelated powers: the social origins and occupational destinations of one's students; the relative balance between one's sources of funding; the prestige of one's faculty; and by the positions assumed by one's competitors, other educational institutions. In America, higher education's consumers, the families and undergraduates of the system, have different qualities and pocketbooks for which education's suppliers offer ostensively distinct brand names and products. Once a type of college has carved out a relationship to a type of curriculum and a particular set of entry requirements, other institutions know that college's market placement; it has a product image aimed at a particular consumer. After private colleges embraced entry exams, and public land-grant institutions adopted high-school certification, then each was investing in a different niche of the market. Yale's commitment to the SAT involved a social and institutional logic of differentiation from public universities and toward an upper-class clientele. The SAT proved to be not very useful until it became clear that it provided a "meritocratic" way to fill the applicant pool with privileged youths. It helped to disguise the amount of socioeconomic privilege there was in the system.

The prestige of the private sector's preference for entry exams eventually won out over the public system's reliance on high-school grades. In the 1960s, public universities were focused on scientific research productivity in the competition for grants and prestige. When it became burdensome for public universities to maintain the system of high-school certification, they adopted standardized tests, the American College Test (ACT) or SAT, for admissions. The triumph of the SAT on both coasts of America boosted for three decades the legitimacy of the test before a public university, the University of California, reexamined the academic validity of the SAT and exposed its socioeconomic underpinnings.

Bourdieu gives us insight into the market behavior of elite colleges in the twentieth century, but he was off on the role those colleges play in the social reproduction of privileged groups. Even though alumni families do very well in raising youths to attend elite colleges, the only social group that successfully combines wealth and occupation with an elite college credential is limited to 2 percent of America's families in the Northeast. Those professional families do rely on elite colleges for the transmission of their privileges to the next generation. Nationally, however, top-income professionals and non-professionals apparently employ other means than elite colleges to ensure the social reproduction of their offspring. Relative to dominant-class social reproduction, the performance of elite colleges is not as insidious as Bourdieu feared, although that is not for lack of effort on their part.

Despite the small regional fraction of Bourdieu's dominant class who are oriented from kindergarten toward elite colleges, those colleges are in Bourdieu's sense of the term *dominant-class institutions*. Nationally, the dominant class provides 42 percent of all applicants to, and 50 percent of all graduates from, our 129 elite colleges. Bourdieu's prediction that elite colleges adjust their admission practices and campus culture to harmonize with families in the top income decile is apparently confirmed. Their excessive involvement with the dominant class affords considerable room for self-improvement.

An Agenda for Reform

What should we do about our current dilemma? In the remainder of this conclusion, I offer thoughts on some of the reforms that might help us. Most of these ideas are being discussed elsewhere; there is little novelty in the list of desirable reforms summarized here. These proposals should move us in the right direction, but the distance to travel between where we are now and where we should be is too great to map in every detail. It is more important for us to understand the mistakes of the past, and to be mindful of today's socioeconomic barriers, than it is for everyone to agree on each step of the way to a proper academic meritocracy.

The most important and fundamental challenge is for elite colleges to directly connect their admissions standards with the academic work of secondary schools. The easy and socially biased option of relying on aptitude tests has been discredited by the University of California. Their research showed that standardized exams on particular academic subjects do a better job than aptitude tests in reducing socioeconomic bias. We could use new tests based on the curriculum taught in public high schools, more like the current ACT than the old SAT. For international examples, we should look to England's experience with ordinary and advanced-level subject exams. We could use national conferences and new national organizations to address the problem. Committees of academics drawn from a cross section of universities and colleges could design, write, and annually monitor the fairness of the tests and their effectiveness in predicting academic performance. Private testing companies that are not obliged to share with the public all of the mechanics of their test-making and data on their results should be boycotted. As California showed, elite universities and colleges have the market power to dictate terms to any test-making organization, if the will is there to do so.

Elite colleges should adopt Berkeley-style socioeconomic-sensitive admissions policies. Much of the intellectual case for class-based affirmative action has been made recently by William Bowen, Martin Kurzweil, and Eugene Tobin.[2] Elite colleges should forego early-action and early-decision admissions, because they systematically favor the affluent over the underprivileged.[3] They should aim for an initial goal of recruiting at least 25 percent of their entering students from the bottom two socioeconomic status (SES) quartiles (see Table 1.1 for reference). The 25 percent target should be pursued with no less vigor than the policies and practices responsible in the late-twentieth century for legacy admissions. Positive incentives, even if only symbolic ones, should be put in place to encourage a competition for low-socioeconomic students. For example, elite colleges could insist as a condition of providing data to ratings groups, such as *U.S. News and World Report* (*USNWR*) or *Barron's*, that a category on social opportunity be created. The category would score each institution based on how many youths from the bottom 50 percent of America's SES scale were matriculating. The "opportunity rating" should not count less in the calculation of an institution's overall score than what is now assigned the "student selectivity" category by *USNWR*. Harvard has taken the lead, under President Lawrence Summers, by making its undergraduate education free to anyone admitted from a family earning $60,000 or less.[4] Now, they just need to reform their admission's criteria to enable them to admit more than a handful of those.

Over the decades, one of the most reliable indicators of college performance has not been the SAT or even high-school grade point average, but rank in class. The top 10 percent of high-school graduates, regardless of type or location of school, should be able to benefit from an elite college education. It should be the joint responsibility of public and private elite universities and colleges to make space for what W. E. B. Du Bois called the talented tenth.[5] As long as our high schools continue to be segregated by social class and race, a commitment to admit the top 10 percent from each school will provide elite institutions with a diverse student body. It would be easy to reach the 25 percent low-SES target if elite colleges expand their national recruitment to a wider than hitherto range of public schools. Elite colleges and universities should send the message to America's youths that anyone who finishes school in the top 10 percent of her or his senior class is admissible. And such a policy would provide a stimulus to local areas for secondary-school reforms across a range of issues, from the equitable distribution of funds and resources to the social composition of each school.

The misinformed search for the best brains and for leaders gave us the institutional pattern of affirmative action for legacies and athletes. Elite colleges should provide public proof of the institutional interests served by the privileged treatment of those two groups, as they did to the Mellon Foundation for race-sensitive admissions,[6] or the advantages of legacies and athletes in admissions should go. We have been told that legacies donate extraordinary amounts of time and money to the service of their alma mater. It is doubtful, however, that this is true. Legacies may be no more willing than non-legacy graduates to contribute small or large amounts of funds or time to the alumni association. It would be a simple matter for elite colleges to present the relevant evidence if legacies are in fact an essential part of the lifeline of private colleges; if not, then they should receive no more consideration in the admissions process than anyone else. And if legacies are such big contributors that elite colleges want to continue granting them odds three or more times better than those facing everyone else, then they should have the honesty to publicize that fact with statistics on legacies in their admission's literature and Web sites.

On athletes, we are told that sports build collective identification with a school, enhancing its attractiveness to potential applicants and donors. We have also been told that sports programs make money for the institution. We know, however, that most universities lose money on their athletic programs. If a winning season captures better applicants or more donations, then that would be easy enough to show. Regardless of the institutional payoff, athletes should not be paid entertainers who are dropped from sight as soon as their eligibility to play is through. We should expect athletes to be students first. Athletes need to accumulate the human capital in college to make of themselves something after the professional draft passes them by. Athletic programs with graduation rates that are one standard deviation or more below the institutional average for non-athletes should be suspended. The poor graduation rates of football and basketball players, often below 50 percent, should not be disguised by hiding them behind the high graduation rates provided by female athletes and low-profile sports. Each sport should be able to justify itself as a student-athlete program, and not as a talent farm for the pros. And universities should publicly reevaluate the educational benefits that justify the non-profit status of athletic programs. How are college athletics different from professional for-profit sports?

Elite colleges should deescalate the application-resume frenzy. They should publicly declare a ceiling of two on how many extracurricular activity items they will look at in an applicant's file. The professional-renaissance-youth prodigy whose resume is stuffed with Herculean feats, a practice that grew out of the elite college search for the leadership class, should be retired. Youths should not feel like they need three or more extracurricular accomplishments to get into an elite college. The professional-student machine, and the parents driving it, should be given a rest. If elite colleges have students who are not pros at filling out the lines on a resume, then who knows what wonders of curriculum improvement and enhancements to the quality and depth of the undergraduate experience are possible?

Another way we could deescalate an unproductive scramble would be to challenge the validity of the ratings industry.[7] We could start by exposing and eliminating the biases in the *USNWR* ratings that systematically favor private over public institutions, because of differences in size, funding, and institutional mission, rather than academic quality. When faculty resources are calculated as salary, student satisfaction is evaluated as percentage who donate money, selectivity counted as percentage of applicants rejected, student quality rated by SAT scores, and retention/graduation rates factored in, then small private institutions with high tuition fees and large endowments will always do better at each of those measures than large public ones. UC Berkeley, Illinois, Michigan, UCLA, and Wisconsin have rarely, if ever, made it into the top 20 of *USNWR*, and never into *Barron's* top tier. Any set of criteria that keeps those flagship public universities out of the top tier should be rejected.

Elite colleges claim to evaluate individuals based on their accomplishments, not on their family backgrounds; yet the effect of asking applicants for information on parent's education is to reward privilege. Admissions officers may say that they hold youths with highly educated parents to tougher standards than underprivileged youths are held to, but the statistics do not substantiate that claim. It is hard to see how the boost in elite college admissions given to offspring of postgraduate degree holders is anything other than a class bias. For the sake of SES affirmative action, youths should be able to identify themselves as first-generation college applicants, but for everyone else, the gathering of information on parent's education should be discontinued.

Finally, elite colleges cannot stand aside from the public political debate about how to improve our public and private secondary schools. It should be a priority for our elite institutions to weigh in with solid empirical research on the full range of issues touched on in the "No Child Left Behind" Act. The trend of legislation, litigation, and policy toward equitable funding and uniform standards needs to be extensively addressed by the nation's top academics. What are the best ways to overcome the barriers to fairness and excellence that may be caused by the disparities of local property tax–based school funding and the curriculum diversity generated by 15,000 sovereign local school boards? Working-class children should not be trapped in failing schools where middle- and upper-class parents would never send their children. Charter schools have immense problems, but Catholic schools and secular independent schools do provide valuable options. The role of socioeconomic inequality in public schools, not just racial disparities, must be solidly addressed. There is scientific and practical evidence that socioeconomic integration lifts the academic performance of racial minorities as well as working-class Whites without lowering the records of affluent Whites.[8] And we must come to terms with providing skills and certifications to those youths who will not go on to higher education. As advocated by William Julius Wilson, we should consider adopting a German-type vocational apprenticeship program that would provide income and skills to teenage youths uninterested in college.[9]

Revamping the testing system, striving to admit the top 10 percent from all secondary schools, practicing socioeconomic sensitive admissions, reforming legacy and athlete admissions, actively challenging the criteria used by the ratings industry, and engaging with the public debate on secondary education are all desirable, non-utopian steps. Taken separately or in combination, they should move us closer to a genuine academic meritocracy, and away from a system in which too many of the measures of merit turn out to be proxies for the privileges of social class.

Notes

NOTES TO CHAPTER I

1. Orlando Patterson, "What Americans Think of Freedom," *David Riesman Lecture Series*, Department of Sociology, Harvard University, 1999.

2. Elanie Sciolino, "Higher Learning in France Clings to Its Old Ways," *New York Times*, 12 May 2006.

3. Anthony P. Carnevale and Stephen J. Rose, "Socioeconomic Status, Race/Ethnicity, and Selective College Admissions," in *America's Untapped Resource*, ed. Richard Kahlenberg (New York: Century Foundation Press, 2004), 101–57, at 102–21.

4. "The Brains Business," *Economist*, 10 September 2005, 3–22.

5. Dan A. Oren, *Joining the Club: A History of Jews and Yale* (New Haven, CT: Yale University Press, 1985); Marcia Graham Synnott, *The Half-Open Door: Discrimination and Admissions at Harvard, Yale, and Princeton, 1900–1970* (Westport, CT: Greenwood Press, 1979); Harold Wechsler, *The Qualified Student: A History of Selective College Admissions in America* (New York: John Wiley & Sons, 1977).

6. James L. Shulman and William G. Bowen, *The Game of Life: College Sports and Educational Values* (Princeton, NJ: Princeton University Press, 2001), 41, 51, 54.

7. Ibid., 34.

8. Lawrence Summers, Speech before the American Council of Education (full text available at www.president.harvard.edu), reported in "Class-Conscious Financial Aid," *Harvard Magazine*, May–June 2004, 62–63.

9. "Harvard Expands Financial Aid for Low- and Middle-Income Families," *Harvard University Gazette*, Press release, 30 March 2006, 1.

10. *Economist*, 1 January 2005, 22.

11. David Brooks, "The College Gap," *New York Times*, 25 September 2005; Patrick T. Terenzini, Alberto F. Cabrera, and Elena M. Bernal, "Swimming Against the Tide: The Poor in American Higher Education," *College Board Research Report, Number 2001–1* (New York: College Board, 2001), 33–34.

12. Dominic J. Brewer, Eric Eide, and Ronald G. Ehrenberg, "Does It Pay to Attend an Elite Private College? Cross Cohort Evidence on the Effects of College

Quality on Earnings," *NBER Working Paper Series, Paper Number* 5613 (Cambridge, MA: National Bureau of Economic Research, 1996); Stacy Berg Dale and Alan B. Krueger, "Estimating the Payoff to Attending a More Selective College: An Application of Selection on Observables and Unobservables," *Quarterly Journal of Economics* 117, no. 4 (2002): 1491–526.

13. Caroline M. Hoxby,"Income Disparities Among College Graduates," Department of Economics, Harvard University, Unpublished Paper, 1998, Table 4; and Caroline M. Hoxby and Bridget Terry, "Explaining Rising Income and Wage Inequality Among the College-Educated," *NBER Working Paper Series, Paper Number* 6873 (Cambridge, MA: National Bureau of Economic Research, 1999).

14. George W. Pierson, *A Yale Book of Numbers* (New Haven, CT: Yale University, 1983), 475–79.

15. "Bulldogs Part of Presidential Ticket for 32 Years Now," *Yale Bulletin and Calendar* 33, no. 9 (29 October 2004), 1.

16. The U.S. presidents or vice presidents with Yale degrees since 1974 are Gerald Ford, George H. W. Bush, Bill Clinton, George W. Bush, and the Yale-dropout Dick Cheney. Yalies who made unsuccessful runs on tickets for the Oval Office include Sargent Shriver, Pat Robinson, Gary Hart, Jerry Brown, Paul Tsongas, Joe Lieberman, Howard Dean, and John Kerry.

17. Warren Goldstein, "for country," *Yale Alumni Magazine*, May/June 2004, 46.

18. "Letters," *Yale Alumni Magazine*, July/August 2004, 4–7.

19. Pete Wilson in California, George Pataki in New York, Bob Taft in Ohio, and George W. Bush in Texas.

20. "Letters," *Yale Alumni Magazine*, July/August 2004, 7. Reaching back to before Yale's unbroken record in the White House, the list of its famous statesmen or politicians includes Dean Acheson, Harry Truman's Secretary of State; Cyrus Vance, Lyndon Johnson's deputy secretary of defense; McGeorge Bundy, national security advisor to Johnson; John Lindsay, mayor of New York; Elliot Richardson, Richard Nixon's attorney general; and, lastly, William Howard Taft, the twenty-seventh U.S. president.

21. "A Record of the Proceedings of the Alumni Officers Convocation, Friday, November 3," *Office of the President, Kingman Brewster Papers* (Yale Archive, Box 10, Folder 10, 1967), 2, 6.

22. E. Digby Baltzell, *Philadelphia Gentleman: The Making of a National Upper Class* (Glencoe, IL: Free Press, 1958); idem., *The Protestant Establishment* (New York: Random House, 1964); idem., *Puritan Boston and Quaker Philadelphia* (Boston: Beacon Press, 1982); Daniel Bell, *The Coming of Post-Industrial Society: A Venture in Social Forecasting* (New York: Basic Books, 1976); Sidney Blumenthal, *The Rise of the Counter-Establishment* (New York: Times Books, 1986); Robert C. Christopher, *Crashing the Gates: The De-WASPing of America's Power Elite* (New York: Simon & Schuster, 1989); Christopher Lasch, *The Revolt of the Elites and the Betrayal of Democracy* (New York: W. W. Norton, 1995); Seymour Martin Lipset and David Riesman, *Education and Politics at Harvard* (New York: McGraw-Hill, 1975); Michael Novak, *The Rise of the*

Unmeltable Ethnics: Politics and Culture in the Seventies (New York: Macmillan, 1971); and Peter Schrag, *The Decline of the WASP* (New York: Simon & Schuster, 1970).

23. This acronym for White Anglo-Saxon Protestants, as Robert Christopher points out (*Crashing the Gates*, 23), was first used in print not by the person it is often attributed to, E. Digby Baltzell, but by Erdman B. Palmore, a Yale sociologist, in the January 1962 issue of the *American Journal of Sociology*.

24. The full quote is from an article by the *Economist* on the 2005 reform of the SAT, driven by the University of California, in which the magazine defends the old SAT and all that it had accomplished to make America a meritocratic land. According to the *Economist*, "The most remarkable thing about the old SATs was that they did exactly what they were supposed to do. They were the brainchild of . . . James Bryant Conant, the president of Harvard . . . and Henry Chauncey, the founder of the Educational Testing Service. . . . Conant looked at the Harvard of the 1930s and despaired. He saw a university dominated by rich Wasps who spent their time lounging around . . . So he asked Chauncey to design tests that would discern people's real ability, . . . The result was both an academic and social revolution" ("In Praise of Aptitude Tests," *Economist*, 12 March 2005, 38).

25. David Brooks, *Bobos in Paradise* (New York: Touchstone Books, 2000), 25.

26. Nicholas Lemann, *The Big Test* (New York: Farrar, Straus and Giroux, 1999), 49. Lemann's last name is pronounced "lemon."

27. Tamar Lewin, "Henry Chauncey Dies at 97; Shaped Admission Testing for the Nation's Colleges," *New York Times*, 4 December 2002, A29.

28. Ibid.

29. Baltzell, *Protestant Establishment*, 350–51; Gerald Grant and David Riesman, "An Ecology of Academic Reform," *Daedalus* 2 (1975): 166–91, at 177–79, 190; and Lipset and Riesman, *Education and Politics at Harvard*, 281–392.

30. Cameron Howell and Sarah Turner, "Legacies in Black and White: The Racial Composition of the Legacy Pool," *NBER Working Paper Series, Paper Number 9448* (Cambridge, MA: National Bureau of Economic Research, 2003); and Angela Tsay, Michele Lamont, Andrew Abbott, and Joshua Guetzkow, "From Character to Intellect: Changing Conceptions of Merit in the Social Sciences and Humanities, 1951–1971," *Poetics* 31 (2003): 23–49;

31. Jacques Steinberg, a Dartmouth graduate and higher education reporter for the *New York Times*, produced a series of front-page articles on elite college admissions, which were subsequently expanded into a book, *The Gatekeepers: Inside the Admissions Process of a Premier College* (New York: Viking Penguin, 2002). Steinberg summarizes the history of elite admissions as, "Until the late 1950s, admission to elite colleges was usually reserved for those applicants who were fortunate enough to have been born into the right family. . . . After inherited privilege was dislodged as a primary credential for elite college admission, the SAT—an aptitude test that was originally intended for limited use as a screener of scholarship applicants at Harvard—was enlisted to fill the void, creating the foundation for the establishment of

a meritocracy" (Ibid., xiii–xiv). And one need only read in the *New York Times* the recollections by Philip Boffey of Philips Exeter Academy's graduating class of 1954, titled, "The College Admissions Scramble: From Sure Thing to Anxious Ordeal" (*New York Times*, 20 June 2004, 12), to hear how the new world of meritocracy has made an older generation of privilege fearful for their progeny's prospects.

32. For example, see Jennie Yabroff, "Money Changes Everything," *New York Times*, 7 May 2006, Section 9: 1, 6. For filler in an article on the challenge unequal paychecks pose to old friends, she quotes the New York University sociologist and director of the Center for Advanced Social Science Research, Dalton Conley, on "meritocratic admissions among elite institutions." The assumption being that meritocracy produces a mix in SES at college that later on yields tensions when divvying up restaurant bills, a crucial challenge to sociability in Manhattan.

33. In a review essay for the *History of Higher Education Annual*, Roger Geiger articulates the current historical consensus, "The transformation of American higher education to selective admissions based largely on academic merit had its inception in the 1950s" (Roger L. Geiger, "Markets and History: Selective Admissions and American Higher Education Since 1950," *History of Higher Education Annual* 20 [2000]: 93–108, at 101).

34. Richard J. Herrnstein and Charles Murray state, "By the early 1960s, the entire top echelon of American universities had been transformed. The screens filtering their students from the masses had . . . changed. Instead of the old screen—woven of class, religion, and old school ties—the new screen was cognitive ability" (Richard J. Herrnstein and Charles Murray, *The Bell Curve* [New York: Free Press, 1994], 42).

35. William Bowen and Derek Bok, *The Shape of the River: Long-Term Consequences of Considering Race in College and University Admissions* (Princeton, NJ: Princeton University Press, 1998); Claude S. Fisher, Michael Hout, Martin Sanchez Jankowski, Samuel R. Lucas, Ann Swidler, and Kim Voss, *Inequality By Design: Cracking the Bell Curve Myth* (Princeton, NJ: Princeton University Press, 1996); James R. Flynn, "IQ Trends Over Time: Intelligence, Race, and Meritocracy," in *Meritocracy and Economic Inequality*, ed. Kenneth Arrow, Samuel Bowles, and Steven Durlauf (Princeton, NJ: Princeton University Press, 2000), 35–60; Steven Fraser (ed.), *The Bell Curve Wars* (New York: Basic Books, 1995); Christopher Jencks and Meredith Phillips (eds.), *The Black-White Test Score Gap* (Washington, DC: Brookings Institution Press, 1998); and Sanders Korenman and Christopher Winship, "A Reanalysis of *The Bell Curve*: Intelligence, Family Background, and Schooling," in *Meritocracy and Economic Inequality*, eds. Kenneth Arrow, Samuel Bowles, and Steven Durlauf (Princeton, NJ: Princeton University Press, 2000), 137–78.

36. Brooks, *Bobos in Paradise*.

37. Pierre Bourdieu, *The State Nobility* (Stanford, CA: Stanford University Press, 1996).

38. Ibid., 136.

39. Alexander W. Astin, Kenneth C. Green, and William S. Korn, *The American*

Freshman: Twenty Year Trends, 1966–1985 (Los Angeles: Higher Education Research Institute, University of California, Los Angeles, January 1987), 89; and Linda J. Sax, Alexander W. Astin, William S. Korn, and Kathryn M. Mahoney, *The American Freshman: National Norms for Fall 1996* (Los Angeles: Higher Education Research Institute, University of California, Los Angeles, December 1996), 70.

40. Karen Aschaffenburg and Ineke Maas, "Cultural and Educational Careers," *American Sociological Review* 62 (1997): 573–87; Paul DiMaggio, "Cultural Capital and School Success: The Impact of Status Culture Participation on the Grades of U.S. High School Students," *American Sociological Review* 47 (1982): 189–201; and Paul DiMaggio and John Mohr, "Cultural Capital, Educational Attainment, and Marital Selection," *American Journal of Sociology* 90 (1985): 1231–61.

41. Jason Kaufman and Jay Gabler, "Cultural Capital and the Extracurricular Activities of Girls and Boys in the College Attainment Process," *Poetics* 32 (2004): 145–68; Joseph A. Soares, "Cultural Capital and Elite Educational Reproduction of Ivy League Families in the 1960s and 1970s," American Sociological Association Conference Paper (2001), Department of Sociology, Yale University.

1. Joseph A. Soares, *The Decline of Privilege: The Modernization of Oxford University* (Stanford, CA: Stanford University Press, 1999).

2. Ibid., 104.

3. Although the U.S. SES scale is not identical to the occupational ranking used to derive the U.K. statistic, the two methods are similar enough to make the comparison meaningful. For the United States, see Table 1 in Chapter 1 of this book, for the United Kingdom, see Vikki Boliver, "Widening Participation and Fair Access at the University of Oxford," *Sociology Working Papers*, Number 2004–02 (Department of Sociology, Oxford University, www.sociology.ox.ac.uk/swp.html), Table II.

4. Soares, *Decline of Privilege*, 112–13. For France, see Pierre Bourdieu and Jean-Claude Passeron, *The Inheritors: French Students and Their Relation to Culture* (Chicago: University of Chicago Press, 1979), 7, 10, 114, 111.

5. Boliver, "Widening Participation"; Anthony Heath and Anna Zimdars, "Preliminary Report: Social Factors in Admission to the University of Oxford," *Sociology Working Papers*, Number 2005-01 (Department of Sociology, University of Oxford, www.sociology.ox.ac.uk/swp.html). The facts on legacy status and admission were reported to me in a personal correspondence from Anna Zimdars, Research Officer, Department of Sociology, Oxford University, on 8 October 2003.

6. Only in 1867 did Congress legislate that an informational department of education should be established; then it took until 1980 for a cabinet-level department of education to be created.

7. Frederick Rudolph, *The American College and University* (New York: Vintage Books, 1962), 250–51.

8. Thomas D. Snyder (ed.), 120 *Years of American Education: A Statistical Portrait* (Washington, DC: National Center for Education Statistics, 1993), 55, Table 19.

9. Ibid., 281–86.

10. Winston B. Stephens, *College Admission and Guidance* (Washington, DC: American Council on Education, 1933), 13.

11. Frederick Rudolph calculates that as early as 1895, fully 41 percent of all undergraduates in America's universities and colleges were public high-school graduates. The percentage continued to rise each subsequent year (*American College*, 284).

12. In 1890, the private sector graduated as many youths as public high schools, but by 1959, they could only produce 192 thousand graduates. The public sector was beating them by a factor of seven (Snyder, 120 *Years of American Education*, 55 Table 19).

13. Dorothy Perry, Barbara Sawrey, Michael Brown, Philip Curtis, Patrick Farrell, Linda Georginanna, Kenneth Burke, Christopher Diaz, Dennis Focht, Karen McNally, and Jane Stevens, "The Use of Admissions Tests by the University of California, A Discussion Paper Prepared by the Board of Admissions and Relations with Schools," 2002, 6. http://www.ucop.edu/news/sat/boars.pdf.

14. Soares, *Decline of Privilege*.

15. Michael S. Schudson, "Organizing the 'Meritocracy': A History of the College Entrance Examination Board," *Harvard Educational Review* 42, no. 1 (1972): 34–69.

16. "Letter dated 25 May 1937 from Harry A. Peters [Esq., Headmaster University School, Shaker Heights, OH—a Yale alum] to James R. Angell," *President's Office: James Rowland Angell Presidential Records, 1921–1937* (Yale Archive, Box 1, Folder 8).

17. "Letter dated 25 March 1937, response from Edward S. Noyes to F. B. Merrels," Ibid.; "Letter dated 29 May 1938 to James R. Angell from Edward S. Noyes," Ibid.

18. Rudolph, *American College*, 261.

19. Frederic Cople Jaher, *The Urban Establishment* (Chicago: University of Illinois Press, 1982).

20. Steven B. Levine, "The Rise of American Boarding Schools and the Development of a National Upper Class," *Social Problems* 28, no. 1 (October 1980): 64.

21. Frank Bowles, *The Refounding of the College Board, 1948–1963* (New York: College Entrance Examination Board, 1967), 23.

22. Richard Farnum, "Patterns of Upper-Class Education in Four American Cities: 1875–1975," in *The High-Status Track: Studies of Elite Schools and Stratification*, ed. Paul William Kingston and Lionel S. Lewis (Albany: State University of New York Press, 1990), 53–74, at 56–60.

23. Paul DiMaggio, "Cultural Entrepreneurship in Nineteenth-Century Boston: The Creation of an Organizational Base for High Culture in America," in *Rethinking Popular Culture*, ed. Chandra Mukerji and Michael Schudson (Berkeley: University of California Press, 1991), 357–73; and Lawrence Levin, *Highbrow/Lowbrow: The*

Emergence of Cultural Hierarchy in America (Cambridge, MA: Harvard University Press, 1988);

24. Levin, *Highbrow/Lowbrow*, 16–24.

25. Ibid., 64–65.

26. Richard Hofstadter, *Social Darwinism in American Thought* (Boston: Beacon Press, 1955); and William Graham Sumner, *What Social Classes Owe to Each Other* (New York: Harper & Bros., 1883).

27. Harris E. Starr, *William Graham Sumner* (New York: Henry Holt, 1925), 373–82.

28. These quotes as well as many of the substantive points made in the following on eugenics in America come from Claudia Roth Pierpont, "The Measure of America: How a Rebel Anthropologist Waged War on Racism," *New Yorker*, 8 March 2004, 48–63, at 51.

29. Ibid., 56–57, 61.

30. Ibid., 58.

31. Ibid.

32. Ibid., 61.

33. Stephen Jay Gould, *The Mismeasure of Man* (New York: W. W. Norton, 1981).

34. Ibid., 149.

35. Ibid., 194.

36. Carl Brigham, *A Study of American Intelligence* (Princeton, NJ: Princeton University Press, 1923), 208.

37. Ibid., 197.

38. Ibid., 210.

39. *Angell Papers* (Yale Archive, Box 2, Folder 26), 14 March 1923.

40. Ibid., 16 February 1925.

41. Schudson, "Organizing the 'Meritocracy,'" 50.

42. Dan A. Oren, *Joining the Club: A History of Jews and Yale* (New Haven, CT: Yale University Press, 1985); Marcia Graham Synnott, *The Half-Open Door: Discrimination and Admissions at Harvard, Yale, and Princeton, 1900–1970* (Westport, CT: Greenwood Press, 1979); Harold Wechsler, *The Qualified Student: A History of Selective College Admissions in America* (New York: John Wiley & Sons, 1977).

43. Farnum, "Patterns of Upper-Class Education," 60.

44. Ibid., 60–61.

45. College Entrance Examination Board, *Twenty-Ninth Annual Report of the Secretary*, (New York: College Entrance Examination Board, 1929), 24–27.

46. Oren, *Joining the Club*, 55.

47. "Standing of Sons of Yale Men in the Freshman Classes, Entering 1920–1923," *Angell Papers* (Yale Archive, Box 2, Folder 16), 14 February 1925.

48. *Angell Papers* (Yale Archive, Box 2, Folder 26), 16 February 1925.

49. George W. Pierson, *Yale: The University College, 1921–1937* (New Haven, CT: Yale University Press, 1955), 477.

50. Ibid.

51. "Board of Admission—Minutes," *Angell Papers* (Yale Archive, Box 2, Folder 26), 17 January 1923.

52. Oren, *Joining the Club*, 63.

53. *Angell Papers* (Yale Archive, Box 1, Folder 13), 7 January 1930.

54. Oren, *Joining the Club*, 54.

55. *Angell Papers* (Yale Archive Box 1, Folder 12), 17 October 1930.

56. Albert Crawford, "Forecasting Freshman Achievement," *School and Society*, January 25 (1930): 125–32.

57. Edwin J. Brown, "A Study of the Facts and Conditions Involved in the Problem of College Admissions," *Studies in Education* 4 (1931), 10.

58. "Table M-12, University Income by Source, 1800–1999," *Office of Institutional Research* (New Haven, CT: Yale University, 2000a).

59. *Angell Papers* (Yale Archive, Box 2, Folder 20), 27 April 1932.

60. Ibid., item dated 29 April 1932.

61. *Angell Papers* (Yale Archive, Box 2, Folder 17), 30 October 1933.

62. Paul Attewell is mistaken when he describes the Ivy League algorithm as a new policy, reacting against past discrimination, "designed to prevent bias" against minority groups today. The algorithm was used along with anti-Semitism for decades (Paul Attewell, "The Winner-Take-All High School: Organizational Adaptations to Educational Stratification," *Sociology of Education* 74, 4 [2001], 274).

63. Paul Burnham, "Letter to Mr. Crawford, 16 December 1947," *Office of Institutional Research* (New Haven, CT: Old Bogey Book, 1950); "Table E-8, Brief Historical Summary of Undergraduate Requirements and Grading Systems" *Office of Institutional Research* (New Haven, CT: Yale University, 2000b).

64. Paul Burnham, "Letter to Mrs. Elizabeth M. Drouilhet, 29 July 1947," *Office of Institutional Research* (Old Bogey Book: New Haven, 1950).

65. *Angell Papers* (Yale Archive, Box 1, Folder 9), 30 May 1935.

66. "Proceeding of the Convocation of the Committee on Enrollment and Scholarships, September 5–7," *Papers of Arthur Howe, Jr.*, 1952–1967 (Yale Archive, Box 1, Folder 5) 1957, 50.

67. Basil Bernstein, *Class, Codes and Control* (London: Routledge and K. Paul, 1971); Betty Hart and Todd R. Risley, *Meaningful Differences in the Everyday Experiences of Young American Children* (Baltimore: P. H. Brookes, 1995); Annette Lareau, *Unequal Childhoods: Class, Race, and Family Life* (Berkeley: University of California Press, 2003).

68. For an example and review of the relevant literature, see Roy O. Freedle, "Correcting the SAT's Ethnic and Social-Class Bias: A Method for Reestimating SAT Scores," *Harvard Educational Review* 73, no. 1 (Spring 2003): 1–43.

69. "Report to the Yale Faculty, 29 September 1960," *Howe Papers* (Yale Archive, Box 1, Folder 8).

70. "Remarks of Dean Arthur Howe addressed to the meeting of the Executive

Committee of the Yale Alumni Board on 6 October 1960," *Howe Papers* (Yale Archive, Box 1, Folder 8).

71. *Brewster Papers* (Yale Archive, Box 11, Folder 7), 1967.

72. Michele Hernandez, *A is for Admission* (New York: Warner Books, 1997), 48.

73. Names of individuals other than public figures, Yale administrators, staff, faculty, and alumni association officers have been excluded from this text.

74. *Angell Papers* (Yale Archive, Box 2, Folder 23), 20 January 1930.

75. Ibid., 24 January 1930.

76. "[Banker's] Western Union Telegram to James Angell," *Angell Papers* (Yale Archive, Box 2, Folder 22), 17 September 1934.

77. "Letter from Alan Valentine to [X]," *Angell Papers* (Yale University Archive, Box 2, Folder 22), 18 September 1934.

78. "Letter from Special Assistant to Secretary of State," *Angell Papers* (Yale Archive, Box 2, Folder 22), 1934.

79. "Letter from Philadelphia Engineering President to James Angell," *Angell Papers* (Yale Archive, Box 2, Folder 22), 1929.

80. "Letter to Dean Percy T. Walden [New York Aumnus]," *Angell Papers* (Yale Archive, Box 2, Folder 22), 1934.

81. Richard J. Herrnstein and Charles Murray, *The Bell Curve* (New York: Free Press, 1994), 30.

82. "Letter from President Griswold to Arthur Howe, 1 October 1953," *President A. Whitney Griswold Papers* (Yale Archive RU 22, Box 5, Folder 32).

83. "Enrollment and Scholarship Convocation," *Howe Papers* (Yale Archive, Box 1, Folder 5), [Speech to the '57 Convocation] 5 September 1957, 2–3.

84. Ibid., 5.

85. Robert Ramsey, Jr., "A Study of Cultural Influence on Academic Performance in College and Law School" (Ph.D. Thesis in Education, Harvard University, 1959), 2.

86. "Enrollment and Scholarship Convocation," *Howe Papers* (Yale Archive, Box 1, Folder 5), [Speech to the 1957 Convocation] 5 September 1957, 6.

87. Burnham, "Letter to Mr. Crawford, 16 December 1947"; Arthur Howe, Jr., "Committee on Admissions and Freshman Scholarships, Annual Report for 1954–55," *Griswold Papers* (Yale Archive, Box 5, Folder 34), 2.

88. "Notes for Talks," *Howe Papers* (Yale Archive, Box 1, Folder 8) 6 October 1960.

89. "Yale Talks Articles," *Howe Papers* (Yale Archive, Box 2, Folder 1) 1, 6, & 8 February 1957.

90. *Office of Institutional Research* (Yale Archive, Box 1, Folder 11), 1971, 13, 15–16.

91. *Office of Institutional Research* (Yale Archive, Box 2, Folder 26), 24 January 1973.

92. Ibid.

93. Roger L. Geiger, "The Competition for High-Ability Students: Universities in a Key Marketplace," in *The Future of the City of Intellect*, ed. Steven Brint (Stanford, CA: Stanford University Press, 2002): 82–106, at 90–92.

94. Verbal SAT scores at Yale did not pass the record set in 1970 until after the SAT was "re-centered" by the ETS in 1995. The re-centering boosts scores by nearly 100 points, making simple numeric comparisons between the pre- and post-1995 cohorts misleading. See "SAT Scores for Freshman Matriculants, 1975–1999," *Office of Institutional Research* (New Haven, CT: Yale University, 1 November 2000), Table D-8.

95. "Yale Reports," *Howe Papers* (Yale Archive, Box 2, Folder 1), [radio transcript for Sunday, 30 September 1956] 5.

96. "Letter to Vice President, Pan American World Airways, Chrysler Building, New York, 11 January 1960," *Griswold Papers* (Yale Archive, Box 6, Folder 44).

97. Ron Rosenbaum, "The Great Ivy League Nude Posture Photo Scandal," *New York Times Magazine*, 15 January 1995, 26–31, 40, 46, 55–6.

98. "Talks 1962–63," *Howe Papers* (Yale Archive, Box 1, Folder 12) 16 September 1963. Pierson could not report on the "heft and height" of the freshman class after 1967 because of the discontinuation of the practice. See George W. Pierson, *A Yale Book of Numbers* (New Haven, CT: Yale University Press, 1983), 120.

99. Michel Foucault, *The History of Sexuality. Volume I: An Introduction* (New York: Vintage Books, 1978).

100. Ramsey, "Study of Cultural Influence," 48.

101. Aihwa Ong, *Buddha is Hiding: Refugees, Citizenship, the New America* (Berkeley: University of California Press, 2003), 8.

102. Ramsey, "Study of Cultural Influence," 48.

103. Joseph Heller, *Catch-22* (New York: Simon & Schuster, 1955).

104. Ramsey, "Study of Cultural Influence," 48, 126–31.

105. "Alumni House report by Arthur Greenfield, II, Executive Secretary," *Brewster Papers* (Yale Archive, [Record Unit 11], Series I, Box 176, Folder 5), August 1969, 2.

106. George W. Bush, "Commencement Address, Yale University, 21 May 2001," www.yale.edu/lt/archives/v8n1/v8n1georgewbush.htm.

107. Sam Chauncey, "Memo to All Corporation Members," *Brewster Papers* (Yale Archive, Box 2, Folder 10), 4 October 1966.

108. Paul Capra, "Alumni School Committee Interview Reports," *Brewster Papers* (Yale Archive, Box 3, Folder 3), 24 October 1969, 2.

109. Table supplied by Russ Adair, Office of Institutional Research, to Author on 7 November 2001.

110. Paul Capra, "Alumni School Committee Interview Reports," *Brewster Papers* (Yale Archive, Box 3, Folder 3), October 1967, 3; John Muyskens, Jr., "Annual Report of the Director of Undergraduate Admissions," *Brewster Papers* (Yale Archive, Box 177, Folder 4), 25 June 1969, Appendix.

111. John Muyskens, Jr., "Annual Report of the Director of Undergraduate Admissions," *Brewster Papers* (Yale Archive, Box 177, Folder 4), 25 June 1969, 5.

112. Robert Sternberg, "Memorandum To: Mr. Henry Chauncey, Jr., Director, University Admissions and Financial Aid Policy, April 1972," *Office of Institutional Research* (Yale Archive, Series 1, Box 1, Folder 12), April 1972.

113. "A Handbook for the Alumni Representatives of the Committee on Enrollment and Scholarships of the Alumni Board," *Howe Papers* (Yale Archive, Box 1, Folder 5), October 1959, 10.

114. Ibid., 11.

115. "Convocation of the Committee on Enrollment and Scholarships, September 5–7, 1957," *Howe Papers* (Yale Archive, Box 1, Folder 5).

116. I have not used precise details, to reduce the likelihood of someone identifying anyone from the files.

117. "Follow-up Report on Sample Admissions Cases," *Howe Papers* (Yale Archive, Box 1, Folder 5), 15 June 1962, 3.

118. Ibid., 2.

NOTES TO CHAPTER 3

1. Arthur Howe, Jr., "From High School to College," *Papers of Arthur Howe, Jr.,* 1952–1967 (Yale Archive, RU 818, Box 2, Folder 1), May 1961, 1, 3.

2. Arthur Howe, Jr., personal interview with the Author, 18 July 2002; Joseph Soares, *The Decline of Privilege: The Modernization of Oxford University* (Stanford, CA: Stanford University Press, 1999), 41–3.

3. "Speech to Enrollment and Scholarship Convocation," *Howe Papers* (Yale Archive, Box 1, Folder 8), 5 September 1957, 19–20.

4. Arthur Howe, Jr., "Harvard's Gamble Project," *Howe Papers* (Yale Archive, Box 2, Folder 1), 1961, 6.

5. Ibid., 6–7.

6. Ibid., 7.

7. Robert Ramsey, Jr., "A Study of Cultural Influence on Academic Performance in College and Law School" (Ph.D. Thesis in Education, Harvard University, 1959).

8. Ibid., 6.

9. Ibid., 7.

10. Robert Ramsey, Jr., "Law School Admissions: Science or Hunch?" *Journal of Legal Education* 12 (1960): 503–20, at 517.

11. Ibid., 518.

12. David Swartz, *Culture and Power: The Sociology of Pierre Bourdieu* (Chicago: University of Chicago Press, 1997), 100–16.

13. Ramsey, *Study of Cultural Influence,* 122.

14. Ibid., 123.

15. Ibid., 122–23.

16. Ramsey, "Law School Admissions."

17. Ibid., 519.

18. Ibid., 519.

19. Ibid., 520.

20. Author interview with Arthur Howe, Jr., 18 July 2002.

21. Staff Study, *What Price Tuition?* (New York: Council for Financial Aid to Education, 1959), 4–8 [found in *Griswold Papers* (Yale Archive, RU 22, Box 207, Folder 1902)].

22. Arthur Howe, Jr., "They're beating the high cost of college, by Arthur Howe, Jr., Dean of Admissions and Student Appointments, Yale University," *Herald Tribune Magazine*, 29 December 1957, Section 7, 4.

23. Office of Institutional Research, "Tuition Rates 1976–1999," Table L-1, Yale University; U.S. Census Bureau, "Median Family Income," *Government Documents*, Washington, DC, 15 November 2000.

24. Ronald G. Ehrenberg, *Tuition Rising: Why College Costs So Much* (Cambridge, MA: Harvard University Press, 2002).

25. Conrad Russell, *Academic Freedom* (New York: Routledge, 1993); Edward Shils, "Great Britain and the United States: Legislators, Bureaucrats and the Universities," in *Universities, Politicians, and Bureaucrats: Europe and the United States*, ed. Hans Daalder and Edward Shils (Cambridge: Cambridge University Press, 1982); Soares, *Decline of Privilege*, 1999.

26. For examples of this view, see "A Record of the Proceedings of the Alumni Officers Convocation, Friday, 3 November 1967," *Office of the President, Kingman Brewster Papers* (Yale Archive, Box 10, Folder 10).

27. Ehrenberg, *Tuition Rising.*

28. "Press Release, 15 January 1957," *Griswold Papers* (Yale Archive, Box 207, Folder 1902), 2.

29. Ehrenberg, *Tuition Rising,* 10.

30. Ibid., 9–11.

31. Arthur Howe, Jr., "Enrollment and Scholarship Convocation [Speech to the '57 Convocation]," *Howe Papers* (Yale Archive, Box 1, Folder 5,), 5 September 1957, 26.

32. Ibid.

33. Office of Institutional Research, "Summary of Financial History, 1700–2000," Table M-15, Yale University, 19 September 2000; Arthur Howe, Jr., "Letter dated 15 December 1962 to Charles S. Gage, Treasurer," *Howe Papers* (Yale Archive, Box 1, Folder 14).

34. *President's Office: James Rowland Angell Presidential Records, 1921–1937* (Yale Archive, Box 1, Folder 12), 26 July 1932.

35. Arthur Howe, Jr., "Enrollment and Scholarship Convocation [Speech to

the '57 Convocation]," *Howe Papers* (Yale Archive, Box 1, Folder 5), 5 September 1957, 4.

36. Arthur Howe, Jr., "Memorandum to the Governing Board," *Griswold Papers* (Yale Archive, Box 6, Folder 44), 19 April 1963, 2–3.

37. Yale University, *Faculty Handbook* (New Haven, CT: Yale University, 2002), 3.

38. Arthur Howe, Jr., "Memorandum to the Governing Board," *Griswold Papers* (Yale Archive, Box 6, Folder 44), 19 April 1963, 1.

39. Morris Hadley, "Report of the Committee on Scholarship Aid," *Griswold Papers* (Yale Archive, Box 6, Folder 45), 9 January 1953, 6.

40. Ibid., 7.

41. Ibid., 10–11.

42. Ibid., 10.

43. Ibid., 11–13.

44. "Report of the Meeting of the Ivy Group Financial Officers," in *Howe Papers* (Yale Archive, Box 1, Folder 28), 1958, 2, 4.

45. "For Restricted Use, Ivy Group Statement of Principles and Policies (As amended to September 1959), Committee on Coordination and Eligibility," *Howe Papers* (Yale Archive, Box 1, Folder 16), 1959, 1.

46. Michael S. McPherson and Morton Owen Schapiro, *The Student Aid Game: Meeting Need and Rewarding Talent in American Higher Education* (Princeton, NJ: Princeton University Press, 1998), 109.

47. Ibid.

48. Bureau of the Census, "Current Population Reports," Series P-60, No. 32 (Washington, D.C. October 22, 1959); and "Harvard College Student Expenses and Financial Aid Policies," *Howe Papers* (Yale Archive, Box 1, Folder 28), 1 May 1958, 1, 4.

49. Jerome Karabel, "Status-Group Struggle, Organizational Interests, and the Limits of Institutional Autonomy: The Transformation of Harvard, Yale, and Princeton, 1918–1940," *Theory and Society* 13, 1 (1984): 1–40, at 24; and Stephen Thernstrom, "Poor but Hopeful Scholars," in *Glimpses of a Harvard Past*, ed. Bernard Bailyn (Cambridge, MA: Harvard University Press, 1986), 125; *Harvard Magazine*, May–June 2004, 62.

50. Lawrence Summers, *Harvard Magazine*, January–February 2005, 83.

51. *Harvard Magazine*, May–June 2004, 62.

52. "Yale University News Bureau, Press Release #393," *Griswold Papers* (Yale Archive, Box 207, Folder 1907), 28 May 1963.

53. Arthur Howe, Jr., "Letter dated 15 December 1962 to Charles S. Gage, Treasurer," *Howe Papers* (Yale Archive, Box 1, Folder 14).

54. Arthur Howe, Jr., "Memorandum to the Governing Board," *Griswold Papers* (Yale Archive, Box 6, Folder 44), 19 April 1963, 5.

55. Should this manuscript change their minds, the document is in *Griswold Pa-*

pers (Yale Archive, Box 66, Corporation Folders, File 633), Education Policy Reports, item dated 1963.

56. "Yale University News Bureau, Press Release #393," *Griswold Papers* (Yale Archive, Box 207, Folder 1907), 28 May 1963.

57. Ralph C. Burr, "Annual report of director of financial aid, submitted by R. Inslee Clark, Jr., Dean of Admissions and Student Appointments," *Brewster Papers* (Yale Archive, Box 176, folder 5), 5 November 1969, 2–3. The report was written by the Director of Financial Aid, Ralph C. Burr.

58. Quoted in Geoffrey Kabaservice, *The Guardians: Kingman Brewster, His Circle, and the Rise of the Liberal Establishment* (New York: Henry Holt, 2004), 264.

NOTES TO CHAPTER 4

1. Nicholas Lemann, *The Big Test* (New York: Farrar, Straus and Giroux, 1999).

2. Geoffrey Kabaservice's Yale dissertation ("Kingman Brewster and the Rise and Fall of the Progressive Establishment" [Ph.D. Dissertation, Yale University, 1999]) is now substantially revised and published as a book, *The Guardians: Kingman Brewster, His Circle, and the Rise of the Liberal Establishment* (New York: Henry Holt, 2004). Unfortunately, the book's broader purview on the "liberal establishment" left little room for the abundant materials marshaled in the dissertation on Yale's history.

3. Kabaservice, "Kingman Brewster and the Rise and Fall," 218.

4. Ibid., 277, 278.

5. Ibid., 8–58.

6. Ibid., 24.

7. Ibid., 32.

8. Ibid., 37.

9. Ibid., 104.

10. Ibid., 94–97.

11. Ibid., 127.

12. Ibid., 157.

13. Ibid., 160–66.

14. Ibid., 188.

15. Ibid., 200, 205, 220.

16. Ibid., 220.

17. Ibid., 225.

18. Ibid., 237.

19. Ibid., 244.

20. "Speech to Alumni Convocation, Saturday, 20 February 1965, at 1:55 P.M.," *Office of the President, Kingman Brewster Papers* (Yale Archive, Box 10, Folder 13).

21. Kabaservice, *The Guardians*, 266–67.

22. "Letter from A.Varick Stout to President Brewster, 2 November 1966," *Brewster Papers* (Yale Archive, Box 3, Folder 5).

23. Kabaservice, "Kingman Brewster and the Rise and Fall," 338.

24. Ibid., 343.

25. The Office of Yale's Secretary funded an oral history project into Yale's past that was conducted by a then graduate student, Geoffrey Kabaservice. The interviews were transcribed and are now in Yale's archive. Kabaservice used them in his dissertation.

26. William Borders, "Ivy League Shifts Admission Goals," *New York Times*, 17 April 1967, 1, 31 (found in *Brewster Papers* [Yale Archive, Box 3, Folder 3]).

27. *Brewster Papers* (Yale Archive, Box 3, Folder 6), 27 April 1967.

28. Ibid.

29. *Griswold Papers* (Yale Archive, Box 6, Folder 42), 3 March 1962.

30. Ibid.

31. Ibid.

32. *Brewster Papers* (Yale Archive, Box 3, Folder 6), 9 June 1967, 1–2.

33. *Brewster Papers* (Yale Archive, Box 3, Folder 6), 15 June 1967.

34. *Brewster Papers* (Yale Archive, Box 3, Folder 6), 23 May 1967.

35. "Letter from Basil D. Henning to Arthur Howe, 6 July 1955," *Griswold Papers* (Yale Archive, Box 5, Folder 34).

36. *Brewster Papers* (Yale Archive, Box 3, Folder 4), 27 October 1963 and 8 November 1963.

37. "Transcription of Question and Answer Discussion with the Alumni Convocation Board and Class Officers meeting of 1966," *Brewster Papers* (Yale Archive, Box 10, Folder 9) November 1966.

38. "Report of the Dean of Admissions and Student Appointments to the President and Fellows of Yale University, 1959–60," *Papers of Arthur Howe, Jr.*, 1952–1967 (Yale Archive, Box 1, Folder 4).

39. "Press release #128 for morning papers of Thursday, 31 October 1968, Alumni Convocation of November 1–2, 1968," *Brewster Papers* (Yale Archive, Box 10, Folder 11).

40. "Yale's role in the education of American Leaders, October 1968," *Brewster Papers* (Yale Archive, Box 13, Folder 11).

41. Established in 1947, the National Football Foundation has as its motto on its Web site for the NFF and the College Hall of Fame, "Building Leaders Through Football."

42. George W. Pierson, *A Yale Book of Numbers* (New Haven, CT: Yale University Press, 1983), 141, 145–46.

43. Dan A. Oren, *Joining the Club: A History of Jews and Yale* (New Haven, CT: Yale University Press, 1985), 23, 70, 80–81, 124.

44. "The Jock-in-Chief," *Economist*, 13 August 2005, 30.

45. Ibid.; J. A. Mangan, *Athleticism in the Victorian and Edwardian Public School* (London: Falmer Press, 1986).

46. "Jock-in-Chief," 30.

47. "Jimmy Jemail's HOTBOX," *Sports Illustrated*, 29 April 1957, found in *Howe Papers* (Yale Archive, Box 2, Folder 1).

48. "Notes on a Meeting on Alumni Communications Held in the Corporation Room, 15 February 1967," *Brewster Papers* (Yale Archive, Box 10 Folder 5), 2.

49. Ibid., 8.

50. Ibid., 7.

51. Ibid., 13.

52. "A Record of the Proceedings of the Alumni Officers Convocation, Friday, 3 November 1967," *Brewster Papers* (Yale Archive, Box 10, Folder 10), 28.

53. Ibid., 29–30.

54. "Letter to Bayard Walker dated 26 June 1967," *Brewster Papers* (Yale Archive, Box 3, Folder 6).

55. "Alumni Board Comparison of Classes of 1952 and 1970," *Brewster Papers* (Yale Archive, Box 3, Folder 7).

56. Pierson, *Yale Book of Numbers*, 101–2.

57. Richard J. Herrnstein and Charles Murray, *The Bell Curve* (New York: Free Press, 1994), 30.

58. Lemann, *Big Test*, 149.

59. The Yale Corporation may have voted on Clark on 2 February 1965 because President Brewster sent a telegram about the vote that day to the chairman of the Alumni Association, William Rockefeller at St. Thomas, Virgin Islands (*Brewster Papers* [Yale Archive, Box 2, Folder 11]).

60. Arthur Howe, Jr., interview with the Author, 18 July 2002.

61. Michael Kinsley, "How Affirmative Action Helped George W." *Time*, 27 January 2003, 70.

62. Herrnstein and Murray, *Bell Curve*, 30.

63. Pierson, *Yale Book of Numbers*, 88; Sam Chauncey, "Memo to All Corporation Members," *Brewster Papers* (Yale Archive, Box 2, Folder 10), 4 October 1966.

64. "Yale College Parents, by JRG," *Brewster Papers* (Yale Archive, Box 2, Folder 10) 4 October 1966.

65. Lemann, *Big Test*, 150–51.

66. There was a change in official Corporation policy on legacies in 1989, a date far on the other side of the meritocratic timeline for when reforms were allegedly implemented.

67. Office of Institutional Research (Yale Archive, YRG 3, RU 173, Series 1, Box 1, Folder 8), 3 September 1971, 1.

68. Ibid., 2.

69. Ibid.

70. John R. Goldin, "Alumni Sons and Daughters in Yale College," Office of Institutional Research, Yale University, December 1977, 1.

71. Ibid., 3–4.

72. Lemann, *Big Test*, 149.

73. Sam Chauncey, "Memo to All Corporation Members," *Brewster Papers* (Yale Archive, Box 2, Folder 10), 4 October 1966, 3, 5. Lemann's factual errors do not end with legacy percentages or the composition of the admissions committee. He also incorrectly claimed that prep-school staff, rather than Yale's admissions staff, decided the ratings in the early admissions notice system, Howe's ABC system (Lemann, *Big Test*, 145).

74. Sam Chauncey, "Memo to All Corporation Members," *Brewster Papers* (Yale Archive, Box 2, Folder 10), 4 October 1966.

75. *Brewster Papers* (Yale Archive, Box 2, Folder 9), 1966, 7.

76. *Yale Alumni Magazine*, October 1966, 31–32.

77. Lemann incorrectly describes this article as coming after the "Muyskens letter," which is impossible since that letter was sent in March 1967. And he claims the article was where Brewster "backpedaled even more openly" than in the Muyskens letter, which is chronologically and, in terms of the points made, inaccurate (*Big Test*, 151).

78. *Brewster Papers* (Yale Archive, Box 2, Folder 9), 1966, 1.

79. Ibid., 2.

80. Lemann, *Big Test*, 151.

81. "A Word To The Y's," *Yale Alumni Newsletter* 21, No. 1 (1971), 5–6, found in *Brewster Papers* (Yale Archive, Box 13, Folder 1).

82. *Brewster Papers* (Yale Archive, Box 3, Folder 6), 9 June 1967, 1–2.

83. *Brewster Papers* (Yale Archive, Box 3, Folder 6), 5 May 1967.

84. *Brewster Papers* (Yale Archive, Box 3, Folder 6), 15 March 1967, 1.

85. Ibid., 4.

86. "Letter from Charles O'Hearn dated 26 July 1967," *Brewster Papers* (Yale Archive, Box 3, Folder 7).

87. "Letter from Howe to Brewster dated 2 January 1964," *Brewster Papers* (Yale Archive, Box 3, Folder 4).

88. Ibid.

89. "Letter from Brewster to Howe dated 9 January 1964," *Brewster Papers* (Yale Archive, Box 3, Folder 4).

90. "Letter from Charles O'Hearn dated 26 July 1967," *Brewster Papers* (Yale Archive, Box 3, Folder 7).

91. *Brewster Papers* (Yale Archive, Box 2, Folder 13), 8 April 1967.

92. "Transcript of Alumni Convocation Meeting, 3 November 1967," *Brewster Papers* (Yale Archive, Box 10, Folder 10), 40.

93. *Brewster Papers* (Yale Archive, Box 3, Folder 6), 15 March 1967, 2.

94. *Brewster Papers* (Yale Archive, Box 2, Folder 14), 18 April 1967.

95. Quoted in Kabaservice, "Kingman Brewster and the Rise and Fall," 345.

96. Lemann, *Big Test*, 152.

97. Kabaservice, "Kingman Brewster and the Rise and Fall," 436.

98. *Brewster Papers* (Yale Archive, Box 13, Folder 13), 15 September 1969.

99. *Brewster Papers* (Yale Archive, Box 10, Folder 4), 3 February 1971.

100. Ibid.

101. *Brewster Papers* (Yale Archive, Box 10 Folder 4), 18 June 1971.

102. Jim Sleeper, "Allan Bloom and the Conservative Mind," *New York Times Book Review*, 4 September 2005, 27.

103. "Yale Class 1950, Twentieth Reunion Report, June 11–14, 1970," *Brewster Papers* (Yale Archive, Box 10, Folder 3).

104. Kingman Brewster, "Interviewed by Kirby Simon," *Griswold-Brewster History Project*, (Yale Archive, YRG 47-F, Box 2), n.d., 17.

105. Yale Alumni Board, "Verbatim proceedings of the meeting of the Yale Alumni Board, held at the Yale Law School on Saturday, 15 June 1968, convened at 9:30 A.M., Mr. David Grimes ('45w), Chairman of the Board, presiding," *Brewster Papers* (Yale Archive, Box 10, Folder 11), 15 June 1968, 9.

106. Yale Alumni Board, "Minutes of the Meeting of the Executive Committee of the Yale Alumni Board, 31 October 1968, held in the Corporation Room, Woodbridge Hall. 10:10 A.M." *Brewster Papers* (Yale Archive, Box 10, Folder 18), item dated October 1968.

107. Kabaservice, "Kingman Brewster and the Rise and Fall," 420.

108. Arthur Howe, Jr., personal interview with the Author, 18 July 2002.

109. Kabaservice, "Kingman Brewster and the Rise and Fall," 424.

110. Ibid., 430.

111. Ibid., 443–44.

112. Vassar-Yale Joint Study Group, *Records*, 1966–68, (Yale Archive, Group 6-J, RU 526, Boxes 2, 4, 7, 8, and 10).

113. Vassar-Yale Joint Study Group, *Records*, 1966–68, (Yale Archive Group 6-J, RU 526, Box 10, Folder 86), "Press Conference, 20 November 1967."

114. Ibid.

115. Kabaservice, "Kingman Brewster and the Rise and Fall," 427.

116. Janet Lever and Pepper Schwartz, *Women at Yale: Liberating a College Campus* (Indianapolis: Bobbs-Merrill, 1971).

117. Kabaservice, "Kingman Brewster and the Rise and Fall," 431.

118. Ibid., 471.

119. "Memo from Coed Steering Committee and Coed Action Group," *Brewster Papers* (Yale Archive Box 60, Folder 11).

120. Kabaservice, "Kingman Brewster and the Rise and Fall," 472.

121. John Muyskens, Jr., "Annual Report of the Director of Undergraduate Admissions." *Brewster Papers* (Yale Archive, Box 177, Folder 4), 25 June 1969.

122. Kabaservice, "Kingman Brewster and the Rise and Fall," 475.

123. Yale Club of New Jersey, "Alumni School Committee Report," *Brewster Papers* (Yale Archive, Box 2, Folder 12), 17 February 1969).

124. Ibid.

125. John Muyskens, Jr., "Annual Report of the Director of Undergraduate Admissions," *Brewster Papers* (Yale Archive, Box 177, Folder 4), 25 June 1969.

126. "Letter dated 27 March 27, 1970," *Brewster Papers* (Yale Archive, Box 60, Folder 15).

127. Soares, *Decline of Privilege: The Modernization of Oxford University* (Stanford, CA: Stanford University Press, 1999).

128. R. J. Sternberg, "Memo on Relationship of Categorization to Admissions Predictors," *Office of Institutional Research* (Yale Archive, Box 1, Folder 5), 16 June 1971, 1.

129. Ibid., 3.

130. R. J. Sternberg, "A Decision Rule to Categorize Yale College Applicants," *Office of Institutional Research* (Yale Archive Box 1, Folder 7), August 1971, 19–20.

131. Fiftieth reunion meetings usually involve a survey of all living members of the class. Yale classes from the 1940s, holding reunions in the 1990s, were regularly asked this question by faculty from Yale's department of sociology who were involved in designing and analyzing the survey.

132. Carter Wiseman, "In the Days of DKE and S.D.S.," *Yale Alumni Magazine*, February 2001.

133. "Letter from Elga Wasserman," *Brewster Papers* (Yale Archive, Box 60, Folder 13), 28 May 1970.

134. Yale does not have "tenure track" for assistant professors, so rather than use "non-tenured" as a faculty designation, it calls its junior faculty "fixed term" faculty.

135. Kabaservice, "Kingman Brewster and the Rise and Fall," 359; Howe interview with the Author 2002.

136. Howe Interview with the author 2002.

137. Kabaservice, *The Guardians*, 174.

138. Howe Interview with the author 2002.

139. Elga Wasserman, "Summary Report of the Chairman of the Planning Committee on Coeducation 1968–1969," *Brewster Papers* (Yale Archive, Box 176, Folder 5), 17 June 1969.

140. John Muyskens, Jr., "Annual Report of the Director of Undergraduate Admissions," *Brewster Papers* (Yale Archive, Box 177, Folder 4), 25 June 1969.

141. Office of Institutional Research, Table D-7, Yale University, 2 November 2000.

142. Kabaservice, *The Guardians*, 288.

143. Ibid., 418.

144. Ibid., 330.

145. Ibid., 328–33.

146. Office of Institutional Research, Table I-3, Yale University, 25 September 2000.

147. Graduate Employees Student Organization, *The Unchanging Face of the Ivy League*, February 2005, 3 (www.geso.org).

148. William Bowen and Derek Bok, *The Shape of the River: Long-Term Consequences of Considering Race in College and University Admissions* (Princeton, NJ: Princeton University Press, 1998); and Douglas S. Massey, Camille Z. Charles, Garvey F. Lundy, and Mary J. Fisher, *The Source of the River* (Princeton, NJ: Princeton University Press, 2004).

149. Bourdieu, Pierre, "The Forms of Capital," in *Handbook of Theory and Research for the Sociology of Education*, ed. J. G. Richardson (New York: Greenwood Press, 1986), 241–58.

150. Michele Lamont and Annette Lareau, "Cultural Capital: Allusions, Gaps, and Glissandos in Recent Theoretical Developments," *Sociological Theory* 6 (1988): 153–68, at 156.

151. Paul W. Kingston, "The Unfulfilled Promise of Cultural Capital Theory," *Sociology of Education*, Extra Issue (2001): 88–99, at 89.

152. Kabaservice, "Kingman Brewster and the Rise and Fall," 332–33.

153. Paul Capra, "Memo to All Alumni School Committee Members Regarding Alumni School Committee Interview Reports," *Brewster Papers* (Yale Archive, Box 3, Folder 3), 24 October 1967, 8, 10, 13, and 12.

154. Ibid., 5.

155. Ibid., 6.

156. Robert U. Redpath, "Correspondence and Clippings," *Brewster Papers* (Yale Archive, Box 173, Folder 3), 1967.

157. Fritz Barzilauskas, "Annual Report of Inter-College Athletics," *Brewster Papers* (Yale Archive, Box 176, Folder 6), 18 June 1969, 4; Soares, *Decline of Privilege*, 1999.

158. A. Whitney Griswold, "The Natural Allies: The Fine Arts and the University," *Atlantic Monthly*, June, reprinted in *The Fine Arts and the University*, ed. Murray G. Ross (New York: St. Martin's Press, 1959), 3–12.

159. A. Whitney Griswold, "Undergraduate Admissions Policy," *Griswold Papers* (Yale Archive Box 3, Folder 7), 9 March 1962, 4.

160. Alexander M. Bickel, Leonard W. Doob, John W. Hall, Basil D. Henning, Louis L. Martz, Thomas A. Noble, Horace D. Taft, Harry H. Wasserman, and John A. Wilkinson, "The Residential Colleges at Yale University an Inquiry Into Their Educational Potentialities and Responsibilities," *Brewster Papers* (Yale Archive, Box 179, Folder 8), 17 January 1968, 2; also see Henri Peyre, "Report to the President of Yale University on the Role of the Arts in Undergraduate Education at Yale," *Brewster Papers* (Yale Archive, Box 177, Folder 8), January 1967.

161. "Transcript of Comments at Alumni Convocation," *Brewster Papers* (Yale Archive Box 10, Folder 10), 3 November 1967, 4.

162. In fact, the fine arts remain central to college life today. Yale's "blue book" states, "Each college celebrates the progress of the academic year with various festivities, concerts, and dramatic presentations" (Yale College, *Yale College Programs of Study*, Fall and Spring Terms 2001–2002), 11.

163. Richard B. Sewall, "Ezra Stiles College Master's Annual Report," *Brewster Papers* (Yale Archive, Box 177, Folder 7), 1 August 1969.

164. Class Secretary, "Class of 1924, Yale College," *Brewster Papers* (Yale Archive, Box 10, Folder 1), 14 October 1966.

NOTES TO CHAPTER 5

1. John H. Hoskins, "Undergraduate Admissions Research Committee, Notes toward program formulation," *Office of Institutional Research Papers* (Yale Archive, Box 1, Folder 2), 4 March 1971, 2.

2. John Meeske, Letter from Yale University Registrar's Office to Author, 29 August 1995.

3. "John Harvard's Journal," *Harvard Magazine* (July–August 1997), 64–65.

4. Meeske, Letter to Author.

5. John H. Hoskins, "Undergraduate Admissions Research Committee Notes Toward Program Formulation," *OIR Papers* (Yale Archive, Box 1, Folder 2), 4 March 1971, 1.

6. Ibid.

7. Ibid., 3.

8. Ibid., 4.

9. Ibid., 5.

10. Ibid.

11. Ibid., 1.

12. *OIR Papers* (Yale Archive, Box 1, Folder 3), 7 May 1971.

13. *OIR Papers* (Yale Archive, Box 1, Folder 5), 18 June 1971, 1.

14. Ibid., 2.

15. Judith Hackman has spent her entire adult life in the Yale administration. In the 1990s, she was a dean in the graduate school, and in 2006 was an official working with alumni.

16. Thomas D. Taber and Judith D. Hackman, "College Criteria Study: A proposal for further study of operational criteria used to distinguish successful college undergraduates from other undergraduate students," *OIR Papers* (Yale Archive, Box 1, Folder 23), 15 November 1972, 39.

17. Ibid., 8.

18. Ibid., 2.

19. Ibid., 2.

20. Ibid., 15.

21. Ibid., 28.

22. Ibid., 18.

23. *Office of Institutional Research Papers* (Yale Archive).

24. Warren W. Willingham and Hunter M. Breland, *Personal Qualities and College Admissions* (New York: College Entrance Examination Board, 1982), 6.

25. Ibid.; Michele A. Hernandez, *A is for Admission* (New York: Warner Books, 1997), 59.

26. Cecilia Capuzzi Simon, "The SAT III?" *New York Times*, 18 January 2004, Education Life, Sunday Section, 15–17.

27. For reviews of the literature see Dominic J. Brewer, Eric Eide, and Ronald G. Ehrenberg, "Does it Pay to Attend an Elite Private College? Cross Cohort Evidence on the Effects of College Quality on Earnings," *NBER Working Paper Series, Paper Number* 5613 (Cambridge, MA: National Bureau of Economic Research), 1996; and Stacy Berg Dale and Alan B. Krueger, "Estimating the Payoff to Attending a More Selective College: an Application of Selection on Observables and Unobservables" *Quarterly Journal of Economics* 117, no. 4 (2002): 1491–526.

28. Benjamin Fine, *Barron's Profiles of American Colleges*, (Woodbury, NY: Barron's Educational Series, 1964); Fine, *Barron's Profiles of American Colleges* (Woodbury, NY: Barron's Educational Series, 1966).

29. William Bowen and Derek Bok, *The Shape of the River: Long-Term Consequences of Considering Race in College and University Admissions* (Princeton, NJ: Princeton University Press, 1998); Brewer, Eide, and Ehrenberg, "Does it Pay to Attend an Elite Private College?"; Caroline M. Hoxby, "Income Disparities Among College Graduates," Department of Economics, Harvard University, Unpublished Paper, 1998; and Caroline M. Hoxby and Bridget Terry, "Explaining Rising Income and Wage Inequality Among the College-Educated," *NBER Working Paper Series, Paper Number* 6873 (Cambridge, MA: National Bureau of Economic Research,), 1999.

30. Bowen and Bok, *Shape of the River*, 128.

31. Brewer, Eide, and Ehrenberg, "Does it Pay to Attend an Elite Private College?," 15.

32. Caroline Hoxby, "The Return to Attending a More Selective College: 1960 to the Present," http://post.economics.harvard.edu/faculty/hoxby/papers.html, 1998), 18.

33. Ibid., 31 Table 4.

34. Hoxby and Terry, "Explaining Rising Income and Wage Inequality," 15.

35. Ibid., 27.

36. Dale and Krueger, "Estimating the Payoff to Attending a More Selective College," 1492.

37. Ibid., 1495.

38. Roger L. Geiger, "The Competition for High-Ability Students: Universities in a Key Marketplace," in *The Future of the City of Intellect*, edited by Steven Brint (Stanford, CA: Stanford University Press, 2002): 82–106.

39. Dale and Krueger, "Estimating the Payoff to Attending a More Selective College," 1493.

40. Ibid., 1523.

41. Ibid.

42. Ibid., 1524–25.

43. Jonathan D. Glater, "Some Parents Letting Children Choose College, and Pay for It," *New York Times*, 10 April 2006. For behavioral evidence of college applicants' awareness of the prestige rankings of top tier colleges, see Christopher Avery, Mark Glickman, Caroline Hoxby, and Andrew Metrick, "A Revealed Preference Ranking of U.S. Colleges and Universities," *NBER Working Paper Series, Paper Number* 10803 (Cambridge, MA: National Bureau of Economic Research, 2004), available at http://www.nber.org/papers/w10803.

44. Warren W. Willingham, Charles Lewis, Rick Morgan, and Leonard Ramist, *Predicting College Grades: An Analysis of Institutional Trends Over Two Decades* (New York: Educational Testing Service, 1990).

45. For a summary of the literature see, James Crouse and Dale Trusheim, *The Case Against the SAT* (Chicago: University of Chicago Press, 1988).

46. Dorothy Perry, Barbara Sawrey, Michael Brown, Philip Curtis, Patrick Farrell, Linda Georginanna, Kenneth Burke, Christopher Diaz, Dennis Focht, Karen McNally, and Jane Stevens, "The Use of Admissions Tests by the University of California, A Discussion Paper Prepared by the Board of Admissions and Relations with Schools," *BOARS*, University of California, 2002: 5. Available at http://www.ucop.edu/news/sat/boars.pdf

47. Ibid., 5.

48. Office of the Director of Admissions and Relations with Schools, "A Comparison of Entrance Requirements at the University of California and at Selected Other Colleges," *UC President Collection* (University of California Archive, Bancroft Library, CU -5, Series 3, Box 13, Folder 6), December 1956, 2. The GI Bill was passed in 1944.

49. "Minutes of meeting of the Committee on Educational Policy, 15 November 1956," *UC President Collection* (University of California Archive, Bancroft Library, CU-5, Series 3, Box 13, Folder 6), 1.

50. Ibid., 2.

51. Ibid., 6.

52. Ibid., 8.

53. Ibid., 7.

54. Office of the Director of Admissions and Relations with Schools, "A Comparison of Entrance Requirements at the University of California and at Selected Other Colleges," *UC President Collection* (University of California Archive, Bancroft Library, CU-5, Series 3, Box 13, Folder 6), December 1956, 1, 4–5

55. In the second report on admissions, the committee made California's peer group more explicit by stating that there were five comparable universities in the United States: Harvard, Yale, Princeton, Chicago, and Michigan. And that of the five, only Berkeley's standards for admitting graduate students were the equal to Harvard's. The rest had lower standards where graduate education was concerned (Committee on Educational Policy, "Second Progress Report on Admissions Stan-

dards," *UC President Collection* [University of California Archive, Bancroft Library, CU -5, Series 3, Box 13, Folder 6], 3 June 1957, 8, 15).

56. Office of the Director of Admissions and Relations with Schools, "A Comparison of Entrance Requirements at the University of California and at Selected Other Colleges," *UC President Collection* (University of California Archive, Bancroft Library, CU -5, Series 3, Box 13, Folder 6), December 1956, 1.

57. Ibid., 1–2, 4.

58. Ibid., 2.

59. Ibid.

60. Committee on Educational Policy, "Second Progress Report on Admissions Standards," *UC President Collection* (University of California Archive, Bancroft Library, CU-5, Series 3, Box 13, Folder 6), 3 June 1957, 4.

61. Michigan also had, for reasons not touched on in the report, SAT data for California to weigh.

62. Office of the Director of Admissions and Relations with Schools, "A Comparison of Entrance Requirements at the University of California and at Selected Other Colleges," *UC President Collection* (University of California Archive, Bancroft Library, CU-5, Series 3, Box 13, Folder 6), December 1956, 3.

63. Ibid., 4.

64. See Chapter 2 of this book on the Harvard's dean's comparison of sixty-nine schools.

65. Office of the Director of Admissions and Relations with Schools, "Excerpt from Schools and Scholarship Committee Handbook Harvard College," *UC President Collection* (University of California Archive, Bancroft Library, CU-5, Series 3, Box 13, Folder 6), December 1956, 1.

66. Ibid., 2.

67. Ibid.

68. Ibid., 2–3.

69. See the first section of Chapter 3 of this book.

70. Office of the Director of Admissions and Relations with Schools, "Excerpt from Schools and Scholarship Committee Handbook Harvard College," *UC President Collection* (University of California Archive, Bancroft Library, CU-5, Series 3, Box 13, Folder 6), December 1956, 3.

71. Ibid., 4.

72. Office of the Director of Admissions and Relations with Schools, "A Comparison of Entrance Requirements at the University of California and at Selected Other Colleges," *UC President Collection* (University of California Archive, Bancroft Library, CU-5, Series 3, Box 13, Folder 6), December 1956, 5.

73. Committee on Educational Policy, "Second Progress Report on Admissions Standards," *UC President Collection* (University of California Archive, Bancroft Library, CU -5, Series 3, Box 13, Folder 6), 3 June 1957. The report was submitted to the president's office on 20 May 1957.

74. Ibid., 3.

75. Ibid., 1.

76. Ibid., 3.

77. Ibid.

78. Ibid., 3–4.

79. Ibid., 2–3.

80. California Postsecondary Educational Commission, "California's Higher Education at a Glance," *Annual Series*, Sacramento, California, December 1996. Statistics on community college transfers to the university are published every year in this series. Interview by Ling Tang with Dr. Warren Fox, Resident Scholar, Center for Studies in Higher Education, University of California, Berkeley, 26 August 2002.

81. Committee on Educational Policy, "Report on Educational Policy and Program at Berkeley and Los Angeles," *UC President Collection* (University of California Archive, Bancroft Library, CU-5, Series 3, Box 13, Folder 26), 19 May 1958, item II, A, 11.

82. *Almanac of Higher Education* (1991), 15, 18.

83. Organization for Economic Co-operation and Development, *Higher Education in California* (Paris: OECD, 1990).

84. Perry et al., "Use of Admissions Tests by the University of California," 5.

85. Ibid., 5–6.

86. "Letter from Kerr, 5 August 1960," *UC President Collection* (University of California Archive, Bancroft Library, Admissions Office and Relations with Schools: Dean of Educational Relations, March 1960–August 1960, Box 76, Folder 12).

87. *UC President Collection* (University of California Archive, Bancroft Library, Admissions Office and Relations with Schools, General, Box 75, Folder 17), 10 January 1962. Confidential Memo from Frank L. Kidner to Members of President's Cabinet and Chief Campus Officers, "Changes in Admissions Requirements in Conformity with the Master Plan."

88. Nicholas Lemann, *The Big Test* (New York: Farrar, Straus and Giroux, 1999), 172.

89. John Douglas, "Setting the Conditions of Undergraduate Admissions: Part III-3," *Center for Studies in Higher Education* (University of California, Berkeley, 2002), 5.

90. Warren Fox, "Higher Education Policy in California," in *Higher Education Policy*, ed. Leo Goedegebuure (New York: Pergamon Press, 1993), 71, Table 2; California Postsecondary Educational Commission, "University of California Fund Sources for Current Operation for Fiscal Years 1967 Through 1997," Sacramento, California, 1997.

91. Quoted in Douglas, "Setting the Conditions of Undergraduate Admissions: Part III-3," 5.

92. *UC President Collection* (University of California Archive, Bancroft Library,

Admissions Office and Relations with Schools, General, Box 75, Folder 18), 22 January 1963.

93. *UC President Collection* (University of California Archive, Bancroft Library, Admissions Office and Relations with Schools, General, Box 75, Folder 18), 12 August 1963.

94. *UC President Collection* (University of California Archive, Bancroft Library, Admissions Office and Relations with Schools, General, Box 75, Folder 20), 23 June 1963.

95. *UC President Collection* (University of California Archive, Bancroft Library, Admissions Office and Relations with Schools, General, Box 75, Folder 20), 13 July 1963.

96. "Remarks of Chancellor Edward Strong on the Occasion of the Initial Meeting of the Board of Trustees, California Alumni Foundation," *UC President Collection* (University of California Archive, Bancroft Library, Alumni Affairs, California Alumni Association: Berkeley, January 1963–September 1963, Box 117, Folder 13), 23 March 1963, Alumni House.

97. Perry et al., "Use of Admissions Tests by the University of California," 13.

98. Ibid., 6.

99. Jerome Karabel, "Freshman Admissions at Berkeley: A Policy for the 1990s and Beyond," *A Report of the Committee on Admissions and Enrollment Berkeley Division,* Academic Senate, University of California, 1989, Table 3, 17.

100. California Postsecondary Educational Commission, "California's Higher Education at a Glance."

101. Karabel, "Freshman Admissions," 13.

102. Ibid., Table 3, 17.

103. Dana Y. Takagi, "From Discrimination to Affirmative Action: Facts in the Asian American Admissions Controversy," *Social Problems,* 37, no. 4 (November 1990): 578–92.

104. Ibid., 583.

105. Ibid., 589.

106. California Postsecondary Educational Commission, "California's Higher Education at a Glance."

107. University of California at Berkeley, Office of the President, Web Site; Nancy Hsu, "UCLA diversity trend continues," *Daily Bruin,* Monday, 22 November 1993, 3.

108. Chronicle of Higher Education, *The Almanac of Higher Education* (Chicago: University of Chicago Press, 1991); Ibid., 1996.

109. Karabel, "Freshman Admissions," Appendix A.

110. The Karabel Report is available at http://academic-senate.berkeley.edu/archives/karabel.html.

111. John A. Douglass, "A Brief of the Events Leading to SP1," Submitted to the Task Force on Governance Panel 2 on Shared Governance, University-wide Office of the Academic Senate, University of California, 28 February 1997.

112. Ibid., 18.

113. Perry et al., "Use of Admissions Tests by the University of California," 6.

114. Ibid., 7–8.

115. Ibid., 6.

116. Ibid., 1.

117. Ibid., 7.

118. Saul Geiser and Roger Studley, "UC and the SAT: Predictive Validity and Differential Impact of the SAT I and SAT II at the University of California," University of California, Office of the President, 29 October 2001: 1–24. Available at http://www.ucop.edu/sas/research/researchandplanning/welcome.html.

119. Perry et al., "Use of Admissions Tests by the University of California," 9.

120. Ibid., 11.

121. Geiser and Studley, "UC and the SAT," 9.

122. Perry et al., "Use of Admissions Tests by the University of California," 13.

123. Ibid., 14.

124. Richard C. Atkinson, "Achievement Versus Aptitude Tests in College Admissions," Office of the President, University of California, December 2001. Available at: http://www.ucop.edu/pres/speeches/achieve.htm.

125. Tamar Lewin, "College Board Announces An Overhaul For the SAT," *New York Times*, 28 June 2002, A12; Barbara Whitaker, "Board Details Plans to Alter College Exam," *New York Times*, 16 May 2002, A21.

126. Betty Hart and Todd R. Risley, *Meaningful Differences in the Everyday Experience of Young American Children* (Baltimore: Brookes Publishing, 1995).

127. Annette Lareau, *Unequal Childhoods. Class, Race, and Family Life* (Berkeley: University of California Press, 2003).

128. Christopher Jencks and Meredith Phillips (eds.), *The Black-White Test Score Gap* (Washington, DC: Brookings Institution Press, 1998).

129. Samuel R. Lucas, "Hope, Anguish, and the Problem of Our Time: An Essay on the Publication of the Black-White Test Score Gap," *Teachers College Record* (1 February 2000).

130. Jay Rosner, "On White Preferences," *Nation*, 14 April 2003.

131. Ibid.

132. Ibid.

133. Roy O. Freedle, "Correcting the SAT's Ethnic and Social-Class Bias: A Method for Reestimating SAT Scores," *Harvard Educational Review* 73, no. 1 (Spring 2003): 1–43.

134. R. Freedle and I. Kostin, "Predicting Black and White Differential Item Functioning in Verbal Analog Performance," *Intelligence*, 24, 1997, 417–44; R. Freedle, I. Kostin, and J. Schwartz, "A Comparison of Strategies used by Black and White Students in Solving SAT Verbal Analogies Using a Thinking Aloud Method and Matched Percentage-Correct Design," *Research Report No. RR-87–48*, Princeton, NJ: Educational Testing Service, 1987.

135. Freedle, "Correcting the SAT's Ethnic and Social-Class Bias," 9.

136. Ibid., 6.

137. Ibid.

138. Ibid., 1.

139. Jay Mathews, "The Bias Question." *Atlantic Monthly* (November 2003): 130–40.

140. College Board, "1996 Profile of College Bound Seniors National Report," (New York: College Board, 1996).

141. Claude S. Fisher, Michael Hout, Martin Sanchez Jankowski, Samuel R. Lucas, Ann Swidler, and Kim Voss, *Inequality by Design: Cracking the Bell Curve Myth* (Princeton, NJ: Princeton University Press, 1996).

NOTES TO CHAPTER 6

1. Joseph A. Soares, *The Decline of Privilege* (Stanford, CA: Stanford University Press, 1999).

2. National Association of College and University Business Officers, "Endowment Study 2003," *NACUBO* 2003. Report available at http://www.nacubo.org.

3. U.S. News and World Report, *America's Best Colleges* 2003, Washington, DC, 2003.

4. Anonymous Interviews with staff at Yale and Harvard.

5. For an approximate list of colleges by tier, please consult any edition of *Barron's Profiles of American Colleges*. We used the 1990 edition since it overlapped with our NELS cohort. All institutions of higher education not classified by Barron's were assigned to the seventh tier. See, Barron's Educational Series, *Barron's Profiles of American Colleges* (Woodbury, NY: Barron's Educational Service, 1990).

6. Pierre Bourdieu and Jean-Claude Passeron, *The Inheritors: French Students and Their Relation to Culture* (Chicago: University of Chicago Press, 1979); Pierre Bourdieu, *Distinctions: A Social Critique of the Judgment of Taste* (Cambridge, MA: Harvard University Press, 1984); and Pierre Bourdieu, *The State Nobility* (Stanford, CA: Stanford University Press, 1996).

7. Bourdieu and Passeron, *Inheritors*, 19.

8. Organization for Economic Co-operation and Development, *Human Capital.* Paris: OECD, 1999.

9. Michele Lamont and Annette Lareau, "Cultural Capital: Allusions, Gaps, and Glissandos in Recent Theoretical Developments," *Sociological Theory* 6 (1988): 153–68, at 156.

10. Paul W. Kingston, "The Unfulfilled Promise of Cultural Capital Theory," *Sociology of Education* Extra Issue (2001): 88–99, at 89.

11. Bourdieu, *Distinctions*, 14–17.

12. Ibid., 99–168.

13. Ibid., 136, 140.

14. Ibid., 120–21.

15. Bourdieu and Passeron, *Inheritors*, 7, 10.

16. "We" refers to the joint labors of Shaughnessy O'Brien, research assistant at Wake Forest University, and me.

17. Lawrence R. Mishel, Jared Bernstein, and John Schmitt, *The State of Working America*, 2000–2001. (Ithaca, NY: Cornell University Press, 2001).

18. Jason Kaufman and Jay Gabler, "Cultural Capital and the Extracurricular Activities of Girls and Boys in the College Attainment Process," *Poetics* 32, 2004, 145–68.

19. Brewer, Eide, and Ehrenberg, "Does It Pay to Attend an Elite Private College?"

20. Richard Kahlenberg (ed.), *America's Untapped Resource: Low-Income Students in Higher Education* (New York: Century Foundation Press, 2004).

21. Consult the 1990 edition, or any current edition of *Barron's Profiles* for a full list of colleges and universities in the second tier.

22. Boudieu, *Distinction*, 124.

23. Judith Blau, *The Shape of Culture* (Cambridge: Cambridge University Press, 1989). From the mid-nineteenth century to the Jazz Age, an institutional field for cultural capital was constructed in the Northeast using Shakespeare, fine art museums, symphonies, concert halls, theater, opera, dance, the Social Register, private boarding schools, and selective admissions in elite colleges. See Chapter 2 of this book, section subtitle: "The School and Highbrow Nexus."

24. Warren W. Willingham and Hunter M. Breland, *Personal Qualities and College Admissions* (New York: College Entrance Examination Board, 1982).

25. Benjamin Fine, *Barron's Profiles of American Colleges* (Woodbury, NY: Barron's Educational Service, 1966). Barron's, *Barron's Profiles*, 1990.

26. Joseph A. Soares, "Cultural Capital and Elite Educational Reproduction of Ivy League Families in the 1960s and 1970s," Department of Sociology, Yale University. Presented at the Regular Culture Session at the American Sociological Association's Annual Meeting, 2001. The data were derived from reunion surveys. Although they do shed light on Yale patterns, we cannot be certain that these results are representative of all Yale graduates for the time period in question.

27. Douglas S. Massey, Camille Z. Charles, Garvey F. Lundy, and Mary J. Fisher, *The Source of the River: The Social Origins of Freshmen at America's Selective Colleges and Universities* (Princeton, NJ: Princeton University Press, 2003), 42.

28. Paul DiMaggio and John Mohr, "Cultural Capital, Educational Attainment, and Marital Selection," *American Journal of Sociology* 90 (1985): 1231–61.

29. James Shulman and William Bowen, *The Game of Life* (Princeton, NJ: Princeton University Press, 2001).

30. There is a NELS question (# F2S59R) asking youths whether they think it is very important, or somewhat important, or not important to apply to the college a parent attended. But that is hardly the same thing as asking those who went to college if they attended the same college as either mom or dad.

NOTES TO CONCLUSIONS

1. Nicholas Lemann, *The Big Test* (New York: Farrar, Straus and Giroux, 1999, 153).

2. William Bowen, Martin Kurzweil, and Eugene Tobin, *Equity and Excellent in Higher Education* (Charlotte: University of Virginia Press, 2005).

3. Christopher Avery, Andrew Fairbanks, Richard Zeckhauser, *The Early Admissions Game* (Cambridge, MA: Harvard University Press, 2003). In September 2006, first Harvard and then Princeton eliminated their early admissions programs, but others are not rushing to follow suit. Stanford, for example, has explicitly declined to discontinue its early admit practices. Harvard and Princeton may be motivated by a genuine desire for reform, but they also do not stand to lose many candidates to rival colleges. See: *Harvard University Gazette*, "Harvard to Eliminate Early Admissions," 12 September 2006; Alan Finder, "Princeton Stops Its Early Admissions," *New York Times*, 19 September 2006; John Etchemendy, "Applied Science," *New York Times*, Op-Ed Contributor, 27 September 2006.

4. Alan Stone, "Harvard Expands Financial Aid for Low- and Middle-Income Families," *Harvard University Gazette*, Press Release, March 30, 2006.

5. W. E. B. Du Bois, *The Souls of Black Folks* (New York: Penguin Books, 1989).

6. William Bowen and Derek Bok, *The Shape of the River: Long-Term Consequences of Considering Race in College and University Admissions* (Princeton, NJ: Princeton University Press, 1998).

7. Ronald G. Ehrenberg, "Reaching for the Brass Ring: The *US News and World Report* Rankings and Competition," *Review of Higher Education*, 26, no. 2, 2. 2006, 145–62.

8. Alan Finder, "Test Scores Jump, Raleigh Credits Integration by Income," *New York Times*, 25 September 2005.

9. William Julius Wilson, *When Work Disappears* (New York: Alfred A. Knopf, 1996).

Index